PSYCHOSOCIAL
THEORIES
OF THE SELF

PATH IN PSYCHOLOGY
Published in Cooperation with Publications for the
Advancement of Theory and History in Psychology (PATH)

Series Editors:
David Bakan, *York University*
John Broughton, *Teachers College, Columbia University*
Miriam Lewin, *Manhattanville College*
Robert Rieber, *John Jay College, CUNY, and Columbia University*
Howard Gruber, *Rutgers University*

**WILHELM WUNDT AND THE MAKING OF A SCIENTIFIC
PSYCHOLOGY**
Edited by R. W. Rieber

HUMANISTIC PSYCHOLOGY: Concepts and Criticisms
Edited by Joseph R. Royce and Leendert P. Mos

PSYCHOSOCIAL THEORIES OF THE SELF
Edited by Benjamin Lee

Conference on New Approaches to the Shelf

PSYCHOSOCIAL THEORIES OF THE SELF

Edited by
Benjamin Lee
Center for Psychosocial Studies
Chicago, Illinois

With the collaboration of
Kathleen Smith

PLENUM PRESS • NEW YORK AND LONDON

Library of Congress Cataloging in Publication Data

Conference on New Approaches to the Self (1979: Chicago, Ill.)
  Psychosocial theories of the self.

  (PATH in psychology)
  "Proceedings of a conference on New Approaches to the Self, held by the Center for
Psychosocial Studies, March 29 – April 1, 1979, in Chicago, Illinois"—T.p. verso.
  Includes bibliographical references and index.
  1. Self—Congresses. 2. Self—Social aspects—Congresses. I. Lee, Benjamin. II. Smith,
Kathleen. III. Center for Psychosocial Studies. IV. Title. V. Series.
BF697.C576 1979   155.2   82-13123
ISBN 0-306-41117-2

Proceedings of a Conference on New Approaches to the Self, held March 29 –
April 1, 1979, by the Center for Psychosocial Studies, Chicago, Illinois

©1982 Plenum Press, New York
A Division of Plenum Publishing Corporation
233 Spring Street, New York, N.Y. 10013

Printed in the United States of America

ACKNOWLEDGMENTS

It remains for me to express my gratitude to those who assisted with this task in so many ways. My thanks to Janine Poronsky, Hedwig Sarnicki, and Phyllis Schneider for typing the manuscript and its interminable revisions, and to Marta Nicholas for her many hours of copyediting. Special thanks to Kathleen Smith, Administrative Assistant of the Center for Psychosocial Studies, without whose skills this volume would never have been completed.

Benjamin Lee

CONTENTS

INTRODUCTION

Benjamin Lee

Center for Psychosocial Studies

On March 29-April 1, 1979, the Center for Psychosocial Studies held a conference in Chicago on "New Approaches to the Self" in which all the authors in this volume participated. Over the years the Center has acted as a communications link and coordination point for interdisciplinary discussions and research. Several years ago, we discovered that there was a renewed interest among psychoanalysts, anthropologists, and developmental psychologists in the investigation of the self, and the reason for this groundswell of activity was the discovery of the importance of problems of meaning and interpretation in each discipline. Since investigators in each of these disciplines were relatively ignorant of developments in the other approaches, we felt that a conference would be a timely catalyst. Each of the authors gave a presentation at the conference, and it is a mark of the success of the interdisciplinary effort that almost all the papers were extensively revised in response to the discussions.

The first three papers by Arnold Goldberg, Ernest Wolf, and Robert LeVine all use Heinz Kohut's psychoanalytic self psychology as their starting point. Goldberg places the self within a broader framework of philosophical and psychoanalytic theories, finally locating it in the types of communicative relationships a person constructs in his interactions with others. Wolf's paper explicates the basic ideas and innovations of Kohut's self psychology. He clearly links Kohut's theory of self-development with its roots in the transferential situation of analysis and the analyst's use of empathic introspection as the method by which analytic data is gathered. Finally, LeVine's paper applies some of Kohut's ideas to the analysis of ethnographic data he has collected over a span of over twenty years among the Gusii of Africa. His results indicate the usefulness of psychoanalytically based approaches to such cultural phenomena as

1

the "evil eye" among the Gusii, while at the same time forc-
ing psychoanalysts to consider a more variable conception of
self-development.

The next two papers by Raymond Fogelson and Anne Straus
are anthropological approaches to the investigation of the
self.   The former author presents a history of the major
approaches that anthropologists have used to study the self.
Its major contribution is to present to other social scientists the variety and richness that only ethnographic example can provide, thereby forestalling premature intellectual
closure or rigidity while expanding our perception of the
range of phenomena which must be included in any theory of
the self. Dr. Straus' paper comes, therefore, as a welcome
example of the points made by Professor Fogelson. She
presents an analysis of the Cheyenne theory of the self,
based upon her own fieldwork, and thereby challenges the
adequacy of Western conceptions of the self to analyze the
Cheyenne.

The final two papers by Milton Singer and Vincent Crapanzano are semiotic approaches to the study of the self.
Professor Singer, utilizing Pierce's dialogic model of seme-
osis (the process of sign generation), erects a foundation
for the study of the self as a sign system which emerges out
of dialogue. He focuses particularly on the child's use of
personal pronouns as being a foundation of self-development,
and then extends his analysis to cultural materials.   Professor Crapanzano's paper approaches the self from a more
Lacanian perspective, although it does overlap with Professor Singer's on several points, especially the importance of
the personal pronouns "I" and "you". He extends previous
semiotic analyses, however, by emphasizing the critical role
of semiotic processes in mediating not only representational
activity, but also desire and motivation.

While these papers represent a healthy diversity in
both emphases and subject matter, they all share one trait
in common. The discussion of one's theory of the self, no
matter what it is, like the self itself, is nurtured and expanded through communication with others.

THE SELF OF PSYCHOANALYSIS

Arnold Goldberg, M.D.

INTRODUCTION

The self has assumed a new popularity, within psychoanalysis as well as in other disciplines. In the former it has given rise to a focus of study called self psychology (Goldberg 1980), which in turn makes claims for certain advantageous positions in both technique and theory. As an expectable counterreaction to these claims, there has been a welcome cry for clarification of the definition and theoretical status of the self—especially one that will delineate the self that is of relevance to psychoanalysis. The following work is an attempt to fashion such a definition and to place it in a developmental perspective.

A SELF DEFINITION

In a masterpiece of linguistic legerdemain, a philosopher (Mischel 1977) writes that one point on which philosophers and psychologists can easily agree is that "the self is not some entity other than the person". This would seem to translate into "the self is the person", but this simple statement probably can generate as much disagreement as any other issue raised by a combination of philosophers and psychologists.

Before a psychology of the self can be fully developed, an attempt must be made to define that elusive word, and to decide whether it is indeed an entity, a structure, or merely someone whom we all know well. Whether or not a definition is possible must also be appraised. Herewith is a start at a disentangling of the selves of other fields, to arrive at the one of relevance to psychoanalysis.

THE SELF AS THE PERSON

The very definition of a person becomes the initial
stumbling block for this consideration. It seems clear that
a person is simply not equivalent to the bodily configuration of an individual; yet philosophers from Feigl (1958) to
Strawson (1979) to Margolis (1977) have long struggled with
whether one should equate mental and physical phenomena, or
should attach mental predicates to a person, or should have
the mind "embodied" in the physical substance of an individual. The resolution of the philosophical muddle will
assist but will not solve the psychological problem--since
the term becomes all-encompassing in the one sense of seemingly including everything about the mental and physical
components and contents of the person, yet woefully ignoring
the unconscious and developmental features.

It would seem prudent to emphasize that psychoanalysis
often pays little heed to the physical attributes of a person, save as they contribute to other psychological considerations which begin to form a definition of the self. To
but touch, at this time, on the problems of defining a person, we must probably grapple with some of the familiar
problems concerning the mind and the body. Strawson (1979)
says that although we clearly talk of ourselves as having
intentions, beliefs, sensations, thoughts, memories, etc.,
we also speak of our having positions such as locations,
characteristics such as weight, and attitudes such as lying
down. It seems that one's thoughts are ascribed to the very
same thing as the physical situation. He feels that a concept of a person must thus include both mental and physical
predicates, and he emphasizes the relationship between these
two. This, of course, is in contrast to the sharp dichotomy
between mind and body in Descartes. Rather than pursuing
and enumerating the many solutions and resolutions of the
mind/body dilemma, we can say that a person seems to consist
of some form of enduring relationship between the two (mind
and body), even if that relationship at times appears to be
identical (identity theory) or totally separate (as in a
physical materialism theory). The self as the person needs
definition in both its corporeal and its psychological manifestations.

The self of psychoanalysis need not fulfill the same
criteria of personhood needed in philosophy or in other disciplines, but must be of particular importance and relevance

to analysis. A psychoanalytic requirement for such a self must include, however, some form of interaction between the mind and the body, and must position the self in the arena of relationships with other selves. This must naturally be extended over time. It should also allow for utilizing the dimensions of analytic inquiry such as seen, for example, in the topographic layers of the mind; i.e., the role of the unconscious must be included. Thus the psychoanalytic self is a person built up over time via relationships with other persons, one who enjoys a multitude of intrapersonal (or intrapsychic) relationships as well.

Despite the efforts of many notable analytic theoreticians who participate in the philosophical debate about the mind and body questions and resolve it in favor of an identity theory (Rubinstein 1965), it is clearly an unsatisfactory resolution for anyone working with psychosomatic disorders. The better resolution for this study, one offered by Margolis (1977), is that of "embodiment". It demands a dualism of sorts while allowing for the fact that the mind, though related to the body, is not identical to it. While the mind exists because of the body, it has only some of its properties as well as properties of its own. As embodied in the physical being of an individual, the mind allows for a total person to be constructed. The particular properties of the mind are of major interest to psychology, the properties of the body to physiology, and the properties of the brain to neurology, or neurophysiology. However, a total person seems to demand a different form of interest in terms of his/her relationships, standards of conduct, and rules of behavior in relation to other persons. As we shall see, these are more than merely one's place or role in the social world.

Theories of the self or the person in a social world are those of interacting individuals. They mainly seem to derive from the work of George Herbert Mead, who felt that the "me" is "the organized set of attitudes of others which one thereupon himself assumes". It is what one feels about himself because of other people's opinions. An advance of this position would include all of the ways in which one incorporates others' views of himself, and would allow for the development of a theory of various roles which are assumed and acted upon accordingly. It is by no means necessary to ascribe to the particulars of Mead's view of the self as a product of others' viewpoints, to consider the

self to be equivalent to the social person. All that is
required of this form of orientation is a commitment to the
perspective of social interaction and social behavior. We
then are what we do and the way we behave; and this need
never be a simple description, since one can carry a highly
complex series of roles at any one time (e.g., husband,
soldier, father, son, liberal, etc.). However, one must
also consider another statement by Mischel (op.cit.): he
says that the problem of the self is a conceptual rather
than an empirical problem. Thus from an initial orientation
from the self as the person and its social implications we
move to that of the person concept.

THE SELF AS THE CONCEPT OF THE PERSON

The movement from the social to the psychological
necessitates the mental examination or personal consideration of the interpersonal. The self therefore is not only
what is made of me but how I in turn consider that product.
One's own inner assessment or concept of one's person and
one's single or multiple roles becomes the determining issue
for a delineation of the self.

That there may be and often are major discrepancies
between the outward manifestations of the social person and
the inner conception of the same seems clear and forces a
consideration of just what makes up the self inside. For
some it is an image or representation of the person, but for
others this is too limiting a perspective. The question
naturally arises as to whether or not a person can consider
himself in a variety of ways without an accompanying pictorial or internal display. Many activities (i.e. actions) of
an individual seem to represent such a self. There are a
variety of descriptions of one's self, usually in the form
of functions (e.g., self control), which depict the inner
self yet seem to command no particular role or form or
image.

The problem extends to or includes that of considering
the self as an entity or thing. Long ago, David Hume noted
his own and everyone else's inability to find one's essence
by introspection; and thereafter, Kant decided the self was
the transcendental subject of any possible experience rather
than an empirical object. There is no doubt that we often
talk of the self as an object; a more careful use of lan-

guage directs us to consider the self more in the category
of functions--more particularly, mental functions. Especially in the concern of exactly "who" is acting and doing
the experiencing, we must avoid the trap of the homunculus
and insist on processes. Even with this proviso, the "self
as the inner idea of the person" may be lacking in preci-
sion.

THE SELF AS THE MIND

Although Piaget (Piaget & Inhelder 1966) describes a
stage of egocentrism wherein the self and the universe are
one, he insists that normal cognitive development involves
decentering and the subsequent distinction between the self
and others. So too does psychoanalysis describe development
that proceeds from a primary, total self-involvement to a
complex arrangement of relationships between the self and
others. However, a case can be made for considering all mental operations as part of the self, conceived of as a supra-
ordinate totality, inasmuch as even the most neutral sort of
relationship survives in the mind only by virtue of its significance to one's self. It is thus in the evaluation of
mental operations, in terms of one's own needs, goals, frustrations, and satisfactions, that one can equate the self
with the mind. However, this removes the physical attributes
of the person from consideration as well as blurring the
distinction between many psychological activities which simply do not seem equal to the whole person. The idea of
agency seems to emerge when we try to envisage someone at
the helm of these many mental functions and activities.
Thus, though the self or person seems involved with
almost--if not quite all--of the mind, it seems necessary to
tease the concepts apart. Persons are not minds, even
though they seem to include the mind and even though they
become represented in the mind.

THE SELF AS THE CONCEPT OF THE MIND

Wollheim (1973) makes the point that one's concept of
one's mind allows for the spatial and organizing principles
that we usually consider in psychoanalysis. This is not to
say that it is necessarily the organization ascribed to the
theory of psychoanalysis (as, for example, in the tripartite
model of the mind), but rather that we conceive of our men-

tal operations in particular ways. For some individuals, the body is the basic and most lasting concept of the operations of the mind; here the Kleinian approach of oral ingestion and ejection seems paramount as an illustration. For some individuals, the arrangement of mental operations in terms of compartments (higher or lower strata, etc.) seems to be of major importance. The particular configurations that we employ to so conceptualize our mind would thus be the logical counterpart of the self as the totality of mental operations, the individual concept of the operations.

Another way of thinking of the self as the concept of the mind is via one or another of the theories of the mind's structure. Thus the self can be seen as a substructure of a mental apparatus—in particular, as a content of the ego. According to Heinz Hartmann (1953), the self is the psychic structure in opposition to objects. Other views of the self seem to restrict themselves to some elaboration of enduring functions of the mind, as noted either in the perspective or the theory of the observer or of the subject. Kohut (1977) has attempted a dual role for the self in this regard; he feels that the self is a content of psychic structure in the narrow sense, as well as the coherent core of the personality in the broad sense.

THE SELF AS AGENT OR OBJECT

Langer (1967) has said that however we may concentrate on acts and action as the basic unit(s) of the mind, once a complex of action occurs, there exists an agent. A system which initiates rather than merely reponds is one involved with motives, purposes, and goals; and this usually characterizes the self of psychology. This agent is capable of action, control, regulation, etc., and thus qualifies for the intentionalistic perspective of human motivation. It also could be extended to the self as recipient, i.e., as an object.

It should be noted that psychoanalysis in particular has stressed three roles for this form of the self. They are the familiar active, passive, and reflexive; and though first elucidated by Federn (1926, 1952 ed.) in terms of ego-states, they have been carried on in that tradition of the manner in which the self treats itself as object—i.e., in the forms above. Others (e.g., Schafer 1968) have dis-

cussed this issue in terms of the self as agent, object, or
place. This, of course, reawakens the thing status of the
self.

THE SELF AS SUBJECTIVE EXPERIENCE

One neat division of mental activities is that of objective versus subjective, or of those having to do with
personal significance—and so experienced as part of the
self—versus those that are impersonally experienced. The
latter would include the pure cognitive or rational components of psychology even if they exist only in an ideal way.
Of course, this would challenge the idea that any mental activity could be without some personal meaning, but it would
allow a continuum for such import. We have managed to reduce or minimize a wide range of perception and/or thinking
to a range of objectivity, and certainly one can reach some
consensus of this in certain scientific activities and/or
mathematical inquiries. Thus, the underpinnings for this
self definition are those of the experience of personal involvement. There need not be a sharp break between the subjective and the objective, but this division opens up a
problem of the term being so all-inclusive as to lose value.
Likewise, one must clarify the use of subjective as not necessarily meaning "biased or relative" as opposed to "objective" true facts. Objectivity also should not be the same
as impersonal, since one should be objective about subjectivity in a scientific pursuit. The use of the subjective
experience does shift the definition from a concept of an
entity or a theory to that of a quality. In language it is
the prefix to a variety of issues such as self-control,
self-esteem, self-hate, etc.

THE SELF AS RELATIONS

Wilden (1972) says:
At both the phonological and the conceptual level, language is constructed on difference....The actual function
of words like 'I', 'me', 'you', 'him', which we commonly
take to refer to entities are, in fact, simply shifters.
The shifter designates only the locus of the sender of
the message; it refers to a relation between sender, receiver, and referent; but it does not, of itself, supply
the context without which it can have no referent other

than itself. 'Me' is not an entity, but is a punctuation
mark. (p. 221)
Later he goes on:
The epistemological line has been drawn in the wrong
place--in the place where it creates a barrier between
sender and receiver....The referent for 'I', which designates the sender, is not the image of the biological organism, separate and different from his fellow human
beings, but rather a locus in the system. (ibid.,
p. 222)

In this framework, the self can be seen as an artificial distinction, or as an attempt to turn a relationship of
a system into an opposition of things. Colin Cherry traces
the history of the word individuum (which originally meant
"indivisible from the community or unit") to its present-day
usage of "separate and distinct". The paradoxes are produced by trying to isolate the self, which in truth must
include the rest of the system--and most particularly the
other.

The self in opposition to objects is a creation of a
theory involving discrete units akin to language and thus to
a digital form of relationship. The self as part of, or
co-extensive with, others is part of a theory involving
wholes or an analogue type of relationship. The latter is
conducive to a theory of meaning; and this necessitates con-
ceptualizing the self as an open system which can, at various points, be wrenched free for examination in one form or
another. The seeming problem of the self as an entity or
not is resolved by this explanation of whether one has a
theory of discrete units or an open system theory.

THE SELF OF PSYCHOANALYSIS

One can collate various words utilized in the psychoanalytic literature to clarify or distinguish the psychoanalytic self. They include structure, pattern, core, unit,
center, concept, abstraction, content, sense, recipient,
time and space axis. With study, one can see that they fall
into two groups: the first is of a general nature such as
abstraction, pattern, or concept; the second is more particular, such as unit or recipient or center. This is somewhat
like the tension between a conceptual and an empirical consideration of the self.

Since much of our research derives from the awakened
interest in self psychology, we can return to it for guid-
ance. Although Kohut initially felt it prudent to confine
the definition of the self to an important content of the
mental apparatus--i.e., as self-representations (images) of
the self that are located within the ego, the id, and the
superego (1971)--it was soon necessary for him to abandon
that restricted definition. The role of the constituents of
the self, the development of the cohesive self, and the
necessity for the comprehension of total configurations in
empathic closures all demanded a larger and wider role for
the self of psychoanalysis. The advancing work of self psychology has thus modified just what the self of psychoanalysis is, and the present version is a far cry from the simple
self image first considered by psychoanalysis.

Heinz Hartmann, in "Comments on the Psychoanalytic Theory of the Ego" (1950), attempted to clarify the psychoanalytic meaning of the self. He felt it necessary to first
distinguish the self (one's own person) as being in contradistinction to objects, and then further to oppose the ego
(a psychic system) in its contradistinction to other sub-
structures of the personality. It also usually seems necessary to remind ourselves that these cathexes were not those
of real people but of representations. As an Editor's note
in Freud's (1905) Three Essays on Sexuality states: "Freud
has in mind the mental presentations (Vofstelleinger) of objects and not, of course, objects in the external world" (p.
217). Next, Hartmann (1953) noted, in the "Contributions to
the Metapsychology of Schizophrenia," that these object relations must proceed from a lack of distinction between objects and activities to a later difference between the activity and the object toward which the activity is directed.
Ultimately, the self achieves a sharp distinction from the
objects as well.

What should have been a fairly clear and simple theoretical statement over the years seemed to lead to a series of
difficulties. In the first place, as we have seen, a person
can and should be considered to consist of both mind and
body as well as a network of social relationships. When
Kohut (1971) discovered the prevalent state of people using
other people as (functional) parts of themselves, he seemed
to corroborate what many non-analysts had said for many
years; and he likewise seemed to underscore the fact that
just as the mental self is by no means equivalent to the

physical self, the question of what a person consists of has
remained. Nowhere was this clearer than in his study of the
emergence of self-object transferences, which by their existence demanded a special definition for the self of psychoanalysis. These are recapitulations of normal development
wherein other people are felt to be functional parts of
one's self.

The second problem that Hartmann's (1953) statement
hoped to resolve, and that has also persisted, is the fact
that development does not seem to proceed to an ultimate
eradication of the continued functional use of objects as
selfobjects. Thus we are confronted with the issue of the
self of psychoanalysis really being the representation of
the person in terms of a multitude of functional and lasting
relationships with others. If we but take the next step
suggested by Roy Schafer (1968) and change the word "representation" (which often seems confused with a miniaturized
replica) to that of "idea", then the self is the idea which
one has of one's relationships with others--those who continue to sustain and support and satisfy.

The theoretician who has previously dealt most exhaus-
tively with the problems of the self vis-a-vis others has
been Edith Jacobson; her major work on The Self and the Object World (1964) was the natural successor to Hartmann's
initial clarifications. For Jacobson, the self was no more
than its representations, both physical and mental; and in
much of her book these representations were equated with
images or inner pictures of the person (perhaps a loose
translation of imago). From fusions with objects and distortions of images, she hoped to develop a clear and realistic inner picture of a separate self. Drives were predomi-
nant factors in self representations, and clear differen-
tiations from others were the goals achieved by drive regulation and neutralization. She faithfully followed the
position of Hartmann (that the self emerges only vis-a-vis
objects), and she is undoubtedly the founder of many object
relation theories which see the self and objects as composed
of a multitude of developing relationships. It is a simple
matter to transpose external happenings into an internal
stage of relationships, and much theory seems content with
the simplicity of this endeavor.

However, as further analytic work on the self was
pursued, it became evident that these self images were but

temporary printouts or readouts of very complex configura-
tions--much as a computer will deliver a reading that is but
a minute reflection of the internal network of activity.
The metaphor of the internal stages and the inner images often could not do justice to some (or most) of the complexities (see below). How, for example, does one picture or image a self which is dedicated to and idealizes the pursuit
of psychoanalytic knowledge? Certainly some complex configurations seem to demand detailed descriptions in language or
other modes of presentation. These complexities further direct one's attention to the very developmental processes inherent in the process of idealization. The advances that
Kohut offered in this area were to both delineate and describe the two major forms of narcissism (the grandiose self
and the idealized parental imago), as well as to detail the
changing steps of maturation of which each form was capable.
Thus representations become, more convincingly than ever,
not mere images but "ideas" about the self or--better, the
various meanings attributed to the self.

The other theoretical questions raised by a burgeoning
field of self psychology have to do with problems that have
long troubled psychoanalysis in that our concepts are felt
to be scientifically weak and tend to propose entities where
none exist. Rather than address this entire issue as it
involves the analytic field, my orientation will mainly concentrate on the supposed reification of the self. Of
course, we must grant any science its use of metaphors and a
corresponding construction of hypothetical entities. We
also should realize that entity-construction is often a later, rather than earlier, stage of scientific growth (Moore
1957). Our initial task is to concentrate on the self of
psychoanalysis and to separate it from those of sociology
and anthropology. As analysts, we must grasp the comprehen-
siveness of the person with both its phenomenological and
its unconscious position; and we must delineate the nature
of the matrix of relationships that leads to the emergence
of this entity. The self of psychoanalysis should be defined on the basis of analytically derived data.

As Loewald (1978) says: "If we use the term object relations for any and all psychic interactions of objectively
distinguishable human beings, regardless of whether or not
instincts and ego are differentiated from object, then the
primary datum for a genetic, psychoanalytic psychology would
be object relations. This relatedness is the psychic matrix

out of which intrapsychic instincts and ego, and extrapsy-
chic object, differentiate." Self psychology, more than any
other aspect of psychoanalytic inquiry, is fundamentally involved with the meaning of these relationships. But self
psychology also insisted on an analytic rather than interpersonal definition of object relationships.

No doubt many psychoanalysts will balk at this growth
of the self in terms of its inclusiveness, as well as its
possible tendency to become a social or interpersonal phenomenon rather than an intrapsychic one. Kohut was among
the first psychoanalysts to insist on the distinction between interpersonal and analytic data, and thus he sharpened
the difference between the self and identity (1971). The
latter is a social phenomenon which is not a focus in analytic treatment, while the self of psychoanalysis reveals
itself only in the analytic experience. Fortunately, psychoanalysis can turn to its own data to focus and clarify
these problems.

The crucial clinical question which analysts must address is whether or not any form of selfobject transference
does exist; it must then be determined whether or not this
is modified by the analytic process. This will determine
the first step of a self formed vis-a-vis others. Some analysts seem to accept the first point; but they insist that
such transferences either are unaffected by analysis or
else, when effectively handled, can move onto a clearer separation of the self from the object. The latter point pre-
serves some distinction between narcissism and object love,
but again one is soon clinically confronted with a change or
maturation in the selfobject relationship without the clear
distinction or separation of the object that was felt theo-
retically essential. Here again one must struggle with the
clinical evidence to support or deny the position of narcissism having a developmental path of its own. Thus the one
problem—that of separation, and eventual autonomous existence—has become modified by self psychology to that of a
maturation of the selfobject, to that of the self as composed of permanent units of relationships.

Other analytic theorists, in their efforts to move away
from the strict conceptualizations of psychic structure as
suggestive of space-occupying entities, have argued for a
grouping of functions which places action and activity in
the forefront of mental life. As Loewald (1978) has stated,

such groupings tend to ignore the fact that we should and do treat structures as organizations rather than as mere collections, and thus we need to insist that our structures have properties which go beyond their individual and grouped functions. The self of psychoanalysis, as considered in self psychology, is thus a collective noun. It includes a variety of functions having to do with self esteem regulation, but it likewise has properties and features of its own. Though it may suffer the popular fate of being reified or anthropomorphized, it is primarily a generalization derived from a wide group of observable empirical data. Of course, an attempt at definition should not lead us to fall prey to the error of believing that a clarification of our scientific language alone can resolve our lack of knowledge. Only further investigations are capable of expanding our vision to make sense of our data.

To recall the empirical versus the conceptual problem of a self definition, most psychoanalysts would seem to agree that self representations are the changing and varied concepts of one's person. We now can reconsider the troublesome question of deciding just what a person (not a physical body) may be. We often are warned against positioning this person as a tiny homunculus inside our head who will direct, as well as experience, life for us. Unfortunately, this latter form of explanation does seem prevalent, especially among object relations theorists; and it has the above-mentioned seductive appeal of merely transposing external events into internal theater. However, relations are not merely what goes on between people, but rather the significances and meanings that become attached to the goings-on.

As noted the use of the metaphor of the internal stage, or the drama of inner persons in interaction, runs the danger of psychoanalysis adopting a form of role theory—albeit an internal one—for its underpinnings. Psychoanalysis never has been content with the position of role theory, which concentrates on overt or manifest roles or behavioral criteria and which thereupon ignores the unconscious components of behavior. Although we do enrich this theory by including unconscious roles, we may still inhibit a comprehension of the range of complexity of the experience. If, for example, a student speaks to a teacher or a patient questions a doctor, usually we can perceive that these obvious roles may conceal the fact that a child-parent relationship also is in

gear. In fact, this insight of the implicit role of a participant in any sort of meaningful relationship was the
first great revelation of psychoanalytic psychology and over
the years has become commonplace. When we add to this very
general orientation those particulars of the relationship
having to do with development, we take the next great step
that analysis has to offer to this picture of the hidden
roles being enacted—i.e., just what sort of a child is
lurking in the shadows? Yet, not until we investigate the
nature of the exchange do we ever feel that we become true
analytic investigators.

Of course, merely watching the person's interacting is
never sufficient. Adding the components of language, nuance, gesture, etc., serves to enlarge the range of comprehension. But we ultimately ask just what effect does one
person have upon another? What are the feelings involved?
How does the one person expect to alter and be altered by
the other? In brief, we ask the nature of the personal experience or the subjective meaning of the interchange. The
hidden role of the child talking to a parent simply does not
reveal the form of data that is of analytic interest; but it
is, rather, an aid to orienting one in the determination of
what this person must feel as both student or patient plus
child in this interaction. Thus, role theory is notoriously
limited for psychoanalysis, and to say that the internal
drama is the real story of the external one still necessitates that one ask just what the story is and not merely who
the actors are. One must take the step demanded by the complexity of this exchange to investigate it as a theory of
meaning which is more comprehensive than that of inner actors who both replicate and complicate the happenings of the
external world. But now that we have given up the use of a
theory of internal roles, we must better explain just what
the relations that comprise the self consist of. As a preliminary to that we will try to clarify the difference between our empirical facts, the generalizations from these
facts, and the thing we employ to organize our facts.

Kohut (1977) says that the self of psychoanalysis is a
generalization derived from empirical observation. One
therefore must first determine the nature of these observations, and only then can one make general statements about
them. Thus, an attempted definition of the self of psychoanalysis first must deal with the question of just what are
the data or the "facts" of this field. Are they observa-

tions, as the word is usually understood? Although analysts
certainly perceive people in interaction, this is not cus-
tomarily what is studied or discovered in analysis.

It may be necessary to begin by differentiating a generalization from an abstraction. The former is a statement
that applies to a number of things and covers them all, to
some extent. It is non-specific but it is immediate. Thus,
a generalization from empirical observation is a grouping of
such observations. The latter term, abstraction, takes a
step away from the immediate experience and has no single
referent at all. "All dogs have tails" is a generalization
that may or may not be true. "The dog of the future" is an
abstraction that may be an ideal or a dream, but is not
readily verifiable. Unfortunately, as we have seen in our
list, psychoanalysis has alternated in the study of the
self, both claiming it to be an object of study or a unit
(i.e., an empirical fact) and simultaneously positing it as
an abstraction--an abstraction of theory. Of course, there
is no reason that it cannot be both, but this is possible
only if a clear differentiation is made first.

The next step is to consider the material or the data
of analysis. Inasmuch as it deals with the inner life of a
person rather than obvious external or behavioral manifestations, one must consider what is examined in terms of the
internal milieu. Ricoeur (1977) initially said that analysis does not deal with facts. He later decided that "reports" are the data of analysis. Modell (1978) states that
analysis deals with affects. Kohut (1971) says that analysis deals with complex mental states. It seems that the analyst gains access to the inner psychology of another person
by responding to what that person experiences or says (s)he
experiences or feels to be the "real" experience. It might
be better put to say that analysis deals with messages, part
of a communicative network. The messages of an analysis are
in the nature of the exchange between the involved parties
and may allow for general statements about them, and/or they
may, in turn, be cast into a series of abstract comments
about them. First there are the generalizations from these
messages, and then the abstractions. The latter stake out
the theory. It also is necessary for us to add the basic
equipment of a theory in order to comprehend how one listens
to or codes or organizes the messages. The suggested way to
think of a theory is as a statement-picture complex (Harre
1976). The required ingredient for such a complex is the

imagining of some kind of a model or pictorial image which helps in the visualization of the process being studied. Of course, psychoanalysis has a variety of such models and these are very much like the use of metaphors which serve to describe and redescribe the examined data.

The models of psychoanalysis are tools of epistemology. They belong to the class of models which Harre (1976, p. 53) calls "modal transform". These are simply those for which the phenomena and the model are identical; they are data restated via a model, or perhaps merely different ways of viewing the world. They usually are not causal models, such as seen in a machine, but rather are of the form "light of a certain wavelength yields a certain color" variety--that is, an interpretation or translation from one mode to another.

Employing a picture to aid in the use of a theory lends the analogue component to the digital message-exchange or digital component; and thus each aspect, sentence and picture, allows us to capture or redescribe the process of the psychoanalytic dialogue.

At another step in constructing a theory for analysis, we may choose a different kind of a theory, one which attempts to model causes of mental states. This usually is a developmental theory which has a sequence of models with the implicit statement of prior models yielding to, or causing, subsequent ones in the sequence. But we always need a theory, a set of data and generalizations about the data.

The self of psychoanalysis thus can be studied as a sequence of models. In terms of the employed models, it is a theory; and in terms of the empirical presentations, it is the primary data of that theory. To fulfill the requirements of the psychoanalytic self, we thus follow--via the data obtained introspectively--the varied presentations of the self as part of a network of relationships. Whenever we break into the system of relations, we use a model and/or a set of sentences; but the elusive self remains but a point in the system of which we are a part, and thus it is always artificially or only partially able to be seen. One needs to conceptualize the psychological self as the functionally or operationally separate focus of various relations, which relations are always part of a psychological matrix. To recapitulate: our models are our theory which enable us to gather data about the self which is posited as composed of

relationships. These are, however, the relationships obtained and formed in, and according to, a psychoanalytic
perspective. The next step in the effort to delineate the
forms of the self of analysis is one of describing the nature of the relationships that compose it.

RELATIONS AS THE SELF MATRIX

Once one enters upon a consideration of relationships
as part of the enormous variety of human interactions, there
seems to be an infinity of such possibilities. Relationships are familial, chronological, spatial, etc. And once
one leaves the arena of concrete relationships for one of
conceptual interactions, the problem seems doubly compli-
cated.

Freud saw relationships between people as based primarily and exclusively on drive satisfaction (i.e., need or
wish and gratification). He also saw objects as being of
two kinds: anaclitic or basically narcissistic. The trans-
position of these general principles to the psychoanalytic
setting involves the analyst assessing how he/she is being
experienced in terms of drive gratification or frustration,
and also in what form of object relationship he/she is
viewed. The additional insights of self psychology have enlarged the vision of the narcissistic object to one experienced as part of the self. It has also switched the consideration of libido to that of an entirely psychological consideration. This is to say that narcissistic libido now is
equivalent to self experience and no longer is confused with
a concrete or measurable form of assessment. Thus, the self
of psychoanalysis becomes one restricted to the analytic
process and whatever one employs as the theory of analysis,
and it thereupon emerges as one basis of analytic data. The
kinds of relationships evoked by this orientation are conve-
niently divided into two categories: similarity or contiguous with the self, or different or separate from the self.
This is no more than a translation of Freud's categories.
This corresponds to the dual types of relationships in communication, which are noted either as supplementary (more of
the same) or complimentary (more of the other). Such a bi-
nary division of relationships runs through much of social
science theory, from Freud to Levi-Strauss, and of course is
only a beginning kind of categorization.

The particulars of these relationships, as seen in psychoanalysis, again depend on the evidence gathered from analysis and again become organized via an analytic theory. Too familiar to be repeated here, these are primarily organized developmentally. For example, if a self experience arising in analysis elicits a mirroring relationship, it is part of the relationship and is posited on a similar childhood experience. Reconstruction of these developmental stages lends itself to a progressive or sequential theory which has causal properties.

The self of psychoanalysis is a construction seen developmentally and arising out of relationships. A theory of such development allows the investigator access to the varied manifestations which are grasped empirically. These are all mental phenomena and lend themselves to psychological studies of meaning. Fortunately or not, the analytic self, however, is not the social person. It is a focus in message-exchange. But these messages are over time, from one physical person to another, and from one psychic system to the next. Thus it becomes the vehicle of meaning; the study of the self allows analysis to travel the road to a psychology of meaning.

Meaning can be followed in a developmental sequence as a series of self models, which are based on relationships, is scrutinized. However, the models of the self must be those that offer a perception of such relations that go beyond a mere repetition of persons interacting in a social sphere. They are psychoanalytic models which serve the data of analysis. Such a task is one which awaits the psychoanalytic investigator who, once satisfied with the place of the self in psychoanalysis, now embarks on the even more formidable effort of determining what meaning is. The combined efforts of philosophy and psychology will once again need to be called upon, but once again the psychoanalyst will need to demonstrate that not all serviceable definitions in one discipline are easily exchanged for another.

REFERENCES

Federn, P. 1926. Ego Psychology and the Psychoses (ed. by E. Weiss), New York: Basic Books.
Feigl, H. (editor). 1958. Concepts, Theories and the Mind-Body Problem. Minneapolis: University of Minnesota Press.

Freud, S. 1905 ed./repr. 1953. Three Essays on the Theory
    of Sexuality. Standard Edition, 7:135-243. Lon-
    don: Hogarth Press.
Goldberg, A. 1980. Advances in Self Psychology. New York:
    International Universities Press.
Harre, R. 1976. "The Constructive Role of Models". In The
    Use of Models in the Social Sciences (ed. by
    L. Collins), London: Tavistock.
Hartman, H. 1950. "Comments on the Psychoanalytic Theory
    of the Ego". In Essays on Ego Psychology. New
    York: International Universities Press, 1964,
    pp. 113-44.
Hartman, H. 1953. "Contributions to the Metapsychology of
    Schizophrenia". In Essays on Ego Psychology.
    New York: International Universities Press, 1964,
    pp. 182-206.
Jacobson, E. 1964. The Self and the Object World. New
    York: International Universities Press.
Klein, M. 1937. Love, Hate and Reparation. London: Insti-
    tute of Psychoanalysis and Hogarth Press.
Kohut, H. 1971. The Analysis of the Self. New York: In-
    ternational Universities Press.
Kohut, H. 1977. The Restoration of the Self. New York:
    International Universities Press.
Langer, S. 1967. Mind: An Essay in Human Feeling. Vol. 1.
    Baltimore: The Johns Hopkins Press.
Loewald, H. 1978. "Instinct Theory, Object Relations and
    Psychic-Structure Formation". Journal of the
    American Psychoanalytic Association, 26:493-506.
Margolis, J. 1977. "Proposal Toward a Theory of Persons".
    In Science and Psychoanalysis (ed. by R. Stern,
    L.S. Horowitz and J. Lyons), New York: Haven,
    pp. 87-102.
Mead, G.H. 1934. Mind, Self, and Society. Chicago: Uni-
    versity of Chicago Press.
Mischel, T. (editor). 1977. The Self. Totown, N.J.: Row-
    man and Littlefield.
Modell, A. 1978. "The Nature Of Psychoanalytic Knowledge".
    Journal of the American Psychoanalytic Associa-
    tion, 26:641-58.
Moore, M.S. 1957. "Some Myths About 'Mental Illness'".
    Archives of General Psychiatry, 33:1483-97.
Piaget, J. & Inhelder, B. 1966. The Psychology of the
    Child. New York: Basic Books.

Ricoeur, P. 1977. "The Question of Proof in Freud's Psychoanalytic Writings". Journal of the American Psychoanalytic Association, 25:835-71.

Rubinstein, B. 1965. "Psychoanalytic Theory and the Mind-Body Problem". In Psychoanalysis and Current Biological Thought (ed. by W.S. Greenfield & W.C. Lewis), Madison: University of Wisconsin Press, pp. 35-56.

Schafer, R. 1968. Aspects of Internalization. New York: International Universities Press.

Strawson, P.F. 1979. Individuals: An Essay in Descriptive Metaphysics. London: Methuen.

Wilden, A. 1972. System and Structure. London: Tavistock.

Wolheim, R. 1973. "The Mind and the Mind's Image of Itself". In Art and the Mind (ed. by R. Wolhelm), London: Allen Lane, pp. 31-53.

COMMENTS ON HEINZ KOHUT'S CONCEPTUALIZATION

OF A BIPOLAR SELF

Ernest S. Wolf,

I

More than twenty years have passed since the publication, in 1959, of Kohut's defining paper "Introspection, Empathy and Psychoanalysis". After that, many developments
had to take place in the growth of psychoanalytic theory and
in the expanding scope of psychoanalytic treatment before
Kohut arrived at what he calls the psychology of the self
and what he conceptualizes as the Bipolar Self. To begin
with, I would like to go back, briefly, to that 1959 paper
on empathy and introspection. For the issues raised at that
time are, to this day, the focus around which pivots the
controversial aspect of Kohut's subsequent work on narcissism and the self. On the one hand, an acceptance of
Kohut's 1959 definition of psychoanalysis makes the emergence of the self and self theory an almost foregone conclusion, a kind of inevitable development; on the other
hand, a rejection of the major defining premises of the 1959
statement on empathy just as inevitably leads to a rejection
of most of the conceptualizations advanced by Kohut during
the last twenty years.

What was the essence of that 1959 paper? It was a
"crucial shift in redefining the psychoanalytic method", as
Ornstein (see Kohut 1978, p. 28) calls it. Ornstein noted
that Kohut's shift of emphasis from the investigation of the
external world with our sense organs to an emphasis of investigating the inner world through introspection and empathy is an innovation. It was innovative, in that it made
explicit and defined the essential core of the psychoanalytic method as it had been created by Anna O., Breuer, and
Freud. And it was innovative in its explicit contrast of
the method of natural science (the collection of data by
extrospective observation of the world around us) with the

23

method of psychoanalytic science (the collection of data by
introspective observation of the world inside of us).

It was no small part of Freud's genius to be able to
combine an essentially idealistic personality--think, for
instance, of Freud's idealization of Moses, Hannibal, Cer-
vantes, Shakespeare, and of the values of truth and beauty--
with the convictions of a committed positivistic and materi-
alistic science. Freud was thus able to shape his introspective psychoanalytic insights into the forms of a nineteenth century positivistic theory. In some of the post-
Freudian theory-building in psychoanalysis, the introspective psychoanalytic core was lost--leaving a shell of highly
intellectual but sterile rationalizations built upon the
master's fundamental insights. The resultant widening gap
between psychoanalytic theory and clinical practice in psychoanalysis was noted by many analysts, particularly by
M. Klein, Winnicott, and the English object-relations school
of psychoanalysts. But Kohut's achievement, starting in
1959, has been to create a new synthesis between the core
data and the basic theory of psychoanalysis, a synthesis
which makes explicit the sine qua non of introspective-
empathic data for any theory that was to be called psychoanalytic.

By positing the central role of introspective-empathic
data-collection in the psychoanalytic method, Kohut has in
fact implied a theory of observation as primary to all other
psychoanalytic theorizing.   This is not the place to spell
out Kohut's theory of observation, but an elaboration of it
would have to include: 1. a statement about man's introspective potential in analogy to the potential that develops into the five extrospective senses; 2. a statement about the
trainability of introspection analogous to the trainability
of the auditory sense (e.g., compare the untutored ear with
that of the musician's) to the trainability of vision (e.g.,
compare what a freshman medical student can "see" when he
first looks into a microscope with what the trained micros-
copist can "see"); 3. a statement about the appropriate cognitive processing of the discriminatively trained perceptions into a systematic classification, into a systematic
theory that is ruled by the senses and yet goes beyond them.
Man is gradually developing such systematic theories in mu-
sic, in literature, in the visual arts, and in psychology.
The latter is called psychoanalysis.   The psychoanalyst's
felt kinship with the artist thus is not based on their sup-

posed common lack of scientific method, but on a common inclusion of introspective-empathic data in their diverse
paths to the truth.

What are the consequences for psychoanalysis of Kohut's
theory of observation, of explicitly positing the introspective-empathic method of data-collection into the center?
Kohut has shown that free association and the analysis of
resistances are not the basic tools of psychoanalysis, but
are to be considered auxiliary instruments employed in the
service of the introspective and empathic mode of observation. These auxiliary instruments—namely, free association
and resistance analysis—free introspective observations
from previously unrecognized distortions, and thus led
Kohut, as early as 1959, to state that in the narcissistic
disorders, persistent introspection leads to the recognition
of an unstructured psyche struggling to maintain contact
with an archaic object or to keep up the tenuous separation
from it. Here the analyst is not the screen for the projection of internal structure (transference) but instead the
vehicle for the direct continuation of an early reality that
was too distant, too rejecting, or too unreliable to be
transformed into solid psychic structures. The analyst is,
therefore, introspectively experienced within the framework
of an archaic interpersonal relationship (Kohut 1959).
Thus, in retrospect, we can see the emergence of what today
we call the psychology of the self.

Let me give a brief clinical illustration to demonstrate the difference between an approach through introspection and empathy and one based on theory. Imagine a
fourteen-year-old girl who had arranged to watch a town-
square procession from the place of business of a couple who
are friends of her father. Upon arriving at the place of
business, the girl found that only the husband was
present—he was a man in his forties—and he asked her to
wait while he went outside to lower the shutters. When he
returned, he suddenly "clasped the girl to him and thrust a
kiss upon her lips".

Now, try to be introspective and empathic with this
fourteen-year-old who had never before been approached, and
ask yourself: What did she experience? Was she startled?
Excited? Sexually aroused? Frightened? Embarrassed? En-
raged? Erotically stimulated? I've asked a number of people—men and women—this question; and the consensus seems

to be that the girl probably would be aware of being startled, perhaps of being a little frightened, perhaps somewhat
embarrassed, and after a short while she probably would be
aware of some anger at the sudden unexpectedness of the
attack, an apparent betrayal by a trusted friend of the
family.

By now most of you will have recognized this little
vignette as the episode of the kiss (Freud 1905, p. 28) from
Freud's famous case history of Dora. Dora told Freud that
she experienced a feeling of disgust. Freud, who usually
was a most introspective and empathic analyst, could not
empathize with Dora. He wrote: "This was surely just the
situation to call up a distinct feeling of sexual excitement
in a girl of fourteen who had never before been approached".
And then he went on to say: "I should without question consider a person hysterical in whom an occasion for sexual
excitement elicited feelings that were preponderantly or
exclusively unpleasurable".

It was clear that Freud was not thinking of a young
girl, of a person, of a self in a particular situation--a
situation which may be experienced as a frightening attack,
or maybe as a humiliating assault, or maybe as a stimulating
intimacy, etc. He was thinking only of a nubile sexual apparatus which, in proximity to an arousing sexual stimulus,
failed to respond with sexual excitement. It is as if the
girl were merely an appendage to her sexual apparatus, and
therefore Freud was bound to diagnose the failure to respond
with pleasurable excitement as a kind of pathology, as hys-
teria. In this rare instance, Freud was not empathic with
the girl; he put theory first, the theory that the sexual
instincts are at the basis of most psychopathology. In all
likelihood, Freud was correct in postulating at least a degree of sexual arousal as a result of a kiss--even under the
most adverse circumstances. But awareness of such arousal
will appear only under favorable conditions. The disgust
experienced by Dora had little to do with whatever sexual
arousal may or may not have occurred. Her disgust was the
appropriate response to the betrayal of her trust. Erikson
(1963) has discussed this issue; and Freud's countertrans-
ference has been noted not only by others but, with his usual honest self-examination, Freud admits that he did not
succeed in mastering the transference in good time (Freud
1905, p. 118).

All that, however, is peripheral to the issue of how best to understand clinical material. We all agree that one cannot make observations without some theoretical commitment to guide the selection and interpretation of data. Classical psychoanalytic theory is a reliable guide for the study of the vicissitudes of sexuality, particularly when distorted sexuality determines the psychopathology, as it does in the psychoneuroses. The psychology of the self however, in studying the total subjective experience of the self, is based on a shift in focus from being empathic with the driveness of sexuality to being empathic with the self. I would venture to say that an empathic listener to Dora would have understood her feeling of disgust as an appropriately angry response under the given circumstances. Freud's assumption of a sexual arousal and his interpretation of the repression (or to be more specific, the reversal of this arousal into disgust) are not necessarily wrong but are peripheral and irrelevant to the issue at hand—to the girl's main concern, to what had brought her into treatment, to what she wanted from Freud.

II

These historical observations may mislead some into assuming that the psychology of the self emerged out of theoretical considerations. However, nothing would be further from the facts. While it is clear that very significant changes in classical psychoanalytic theory have become necessary, and while the psychology of the self is developing a body of new theory, the initial impetus for the new conceptualizations grew out of clinical experience—and, specifically, clinical difficulties. Kohut noticed that some patients just did not respond as expected to the interpretation of their defenses and of their drives. They continued to resist and insist that the analyst did not understand them or that he did not really listen. Finally, after some intense internal struggle, Kohut recognized that these patients were actually telling him something to which he had not really listened yet; and empathically he began to notice the fragile self-esteem of these analysands, their great vulnerability and sensitivity which made them become so guarded against extending the expected libidinal transferences to the analyst. He also began to note a different, more archaic, kind of attachment these analysands had to the analysts—very much like transferences in that they were also reactivations of infantile patterns of relationships transferred from the parent of infancy to the analyst of the here-and-now.

These observed transferences clustered themselves into two groups: the mirror transferences and the idealizing transferences, as Kohut designated them. The common aim of all of these transferences was to elicit from the analyst responses which would result in the analysand's narcissistic enhancement. Therefore, collectively, Kohut designated them the narcissistic transferences. The variety of mirror transferences are the revival of a childhood need for confirmation of the child's innate sense of vigor, greatness, and perfection; the idealizing transferences are the reactivation of a childhood need to look up and merge into a source of calmness, infallibility, and omnipotence. For example, in the mirror transference, the child reactivates his need to have experienced himself as the apple of his mother's eye; while in the idealizing transference, the child reactivates the need he had to feel himself part of that god-like parent.

For example, an analysand's constant demand for attention was expressed by him in the obviously unusual patterns and colors of the clothes he wore; another manifestation was his habit of compelling my attention by frequently starting the analytic hour with an arrogantly depreciatory comment about me or my office. Yet, at the same time, he was also always very fearful that I might not be listening to every word. He would accuse me of inattention when I moved my chair; and frequently, if I were silent too long, he would directly ask me what I was thinking. To think that my mind was off somewhere, or on someone else, was terribly upsetting to him. Only gradually did we begin to understand that this imperative need to be constantly looked at and listened to was a reassertion of a childhood need that had been distorted and amplified by a maternal hostility and neglect.

He had been born in Central Europe, the second son of a very unhappy mother. Before her marriage to a wealthy businessman, she had been an entertainer; and to her children she was always a beautiful, glamorous, but flighty and self-centered, woman. The upheavals of World War II forced an emigration into poverty and loss of social position. In the surroundings of the new country, the youngster experienced his father as weak, ineffectual, and incompetent—yet

puritanically moralistic. As an idealizable model of manli-
ness or as a source of warmth and closeness, the father was
no longer available to his children. The mother reacted to
the changed circumstances not with collapse, like the
father, but by increasing concern for herself, for her own
psychic wounds, and for her need to be the center of attention in rebuilding a social position. Neither parent was
able to mobilize much empathic insight for the other nor for
the needs of their children. As far as my analysand is concerned, the details of isolated incidents during his childhood are not nearly as important as the chronic, pervasive
milieu that denied him the confirmation of his worth by pa-
rading in front of him his father's impotence and his mother's attention-getting flashiness, while at the same time
ignoring his own legitimate strivings for recognition and
for merger with some idealizable strength. The patient and
I learned to understand this very well, and we also learned
to understand the meaning of his insistent need to get from
me what he had missed as a child. I have mentioned the manifestation in the transference of his need for mirroring recognition. Gradually over several years of analytic working
through, which included my acceptance and understanding of
his need without gratifying it, we slowly saw a change oc-
curing so that eventually he could feel comfortable even if
I didn't hear something he had said or even if I didn't
smile when he first greeted me.

At a later stage in this patient's analysis, an idealizing transference became prominent. The father's collapse,
after emigration, into a moralistic but weak and ineffectual
husband and father had robbed this youngster of a needed
masculine imago to look up to and to make part of himself.
Gradually, and again against the fiercest resistance motivated by fear of eventual disappointment in me, he began to
secretly endow me with some of the qualities that his father
lacked--all the while hiding his idealization under a cover
of scathing criticism of my bourgeois tastes and my non-
aristocratic lineage. Yet, in his speech and manner of
dealing with people, he began to imitate me by incorporating
into his own behavior and thinking my style and what he believed to be my attitudes and ways of thinking. Begrudging-
ly, as he began to feel better and function better, he
granted that perhaps I might really be helping him. One
small incident, by itself unimportant, was rather revealing.
We were making vacation plans, and he could not understand
my rigidity about the date of my departure on vacation until

I mentioned my being constrained by the schedule of the
charter airline I had planned to use. This little piece of
knowledge about me precipitated an outburst of contempt and
rage. He felt deeply disappointed in me because, by using a
charter rather than a regular airline, I had suddenly become
weak and incompetent in his eyes. Charters are for poor
people, for people who have lost their freedom of action;
and in his eyes I had suddenly become like the collapsing
weak father who was no longer available to his son as a
source of needed psychological strength. The disruption of
the idealizing transference that had occurred was rather
typical of the inevitable transference disruptions that
characterize the analytic process in the disorders of the
self. Such disruptions provide the opportunity for working
along with the opportunity for transmuting internalization
which lead to the gradual accretion of new psychic structure
that repairs the defects in psychic structure acquired during childhood and thus restores strength and cohesion to the
self.

I have gone into some detail to avoid some rather
common misunderstandings. Let me stress that acceptance,
explanation, and interpretation of a transference to the an-
alyst--whether the transference is narcissistic or whether
it is libidinal--does not constitute gratification. I have
heard, for example, that some colleagues believe that analysts working within the Kohutian framework gratify their
patients' grandiosity with praise and that their own grandiosity is gratified by encouraging the patient's admiration
of the analyst. I have also heard that because we are attempting to be empathic and understanding, we make it difficult for negative, hostile transference reactions to come to
the surface. Some people seem to worry that analytic abstinence has been replaced by a love-thy-patient morality. I
hope in the above example to have succeeded in laying to
rest some of these misunderstandings. To understand and to
accept an intense transference reaction as a revival of a
then-legitimate childhood need means neither approval nor
gratification, nor does it mean that the analyst attempts to
make up for what was missed earlier in life. It simply
means that the analyst understands the inevitability of the
need, given the specific historical circumstances, and
therefore the analyst does not add insult to injury by lec-
turing about or even condemning it. While one may question
the accuracy and even the actuality of the reconstructed
historical events of the analysand's childhood, the analyst

and the analysand at the same time gain a conviction about
the power and about the significance of the experienced past
as it emerges from memory and associations into a reconstructed whole.

Let me now return to Kohut's discovery of the narcissistic transferences. He also noted that when he began to
understand his patients' reactions as the revival of archaic
infantile needs, the patients began to calm down and there
was a diminution of symptoms together with an increased
feeling of well-being and of self-esteem as well as improved
functioning. To put it colloquially, the patients felt like
themselves again. Kohut explained these observations by
postulating that these analysands had come into analysis
with a deficient psychological structure at the center of
their personalities, i.e., with a deficient self. The analyst (through his interest, his empathy, and his understanding) creates an ambiance in which the analysand's self feels
confirmed and restored to a former state of completeness and
cohesion. The patient has formed a relationship to the analyst in which aspects of the analyst are experienced as part
of the patient's self. Objects which are experienced as
part of the self are termed selfobjects by Kohut. Thus the
analyst becomes the selfobject for the analysand.   Selfob-
jects--by virtue of their being experienced as part of the
self--lend cohesion, vigor, and harmony to the self.   The
mirror and idealizing transferences are transference relationships in which the analyst has become a selfobject for
the analysand. Kohut, therefore, now terms these selfobject
transferences.

When selfobject transferences are firmly established,
the analysand's self feels strengthened and his feeling of
well-being improves. When the inevitable lapses in empathy
on the part of the analyst (or other vicissitudes) disrupt
the selfobject transference, then the analysand experiences
an increase in symptomatic discomfort since the disrupted
relationship is experienced also as a fragmentation or depletion of the self. A diligent and empathic examination of
the psychological situation of both analyst and analysand
will usually reveal the causes for the disruption of the
transference and restore it to its previous level of selfobject tie concomitant with a restoration of the self's cohesion. Working through consists of repeated episodes of disruption and restoration, with a gradual accretion of new

structure to the self by the process of transmuting internalization.

It is through this same process of transmuting internalization associated with the vicissitudes of the selfobject's transactions of childhood that the self first emerges during the second year of life, goes through a phase of fragile vulnerability, and, finally, through accretion, gains enough strength to reach a level of relatively irreversible cohesion around the age of eight years. The selfobjects of childhood are, of course, usually the parents--and specifically during the earliest months, usually the mother. When reconstructing the early history of patients during analysis, one always finds instances of failure in the parental selfobjects to respond appropriately to the selfobject needs of the child. Probably one would find, in the history of any person, such failures of the parental selfobject to respond appropriately. However, such failures, even the grossly dramatic ones, by themselves are not what is most important in the pathogenesis of disorders of the self. Rather, it is the chronic, pervasive attitudes of the selfobject that constitutes a selfobject milieu which is decisive here. Occasional failures are not destructive; on the contrary, they may well turn into the episode of "optimal frustration" that stimulate the youngster to stretch his resources to the limit and himself take over some of the functions that had been performed by the selfobject.

But such wholesome experiences of optimal frustrations followed by expansion of the self through transmuting internalization require that the selfobject failure occur against a background of a generally healthy selfobject milieu, which means: 1. That the frustrating incident had been preceded by a period of experiences in which the child's need for mirroring and idealizable responses had been satisfactorily met, and 2. That the trauma of frustration is quantitatively within the bounds of stimuli that the child's still-fragile psyche can cope with--i.e., that the internal harmony becomes only slightly unbalanced, without bringing total functioning to a disruptive halt. It follows that one cannot give specific directions to parents or their surrogates about how to create an optimal ambiance in which their offspring can flourish. Rather, one has to leave it to the empathic perceptivity of the parent to judge the child's needs. Similarly, it is also quite clear that the parents' judgement, or lack of it, depends primarily on the harmonious balance of their own narcissistic strivings, on their own state of self. That is why Kohut stresses the importance of what the parents are over what the parents do, in analogy to what I said earlier about the analyst as a self-object.

Let me try to illustrate. Imagine a toddler running barefoot about the room; he stumbles over his shoes, falls, and painfully hurts himself. The sudden impact of stimuli overwhelms his fragile self and, to put it colloquially, he appears to come apart at the seams as he cries and struggles in seemingly uncontrolled and uncoordinated movements. His fragmenting self makes him a very frightened child. An equally frightened or a very self-involved mother might fail to respond appropriately to the child's need for a calming selfobject: a very frightened mother might herself become so disorganized by the sight of the hurt child that, unable to get herself together enough to pick him up soothingly, she only conveys to him her equally disorganized state of anxiety; the self-involved mother might not even notice the child's need, and show her annoyance because the child's crying threatens to invade the privacy of her own reverie. Each of these mothers, because of who she is, deprives the child of an opportunity to restore the cohesion of his self through interaction with an appropriately responsive selfobject. The mother who is appropriately in tune with the child, and whose own equanimity has perhaps been alerted but not destroyed by the child's distress, will pick up the youngster and hold him close so that the youngster will feel lifted up by strong arms and will experience the gentle calmness of her voice and the firm strength of her body infusing him until his own self acquires similar strength and calmness: he feels merged with the omnipotent parent image, the idealized selfobject.

Wholesome as this experience is for the child, it is perhaps too traumatic to illustrate the optimal frustration that leads to transmuting internalization. But let us follow the situation a little further. The mother now puts him down on the floor; and perhaps the youngster also feels put down figuratively, in the sense of a narcissistic injury, as the mother tries to put on his feet the very shoes over which he had stumbled. To the youngster, at that moment, the shoes may be the instruments of his humiliation; the destroyers of his newly acquired ability to walk, of his illusory omnipotence; the cause of his downfall. (I could not

resist the pun.) So, at the sight and touch of his shoes he
reexperiences, to a smaller degree, the frustration of his
omnipotent strivings; and he cries out in an explosion of
narcissistic rage. It is now that we get a glimpse into the
childhood milieu, a sample of the genetic ambiance in which
the child's self may either flourish or flounder. Leaving
behind the traumatic event of the child's fall, can the
mother now, through the quality of her relationship with her
child, convert the traumatic frustration associated with
putting on the shoes into an optimal frustration in which
the child can partake of some of her strength and make it
his own?

This illustration of some of the basic concepts of the
psychology of the self was perhaps excessively long. But
you may have noticed that there are certain parallels between the restoration of a child's feeling of well-being and
that of a patient in treatment. A child grows and develops
in interaction with the empathically tuned-in and responsive
parent. A patient may be restored to a feeling of well-being through the experience of the often silent selfobject
transference that is established by the mere presence of
the calm and empathic analyst. But, for the patient, such
transferences only establish the condition for the restoration of the patient's self. In order to fill in the structural defect, in order to heal the hurts of the past, there
also needs to be a working-through process which depends on
the ability of the patient and the therapist to convert the
inevitable traumatic frustrations of transference disruptions via interpretations and explanations into the optimal
frustrations that facilitate the formation of new psychic
structure.

                                III

The emergence of the self in childhood depends to a
great extent upon the quality of the interactions between
the child and his selfobjects. The self may emerge as a
healthy and firm structure or, if the interactions with the
selfobjects are chronically faulty, the self will emerge
either diffusely damaged or more seriously damaged in one or
more of its constituents. Even the very emergence of a self
depends at least partly on the interactions with the earliest selfobjects. One must assume that a newborn as yet possesses no self but only potentialities that may expand and

consolidate into a self. Yet the mother of the newborn relates to her baby as if he were already a virtual self, addressing the child in harmony with her fantasies and expectations. In this process, she encourages the development of
certain potentialities while causing the retardation and
even discarding of other self possibilities. The nuclear
self that emerges around 18 months, more or less, therefore,
is as much a creation of the interplay with the selfobject
milieu as it is a realization of inherent potentials. The
vulnerability of the emergent fragile self diminishes gradually, and normally the self attains a stable state of irreversible cohesion in early latency. Yet potentially destructive crises may still occur, particularly in adolescence and mid-life.

The adult self, depending on its selfobject history,
may thus exist in varying degrees of coherence, from cohesion to fragmentation; in states of varying degrees of vitality, from vigor to depletion; in varying degrees of harmony, from order to chaos. And the stability of the overall
self configuration may sometimes be bought at the price of
giving one of the constituents of the self undue weight and
emphasis, with the result of a distorted self-structure.
Examples of such persons with a strong but distorted and
perhaps brittle self, who would be considered pathological
only in a limited, perhaps nonclinical sense, are certain
charismatic or messianic leaders like a Churchill or a
Ghandi––the former self with an over-expanded pole of ambition, the latter self with an over-expanded pole of ideals.
Kohut finds that the self is made up of three major constituents: 1. a pole of ambition, from which emanates the basic
strivings for power and success; 2. a pole of values, which
harbors the basic ideals, and 3. an intermediate area of basic talents and skills. I have already mentioned charismatic and messianic personalities that represent hypertrophy of
one of the two poles of the bipolar self. However, I feel
that in contemporary society we facilitate the emergence of
selves whose poles are atrophied but whose mediating skills
and talents are in a state of overgrowth.

Western culture seems to have become a breeding ground
for corporate man, for the technologist who is neither very
ambitious for personal acclaim nor very much burdened by
values and ideals, whose sense of fulfillment is derived
from the competent exercise of skills and talents. Perhaps
we are witnessing the emergence of the man of the future.

However, I note the passing of the eccentric character with
some regret and some apprehension about the danger that a
society made up of skilled technocrats will lose much of
what humanity has valued in the past; I wonder whether such
individuals will also become an easy prey for the demagogic
leader who, by his charisma or messianism, fills the void at
the atrophied pole of this modern man's self.

But to return to our discussion of the structure of the
self, let me paraphrase Kohut's description of what the self
is. He describes the self as a generalization based on introspectively and empathically perceived mental phenomena,
not a concept of abstract science but a generalization from
the empirical data of depth psychology. The essence of the
self, its nature, is unknowable since the essence cannot be
differentiated from its manifestations by introspection.
But on the basis of the observable manifestations, one can
collect data and construct theories about the development of
the self, about types of the self, about the component constituents of the self, and about the vicissitudes of the
self.

The main vicissitude of the self is a faulty selfobject
milieu. When, as a result of such pathogenic selfobject relationships, the self fails to achieve cohesion or vigor or
harmony--or loses these qualities after they have been es-
tablished--then a state of disorder of the self may be said
to exist. Self disorders may be classified into primary and
secondary disturbances of the self. Secondary disturbances
of the self are the reactions of an essentially undamaged
self to the adversities of life, the victories and defeats
that bring joy or despair. Among the primary disturbances
of the self are the psychoses and borderline states which
are characterized by serious and protracted damage to the
self. Inherent biological factors combine with psychogenic
selfobject experiences in the etiology of the psychoses.
Schizophrenia probably is associated with a lack of even
minimally effective mirroring responses early in life.
Serious deprivation of joyful responses to the child's
aliveness will deplete it of self-esteem and leave a residual disposition toward severe empty depression of adult life.
Almost total deprivation of the experience of participating
in the calmness of an idealized adult will leave the person
without the psychological structures that can control inner
excitement, and he thus remains prey to the over-stimulation
of manic excitement.

The borderline states differ from the psychoses in that the central defect is covered over by defenses that make some selfobject relations possible while excluding those which would be experienced as excessively noxious or traumatic. Thus, while some borderline personalities protect themselves against the threatening traumatic closeness of others by withdrawal behind schizoid defenses, others protect themselves by surrounding themselves with the typical aura of suspicion and hostility of the paranoid.

The damage to the self is less severe and sometimes only temporary in the narcissistic behavior disorders. However, serious symptoms such as delinquency, perversion, or addiction expose these individuals to grave dangers.

Very similar but less dangerous to the patient are the narcissistic personality disorders. Here the self damage also is temporary, and the symptoms (such as hypochondria, depression, hypersensitivity to slights, lack of zest, etc.) are more related to the psychological state of the self than to the person's actions.

Of all the primary disorders of the self, only the last two groups--the narcissistic behavior disorders and the narcissistic personality disorders--are treatable by psychoanalysis, since their selves have sufficient cohesive capacity to tolerate, without serious reactions or fragmentation and depletion, the frustration of the working-through process with its potentially therapeutic optimal frustrations and disruptions of the transference.

Disorders of the self can also be classified according to the type of self pathology and its relationship to early selfobject experience.

Understimulated selves were deprived of stimulating responses from the selfobjects of childhood; they experience themselves as boring and are prone to use any means to create a pseudo-excitement to ward off feelings of deadness. Head banging among toddlers, compulsive masturbation in later childhood, daredevil activities of adolescence, frenzied sexual activities or lifestyles in adults, are examples of this. The substitution of pleasurable sensations in parts of the body is used to cover the core of empty depression.

Fragmenting selves lack sufficient integrating responses from the selfobjects of childhood; they experience
themselves as poorly coordinated, awkward, disoriented, perhaps hypochondriacal, generally anxious—especially after
rebuffs or slights, even minor ones.

Some overstimulated selves, because of the excess stimulation by the selfobjects of childhood, are fearful of the
excitement associated with their intense ambitions and fantasies of greatness. Therefore they are on guard against
the stimulation of being the center of attention. Other
overstimulated selves feel their intense need to merge with
an idealized selfobject and guard against the feared closeness to admired people. They also find it is difficult to
become enthusiastically interested in goals and ideals.

Overburdened selves are deficient in self-soothing capacity, due to early deprivation of opportunities for mer-
gers with calming selfobjects. Such individuals experience
the world as hostile and dangerous, and they react to noxious stimuli with narcissistic rage.

IV

In my discussion of psychoanalytic self psychology, I
have said hardly anything about libido, drives, and defenses. I have not mentioned the psychic apparatus with its
id, ego, and superego. You may well ask how the theories of
the self relate to classical psychoanalytic drive-and-de-
fense psychology, to narcissism, and to infantile sexuality?
What is the relationship between the disorders of the self
and the psychoneuroses and the character disorders?

Classical psychoanalytic theory postulates a basic biological substratum from which emanate the basic psychological drives. In particular the sexual drive (designated libido) and the aggressive drive are seen as the basic motiva-
tors of action in their striving towards discharge. The
psychic apparatus (conceptualized in id, ego, and superego)
tames and controls the primitive drives. Psychoneuroses are
conceptualized to result from failures and distortions of
this drive-versus-defense patterning of the psychic apparatus.

In the psychology of the self, biologically based drives are not seen as the basic psychological unit. Rather, the biologically based drives are conceptualized by Kohut as belonging to the pre-psychological elements that enter into the formation of the structured self. It is only when the self is unable to keep its component elements integrated within its complex structure that drive components emerge psychologically as a disintegration product of the self. It is then that the afflicted person experiences himself as driven by sexual or aggressive impulses. The phenomena of drives and defenses and the vicissitudes of neurotic illness are, therefore, viewed as secondary to the breakdown of a cohesive self.

This does not mean, however, that self psychology ignores the manifestations of the Oedipus complex that normally occur within the healthy cohesive self during the child's traversing the Oedipal phase. The normal healthy child with an integrated and cohesive self experiences the vicissitudes of Oedipal conflict as joyous and lustful, even when somewhat tense and anxious. From the point of view of the psychopathology of the disorders of the self, it is the excessive counter-sexuality or counter-aggression directed by the selfobjects in response to the normal manifestations of infantile sexuality which overstimulates and fragments the still fragile infantile selves. As a result, the components of healthy sensuality and self-assertiveness are torn out of the integrating matrix of the total self, and appear as overstimulated and distorted disintegration products. It is against these disintegration products that neurotic defenses come into play as the overstimulated self attempts to reconstitute its self around these fragments of driveness. In contrast, the understimulated self, far from defending against the sensual components of the disintegration products, uses sexuality to create a sense of aliveness--e.g., by perverse behavior.

I shall illustrate with an example. Let us assume a child whose mother has been attempting to train him to use the toilet for his bowel movements. Let us also assume that this is a healthily developing normal child and that within his young and still vulnerable self there are integrated the biologically based sexual and aggressive impulses that have reached an age-appropriate level of maturity, including the experience of pleasurable sensations in connection with the stimulation of his anal mucosa. One day this child deposits

some feces in the toilet, and proudly he calls his mother to
show her his great accomplishment. At this stage of the development of his self, the mother is still needed as a selfobject that confirms the child in its sense of perfection,
greatness, and value. The mother who is appropriately in
tune with her child's needs will probably acknowledge and
praise the new accomplishment. She will not be shocked by
the assertiveness of the child's behavior nor by the sensuality of his obvious pleasure. The child's self is
strengthened in interaction with the attuned mother; and the
child feels accepted, with the sense of well-being. However, a different sequence of events may ensue if the mother
is not properly attuned to the child's selfobject needs.
She may tell the child that she's too busy to come, and order him to flush the mess; perhaps she will come, and her
expressing disgust at the production will traumatically
shame the child; or perhaps she will just come, busily do
what is necessary to dispose of the matter, and return to
her other pressing responsibilities without much attention
to the proud achiever.

Decisive for the child's future, for the possible pre-
disposition to future neurotic illness, is whether the mother's responses injure the child's fragile self or strengthen
it. If the child's self is injured by the mother's lack of
responsiveness, the child's tendency to substitute anal
pleasures may fill the void. If the child's self is injured
by the mother's over-reaction, a different kind of anal fix-
ation may occur--for example, if the mother tries to get
control by the frequent administration of enemas. Perhaps
the child's self becomes so overstimulated, in that case,
that it takes recourse to neurotic defenses. Whether the
child can eventually enjoy the tensions of either normal or
perverse sexuality depends on many factors, among which the
cohesive strength of the self is an important one. But it
needs to be stressed again that it is not single selfobject
incidents but the pervasive selfobject milieu that determines the outcome.

The same general principles pertain, of course, also to
the normally occurring Oedipal phase of a child. The Oedipal phase will not become a pathological Oedipus complex--
i.e., the Oedipal phase of the child will not lead to a psy-
chopathological development--unless the selfobject milieu of
the child responds to the appropriate manifestation of the
child's aggression and sexuality with excessive counter-ag-

gression and excessive counter-sexuality instead of accepting the exuberance and sensuality as a step in the psychological development which may be controlled but should not
be crushed. The father who can see in his Oedipal son a
"chip off the old block" or a mother who can vicariously enjoy some of her Oedipal child's seductiveness are not likely
to sow the seeds of future neurotic illness.

In the foregoing, I have outlined some of the aspects
of the continuity of psychoanalytic psychology of the self
with classical psychoanalysis. I wish I could similarly
outline the relation of Kohut's contribution to the many
other contributions to self psychology that have been made
by Adler, Jung, Rank, Hartmann, Bibring, Horney, Sullivan,
Winnicott, Rapapport, Lichtenstein, George Klein, Annie
Reich, Edith Jacobson, Jacques Lacan, Mahler, Kernberg, and
many others. I hope the length of this list is sufficient
justification for not attempting to place Kohut's work into
contextual relation to other psychologists of the self.
Like any scientist, Kohut has built on the shoulders of his
predecessors. I will venture the view, however, that Kohut
has created a new and original synthesis, a systematic integration into a new theoretical framework which gives new
impetus to our struggling but very much alive young science
of psychoanalysis.

REFERENCES

Erikson, E. 1950. Childhood in Society. 2nd ed., 1963,
        New York: Norton.
Freud, S. 1905. "Fragment of an Analysis of a Case of Hys-
        teria". In Standard Edition, VII (1957, London:
        Hogarth Press), pp. 15-122.
Kohut, H. 1959. "Introspection, Empathy and Psychoanaly-
        sis". Journal of the American Psychoanalytic
        Association, VII:459-83.
Kohut, H. 1971. The Analysis of the Self. New York: In-
        ternational Universities Press.
Kohut, H. 1977. The Restoration of the Self. New York:
        International Universities Press.
Kohut, H. 1978. The Search for the Self. Selected
        writings (ed. by P.H. Ornstein). New York:
        International Universities Press.
Kohut, H. and Wolf, E.S. 1978. "The Disorders of the Self
        and Their Treatment". International Journal of
        Psychoanalysis, LIX, Part IV:413-25.

Ornstein, P.H. 1978. Introduction to Kohut 1978.
Tolpin, M. 1971. "On the Beginnings of a Cohesive Self".
        The Psychoanalytic Study of the Child,
        XXVI:316-54.
Tolpin, M. and Kohut, H. The Disorders of the Self: The
        Psychopathology of the First Years of Life, (in
        press).
Wolf, E.S. 1976. "Ambience and Abstinence". Annual of
        Psychoanalysis, 4:101-15.
Wolf, E. S. 1978. "The Disconnected Self". In Psychoana-
        lysis, Creativity and Literature (ed. by A. Ro-
        land, New York: Columbia University Press), pp.
        103-14.
Wolf, E.S. and Wolf, I. 1979. "We Perished, Each Alone: A
        Psychoanalytic Commentary on Virginia Woolf's To
        a Lighthouse". International Review of Psycho-
        analysis, VI, Part I: 37-47.

THE SELF AND ITS DEVELOPMENT IN AN AFRICAN SOCIETY

A PRELIMINARY ANALYSIS

Robert A. LeVine

Laboratory of Human Development
Harvard University

This chapter is a brief report on findings from a long-term study of the Gusii of western Kenya and a preliminary exploration of the developmental formulations of Heinz Kohut in the context of Gusii culture.

The Gusii are a Bantu-speaking, largely agricultural people numbering close to one million and inhabiting a high-land area over 5,000 feet above sea level just east of Lake Victoria. I worked there first during 1955-57, conducting an anthropological study of their culture, family life, and methods of child rearing.[1] In the 1960s I made several brief visits, investigating historical and demographic questions.[2] The present chapter is based largely on fieldwork from October 1974 to July 1976, which was organized around a study of infant development and involved setting up a pediatric clinic in the area and conducting longitudinal research on infants and their families.[3] The infant study and pediatric clinic constituted the context for our contemporary relationships with all the people of the area.

STUDYING THE SELF THROUGH GUSII CULTURE

We approached the individual experience and psychological functioning of the Gusii through four avenues: first, the infant study itself, aimed at monitoring the normal growth and development of 28 children during the first and second years of life in their environmental context. This was an ambitious program of data collection that brought members of our team into continuous contact with the sample families, and provided a close acquaintance with them as well as a large body of quantifiable observations of infant

social behavior on which to base an understanding of
infantile experience. Second, there were the observations
and case studies of Sarah LeVine, a psychiatric social work-
er who learned to speak the Gusii language effectively and
conducted regular home observations of mother-child interactions on each of the 28 infants. She formed a closer relationship with seven of the mothers, each of whom she visited
weekly for 15 months, conducting open-ended conversations in
which the mothers usually talked about their current lives
and often reported their dreams; toward the end she visited
each of their original homes, thereby gaining an impression
of the families in which they grew up. This body of case
material (S. LeVine 1979), with 50-70 sessions per woman,
represents our most clinical approach. Third, Sarah LeVine
and I collaborated in a series of case studies of family
crisis centering around events occurring during 1974-76,
some of which had their origins during the period of fieldwork twenty years before. These crises--precipitated by in-
fertility, psychosis, land disputes, crime, and sudden
death--reveal a great deal about the sources and management
of interpersonal conflict and other types of stress.
Finally, I conducted ethnographic investigations of social
interaction, folk medicine and ritual, the results of which
I shall report in a preliminary way in this chapter.

     In these four ways, then, we attempted a psychosocial
understanding of the Gusii. The overall research strategy
as it developed in the field was to collect from this one
population data in depth and over time, using a multiplicity
of methods, observational settings, and persons observed.
This diversity of perspectives provides a basis for cross-
validating inferences regarding the cultural and personal
meanings of particular patterns and their place in personality development.

     In the following sections I shall illustrate the
approach of what I call 'person-centered' ethnography to the
understanding of personality among the Gusii. This is
ethnography conducted largely as Malinowski developed it
more than 60 years ago, to gain the insiders' view of their
institutions through field observation and interview, but
specifically focused on the individual's social life and
conscious experience. This approach does not reach the
deepest levels of psychological functioning (at least,
directly) but it resembles psychoanalytic investigation in

being a method of empathic understanding, guided in its search by what is salient to those who are being studied, and following their interests and their ways of communicating their thoughts and feelings. At its best it can clarify the surface of conscious experience, exposing specific vulnerabilities, motivational conflicts, and defenses used by a people and yielding insights into how certain aspects of their culture may be shaped by their emotional needs. By clarifying the conscious surface of individual experience in cultural context we are able to generate hypotheses about psychological dynamics, structure, and development that can and must be tested in direct studies of individuals. This ethnographic material, however, is valuable not only as context for other investigations but also because it can reveal the operating standards of and expectancies about individual functioning within a particular community.

The focus of this ethnographic approach is the self as presented in social interaction and as represented in private introspection and public ritual. The self is a universal category of experience, however variable the meanings assigned to it by different individuals and cultures (Hallowell 1955). As a social science concept it has been widely used in sociology, anthropology, and social psychology. The work of Kohut (1971, 1977) represents a major attempt to reorganize psychoanalytic theory around a conception of the self in normal and abnormal development. I regard this as a promising conceptual bridge between psychoanalysis and the social sciences.

The phenomena of self-presentation in social interaction and symbolic self-representations in ritual have usually been analyzed in the social sciences from the sociological perspective of the Durkheimian school of which Erving Goffman (1971) and Victor Turner (1967, 1969) are exemplars. The psychological aspects have been neglected. In attempting to deal with these aspects, I accept the dramaturgical metaphor used by Goffman and Turner, who treat interpersonal encounters and public ceremonies as dramatic events in which a sequence of appearances is produced in accordance with collective standards. From a psychoanalytic perspective, however, the drama serves a function for the individuals who enact it and those who watch it, and its meanings for them, conscious and unconscious, are indicated by the most repeated sequences of ideas concerning the self. In other words, the sequences of ideas concerning the self in the natural dramas of public life can be analyzed as if they were free associations; and their recurrence in diverse dramatic contexts can be treated as if they were the repetitions of a patient--i.e., as evidence of motives motivational conflicts, and defenses. This approach may seem to resemble what David Rapaport (1967, p. 181) called "as if" analysis, but it is applied not to decontextualized myths and folktales but to the actual behavior of individuals in the routine and ritual contexts that make up their social lives.

FACE-TO-FACE INTERACTION

Let us begin with Gusii conventions of face-to-face social interaction. In all societies there are institutionalized rules or norms of face-to-face interaction which contribute, as Goffman shows, to the maintenance of public order, social solidarity and social relationships. From a psychological viewpoint, such norms are involved in the regulation of the individual's sexual, aggressive, and self-assertive tendencies, which are highly motivated but potentially dangerous to himself as well as others. Every culture has (1) norms of propriety that regulate sexual behavior in social situations and proscribe, in specified types of encounters, behaviors that tend to elicit sexual arousal, embarrassment, and disgust in other persons; (2) norms of conviviality that prohibit aggressive displays in many social situations and prescribe friendly communications--as in greetings, rules of hospitality, and the varieties of ritual politeness Goffman calls supportive and remedial interchanges and tie-signs; (3) norms of humility that regulate boasting, gloating, and conversational dominance, and specify face-to-face standards of respect for social statuses. Most individuals on most occasions try to maintain an appearance of propriety, conviviality, and humility; i.e., they attempt to present themselves as persons who are appropriately restrained, friendly, and respectful according to the standards of their culture. In so doing, they participate in a form of social censorship, concealing from public attention facts about themselves (including their emotions and intentions) which they experience as too dangerous to disclose. By examining these norms at one point in time, we can discover what a people seek to conceal and what style of concealment they use. By examining them over time, as in the two decades that separated my periods of fieldwork among

the Gusii, we can see how the selective conformity of a particular generation has re-shaped the unwritten rules in
accordance with their own standards of social appearance.

The traditional Gusii norms of propriety are very explicit, elaborate, and morally salient. They form part of a
cultural system of kin avoidance and joking norms so extensive that in the past, and to a lesser extent even now, a
large proportion of each individual's daily encounters were
governed by them. These norms, including the mother-in-law
avoidance to which Freud devoted so much attention in Totem
and Taboo, are prohibitions on sexual contact, intimacy, and
in some cases face-to-face interaction between persons whose
kin relationships are defined by parenthood--real, classificatory, or through marriage. Avoidance between adults of
contiguous generations extends to talking about sexual and
excretory matters, seeing nakedness or anything else potentially sexual in each other's presence, touching, and physical proximity. This core set of proscriptions has generated
secondary norms regarding the use of euphemistic vocabulary,
the proper conduct of courtship, the design of housing, and
the arrangement of guests on social occasions--all intended
to avoid the embarrassment resulting from improper contact
between "parents" and their "children." It is hardly an interpretation to call this a drama of incest avoidance, particularly as its most salient aspects for the Gusii are the
exclusion of the adult son from his mother's house, especially its sleeping area, viewed as a space for sexual intimacy, and the exclusion of the father from his married son's
house (as the Gusii see it, the house of the son's wife).
These norms of propriety were sources of great pride for the
Gusii, who saw them as the basis of their moral superiority
to that of neighboring peoples. But there is another side
to them, suggested by their reversal in prescribed relations
between alternate generations, "grandparents" and "grandchildren", who are supposed to engage in joking sexual
abuse, providing a measure of relief from the avoidance
taboos.

In contrast with their standards of propriety, Gusii
norms of conviviality are not very extensive and elaborated,
are often violated with impugnity, and are only laxly
enforced--particularly by comparison with many other African
peoples. Greetings are relatively brief, and hospitality
norms are honored in the breach these days without giving
offense. On the other hand, however, one aspect of convivi-

ality is absolutely mandatory: maintaining the appearance of
friendly relations in casual neighborhood encounters through
the prescribed formula of a handshake, a smile, a greeting,
and a few pleasantries--regardless of one's mood, acquaintance with the person greeted, or actual feelings about him.
Deviations are interpreted as intentional affronts and can
give rise to the suspicion that the violator is a witch.

The salience of this norm for contemporary Gusii is indicated by the increasing prevalence of handshaking even to
the point of overriding norms of propriety. In 1957 shaking
hands with one's parents and parents-in-law was forbidden;
by 1974 it was required. Whereas earlier one would have
been embarrassed by the incestuous implications of physically touching a "parent", now Gusii would be more embarrassed to exhibit differential behavior toward a special
category of kin. In these days of increased mobility and
expanded contact with strangers, handshaking has become the
uniform display of conviviality, extended indifferently to
kin and non-kin, friends and strangers alike. However great
the discrepancy between actual feelings of hostility among
kinsman and neighbors and the appearance of friendly relations, most Gusii adhere tenaciously to this superficial
conviviality in their face-to-face behavior. Some of them
say it keeps the enemy at a distance and is intended to conceal from him the antagonistic feelings that might provoke
him to some form of attack. The individual feels safer having denied, in an encounter, the ill will he really feels
toward those around him. This adaptive strategy is by no
means limited to handshaking but encompasses most ordinary
social intercourse; one avoids making any face-to-face communication that will antagonize or upset another person,
even if it is a matter of simply conveying bad news. Thus
Gusii conviviality norms require a repetitive public drama
of cheerful friendliness, and nothing is permitted to inter-
fere with its friendly or cheerful aspects.

Gusii norms of humility are also less elaborated than
those of many African societies, particularly those with
monarchical political traditions. The display of deference
was not heavily developed in traditional Gusii culture; its
etiquette was conspicuously egalitarian. Pronounced differences in status by age, sex, and wealth were not recognized
in gestures such as bowing, prostrating, kneeling or curt-
sying which are quite common elsewhere in Africa. Deference
was given, but it tended to be subtle and not accessible to

casual observation; and this remains true. Persons of higher status generally exert themselves less in face-to-face
interaction (others come to them and bring them things), and
they have greater control over the termination of encounters. The maintenance of these respectful relationships is
considered important, but people do not invest energy and
effort in displaying deference.

The primary concern of the Gusii is with the suppres-
sion of self-assertion rather than the presentation of
respect. Their norms prohibit the presentation of a self-
aggrandizing appearance through any behavior remotely inter-
pretable as boasting, gloating, or flaunting. The people we
knew tended to overconform to these norms, withholding from
their closest associates information concerning their own
good fortune. For example, women usually did not announce
being pregnant, or men tell of having gained employment or
passed an important examination, to anyone in the family or
neighborhood--claiming that such self-disclosure would be
considered boastful and would provoke malevolent jealousy in
the hearer. Since they withheld the information even from
those whose fortune in that particular respect was mani-
festly greater than their own, it became clear that the
probability of a jealous reaction was less directly feared
than presenting a boastful appearance by initiating the
self-disclosure. A woman might quietly concede when closely
questioned that she was pregnant, or a man that he had been
employed or passed an exam; but an appearance must be maintained that the facts had been wrested from an unwilling informant. To boast about one's good fortune by announcing it
even to intimates is regarded as making oneself dangerously
vulnerable, exposed to the ubiquitous jealousy that can kill
through witchcraft, sorcery, and poisoning.

The investigation of Gusii conventions of face-to-face
interaction resulted in several conclusions of psychoanalytic interest. First, in examining such norms ethnograph-
ically, we reveal the operation of a social censorship system operated by individuals who seek to maintain public
appearances that conceal indications of their lusts,
hatreds, and ambitions. The Gusii style of concealment in
all areas tends to be severely inhibitory--avoiding even
disguised expression of the censored motive, and enacting
dramas of disavowal. Despite the cover of public appearance, however, everyone is intensely aware of the motives
that lie underneath, a phenomenon which elsewhere in Africa

has given rise to the observation by anthropologists that
Africans had discovered defense mechanisms such as projection and displacement before Freud. Indeed they had, but
their insights and interests are directed toward social interaction, not introspection. In the Gusii case, their pro-
scriptive attitude toward self-disclosure of affect, positive and negative--even to intimates--does not favor psychoanalytic work of the usual kind. Individuals monitor and
discuss the affects and intentions of their neighbors rather
than their own. The goals of social interaction among the
Gusii are the maintenance of friendly and modest appearances
that will protect one from the ill will of others. Self-
disclosure has no place in this structure of goals. Ban-
ished from the face-to-face domain, the discussion of motivation is richly developed in the darker recesses of gossip
and rumor. The Gusii system of social censorship, taken as
a whole, reveals specific vulnerabilities experienced by
Gusii individuals, viz. their sense of being endangered by
the hostile and jealous feelings of their neigbors--an
aspect of experience we encountered in many other bodies of
data.

THE LIFE COURSE AND RITUAL

Another line of ethnographic investigation was conducted into the lives of adults--their careers, so to speak,
in subsistence, parenthood, and religion. I attempted from
a wide variety of materials, to explicate what I call the
"life plans" of Gusii men and women: their long-range goals;
their standards of success and failure, and their reactions
to failure (LeVine 1980). In carrying out this study and a
related one of Gusii folk medicine I discovered a relationship between the several "career lines" along which long-
range goals are pursued. All Gusii men and women pursue
economic and reproductive goals. When they are seriously
thwarted in the attainment of these goals--through chronic
illness of self or child, disability, or infertility--they
seek help from indigenous healers; and if they are indeed
cured, they frequently become trained in the curative pro-
cedure and embark on a new career as a practitioner. The
pattern of the patient becoming the curer is widespread in
Africa, but what was more surprising was to find that a considerable proportion of the adults over 40 in our area had
become practitioners of one sort or another: diviners, herb-
alists, surgeons, sorcerers, performers of protective cere-

monies. Most of them were cured patients; some were the children of cured patients. Most who had gone through the transformation from patient to curer enjoyed telling the story (in contrast with the usual attitude toward self-disclosure) and spontaneously repeated it to us on several occasions. It was clear that this spiritual career was experienced as compensation for failure in the other career-line, a compensation that in some cases--though not all--led to further mastery or success. I came to think of the stories they liked to repeat as dramas of personal potency in three acts. Act one: potency diminished; the sufferer seeks help. Act two: potency restored; the sufferer is cured. Act three: potency augmented; the former sufferer gains the power to cure others and with it a sense of being generally less vulnerable to the dangers in his social and spiritual world. There is here as in the material on social interaction an individual who feels threatened by outside forces and is in need of protection; the culturally constituted drama provides that protection, in this case much more effectively.

My third ethnographic study was of the Gusii ritual system--observing rituals of birth, initiation, marriage, death, and sacrifice; no more than a brief overview is possible here. Except for visits to diviners, all Gusii ritual takes place at home, in specified locations within and outside the house. The traditional Gusii house and its normal activities are the central sources of imagery and metaphor for the ceremonies that occur there. The rooms and doors of the house, the hearth, the roof, the cooking pot, the cattle pen--these and the activities of eating, drinking beer, slaughtering goats, sleeping, and entertaining visitors, constitute the basic symbolic elements in most Gusii rituals. Each house is identified primarily with a married woman for whom it is her only home, and secondarily with her husband who may have several wives and thus claims to several houses. The importance of the house in ritual is illustrated in the extreme case of an eighty-year-old woman who died without a house of her own; a special house had to be built of grass to permit her funeral ritual to be carried out.

For the Gusii as for the Nyakyusa (several hundred miles to the south), described by Monica Wilson (1957), the primary ritual drama is seclusion. This occurs in initiation ceremonies, following male circumcision and female

clitoridectomy; in birth, particularly after twins and premature and breech deliveries; and when lightning strikes the
house or certain other omens of spiritual danger occur.
There is also a modified seclusion for widows following the
death of the husband. Seclusion is always at home. In the
case of the male initiation ceremonies, a special house is
built, though it is in the paternal homestead a short distance from the mother's house. In all other instances
seclusion is in one's own residential house or that of one's
mother. The drama of seclusion common to these different
ceremonies portrays the person to be secluded as being in a
weakened physical or spiritual condition and particularly
vulnerable to dangerous forces in the immediate environment
that might kill him or her. The house is portrayed as a
haven affording protection from these dangers while the person is strengthened through feeding and other measures during the period of seclusion. Once strengthened, he or she
is ready for the ceremony of emergence (ekiarokio), which
involves special practitioners, ritual sacrifices and beer
drinking, and the administration of protective medicines.

Although the details vary greatly according to whether
the seclusion follows the circumcision of ten-year-old boys
or the birth of twins, for example, the ritual drama has
this same basic form. It is a drama of potency diminished,
followed by potency restored; in the case of unusual birth,
the mother may eventually become a practitioner (omokorer
ani) who performs ceremonies like the ones done for her and
her babies, thus adding the last act of potency augmented.
For the initiated boys and girls the normal processes of
growth are assumed to augment their vitality, which was tem-
porarily but necessarily threatened by the genital operation.

In the context of life-transition rituals, as with the
norms of social interaction and the life histories of cur-
ers, we can observe the Gusii sense of personal vulnerability to dangers from the immediate world of living and dead
persons, and the tendency of their cultural forms to provide
protection through the prescriptive enactment of a public
drama of strengthening. To say, as Monica Wilson does, that
emergence from seclusion is experienced as rebirth, fits the
Gusii material as well as the Nyakyusa, in the sense that
the threatened person retreats to the protective maternal
house for an additional period of development before being
exposed to the outside world again. There are numerous

ritual details, particularly the role of the placenta as a symbol in twin rituals, that could be brought to bear in support of such an interpretation, but I must forego the lengthy exposition that would entail.

We have examined briefly Gusii social conventions, life plans, and rituals--viewing them not as imposed on Gusii individuals from without, but as aspects of their own lives which they voluntarily and strenuously maintain and redesign to their own desires. These are, after all, unwritten codes not enforced by any bureaucracy, surviving without institutional support--and, in the case of indigenous ritual, in the face of opposition from the church. Conformity to these codes is thus as validly seen as an expression of individual motives as it is a reflection of the social environment. That the contemporary Gusii choose to enact these dramas tells us as much about them psychologically as it does about their socio-cultural traditions. We learned that they feel threatened by the jealousy of those around them and vulnerable physically to their ill will. We saw that their current culture caters to this sense of vulnerability, eliminating what is most disturbing from the visible arena of social life and replacing it with a reassuring veneer of bonhomie and with highly prescriptive performances designed to strengthen and protect. The Gusii we worked with, I believe, are individuals in need of social support and regulation for their intrapsychic adjustment, adapting to a decaying community structure that no longer resolves disputes, regulates competition or reinforces moral norms; and they get that support and regulation from ritual. Through ethnography (i.e., using cultural materials, nonverbal as well as verbal, to de-code messages of psychological significance), we have been able to clarify the outer contour of that intrapsychic adjustment, identifying the cultural terms in which Gusii experience inner anxiety, conflict, and defense. To confirm these interpretations and achieve a deeper psychological and developmental understanding of these trends requires an analysis of our data on individuals and families.

VISUAL INTERACTION IN EARLY EXPERIENCE:
KOHUT'S THEORY AND GUSII DATA

As an illustration of how material from our infant study bears on the development of the self as revealed in

ethnographic investigation, I have chosen visual interaction. Eye-contact or mutual looking is a universal category
of communicative behavior that can be observed throughout
the life-span and acquires varying meanings in diverse cultures. Interocular contact is emotionally arousing, probably for all humans (Tomkins 1963); and it has recently
received a good deal of attention from psychological investigators (e.g., Argyle and Cook 1976), who have shown differences by age, sex, social situation, and cultural background in tendencies to engage in eye-contact or gaze-aver-
sion. Developmental researchers (e.g., Stern 1974) have
argued that mutual looking and the aversion of gaze between
mother and infant play an important role in the establishment of the earliest reciprocity and interactive rhythm for
the child, one that foreshadows and influences later social
interaction.

Kohut's account of early development is independent of
these experimental and observational studies, but he also
assigns a potentially significant role to visual interaction
between mothers and young children. Rather than attempt to
summarize his theory here, I shall call attention to certain
of its most relevant features. According to Kohut (1977),
empathic mothering that takes account of and responds appropriately to the child's emerging emotional needs is essential for normal psychological development during the first
three or four years of life. The mother or another caretak-
ing person acts as the "joyful mirror to a child's healthy
assertiveness" (1977, p. 130), providing "self-esteem-
enhancing acceptance and approval" (p. 61). Later, through
a series of "optimal failures" of empathy by the mother, the
child internalizes her approval as self-esteem, thereby laying the basis for a cohesive self. A mother's chronic
self-absorption or other gross failure of empathy during the
child's early years (as when she is affected by severe physical or mental illness) deprives the child of the joyful
mirroring needed for a cohesive self and can lead (if later
developments do not compensate adequately) to a narcissistic
personality disorder, involving deficient self-esteem and
other symptoms of a fragmented self. In such cases, psychoanalytic treatment often unearths the remembered image of

the "cold unresponding, nonmirroring face" of the mother throughout the early years, or after the birth of a sibling, as a factor in the etiology of the disorder.   This sketch does not do justice to Kohut's rich and systematically elaborated formulation, but it does suggest the salience in it of "the gleam in the mother's eye".

Let us turn now to material from our longitudinal study of infants among the Gusii of Kenya. Our observations there were designed to make possible a "psychoanalytically informed examination of the child's environment" (Kohut 1971, p. 254) in an African cultural context. The focus here is on the affective meanings acquired in the early years for one type of communicative signal, viz. looking and being looked at. Table 1 shows some data on patterns of reciprocal looking during the first 26 months, taken from home observations of 1-2 hours in length made by an educated Gusii woman whom I trained. (This was one of three bodies of home observations on these babies and their caretakers.) Though the numbers of individuals is small and the variation from one individual to another great, there are some patterns. The column on the left shows the percent of minutes mother looks at baby in the same minute baby is looking at mother, while the right-hand column shows the proportion of minutes baby is looking at mother in the same minute mother is looking at baby. The large number of 100s in the latter column and the smaller numbers in the former suggests that the babies are looking at their mothers much more than they are getting looked at by them, in all of the age periods. The gap is smallest at the earliest age (6-7 months), when the four mothers shown are looking at baby in one-quarter to two-thirds of the minutes the babies are looking at them (the mean is 42.8%, median 39.8%). This can be taken as the peak period of maternal looking-reciprocity, for the sample as a whole. After that, there seems to be little reciprocation, by the mother, of the baby's looks; though individual differences are considerable, the mean or median never rises above 20%. This means that, insofar as these data are indicative, Gusii infants and toddlers are unlikely to acquire the expectation that looking at their mothers will result in being looked at in return.

TABLE 1

RECIPROCAL LOOKING BETWEEN MOTHERS AND INFANTS

Age in months	Percent of minutes that Mother looks at baby in the same minute that baby is looking at mother*		Percent of minutes that baby looks at mother in the same minute that mother is looking at baby**	
6-7 n=4	66.7	(3)	100	(2)
	54.6	(11)	100	(6)
	25.0	(20)	100	(5)
	25.0	(8)	66.7	(3)
8-9 n=7	0	(2)	—	(0)
	0	(4)	0	(1)
	25.0	(4)	100	(1)
	9.1	(11)	100	(1)
	20.0	(10)	100	(2)
	0	(1)	0	(2)
	8.3	(12)	100	(1)
11-12 n=4	33.3	(12)	100	(4)
	30.0	(20)	100	(6)
	0	(9)	—	(0)
	0	(4)	—	(0)
15-16 n=5	0	(6)	0	(2)
	40.0	(5)	100	(2)
	20.0	(5)	100	(1)
	28.6	(14)	100	(4)
	12.5	(16)	100	(2)
17-18 n=2	14.3	(7)	100	(1)
	0	(4)	—	(0)
23-24 n=4	0	(1)	—	(0)
	0	(1)	—	(0)
	33.3	(9)	100	(3)
	0	(4)	—	(0)
25-26 n=3	45.5	(11)	100	(5)
	8.3	(12)	100	(1)
	0	(2)	—	(0)

*Number in parentheses refers to the number of minutes in which the baby looks at the mother.
**Number in parentheses refers to the number of minutes in which the mother looks at the baby.

THE MEANING OF BEING LOOKED AT FOR GUSII ADULTS

How does this pattern of early experience influence the development of the self among the Gusii? The data from person-centered ethnography in the three arenas discussed above—routine encounters, autobiographical narratives, and ceremonies considered as social performances—show a common theme: the dangers of being seen. More specifically, we have discovered that the representation of self in each of these arenas is partly organized around the idea that the greatest threats to one's physical, as well as mental, well-being have their source in other people's eyes.

Although it is not possible in this paper to present the material that lies behind this statement in adequate detail, I shall indicate its nature:
1) The social conventions regarding face-to-face interaction in routine encounters. We found that it was considered personally necessary as well as conventional to conceal from others any information about one's advantages, good fortune, or other positive events that would portray the self in favorable terms. At the most superficial level, this attempt to eliminate social visibility as a favored person has its roots in a fear of envy that is widespread in peasant and primitive societies. For the Gusii, however, it goes far beyond the simple fear of envy. When a woman states that she would not volunteer the fact of being pregnant to a friend or relative who has more living children than herself (even though the other will soon know) on the grounds that it would be dangerously boastful, she is indicating more than a fear of jealousy. This extreme reluctance to take pride in a natural and desired bodily event, the interpretation of it as boasting or gloating, and the explicit assumption that it could lead to destruction of oneself through the potential resentment of others—these show a diffuse and deep-seated fear of portraying one's self-assertive tendencies (Kohut's "grandiose self") that might be expected from someone who did not receive the mirroring approval of a mother in her early years. In other words, without that early maternal approval and acceptance

These figures are in accord with our observational experience that Gusii mothers are more attentively involved in
infant care during the first few months of the baby's life.
After that, though breast-feeding continues until 16 months
and co-sleeping until two years, the mother spends much of
the daytime in agricultural and domestic tasks, and a child
of 5-12 years old takes care of the infant. At home, the mother responds primarily and rapidly to the baby's cry rather
than to social signals like looking, smiling, and babbling;
she rarely looks at her infant while breast-feeding. As the
infant grows older, mother pays less visual attention to
him, though her domestic tasks would permit her to do so.

At about two years of age, the child begins learning to
fetch and carry obediently under maternal supervision. From
now on, the mother is vigilant concerning the child's performance of tasks. There is no praise for good performance
but there is predictable correction or reprimand for inadequate or neglectful performance Under these circumstances,
the child adopts what we call a "low-profile strategy"--
i.e., the tendency to avoid being seen by the mother, and
other adults, as a means of avoiding being commanded or
chastised. In Children of Six Cultures, the Whitings (1975,
p. 64) found that among American children of 3-10 years of
age, attention-seeking was more than three times as frequent
as among Gusii of the same age.

What does this suggest about the meaning of looking and
being looked at? Our hypothesis is that Gusii infants after
six months learn not to expect their mothers to look at them
or to engage in visual reciprocity, regardless of what they
do. In the third year of life, they learn to expect that
maternal attention signals the onset of a demand for obedience or a reprimand for misbehavior. Instead of a gleam in
the mother's eye, they expect a glare. In this context, the
affective meaning of being looked at by the mother is negative rather than positive.

for self-assertiveness, the individual might well, if Kohut is right, lack the self-esteem necessary to attract positive attention without expecting disastrous consequences.

2) Autobiographical narratives in relation to Gusii life-plans. When Gusii individuals talk about their lives, they never fail to mention their afflictions (see S. LeVine 1979). In fact, the afflictions frequently provide the central drama of autobiographical discourse. Three of the major sources of affliction involve the dangers of being seen. There are two forms of the "evil eye", i.e., dangers inherent in specific persons whose gaze is believed to harm and kill, primarily by magical penetration--into the visceral organs--of particles that were on the skin prior to being looked at. Anecdotes about these afflictions portray the afflicted as highly vulnerable to penetration; the only ways to avoid being affected by the evil eye are to avoid meeting the person who has it or to use red objects (clothing, plants) to distract his/her gaze. The third source of affliction involving eyes is witchcraft, which--though it operates through medicines of magical potency--is also signaled by the malevolence in the witch's eyes; her looking at you intently indicates you are her victim. These narratives are elaborated, and are remarkably consistent across individuals. There can be no question that a great deal of mental and physical disease among the Gusii is attributed to malevolent forces mediated through the eyes of persons, acting upon a person who describes himself as vulnerable.

3) Public ceremonies. The seclusion which I have described earlier as the central drama of the Gusii ritual system is in fact understood primarily as a protection from the eyes of neighboring kinsmen. A great deal of evidence supports this. For example, the person in seclusion must go outside to excrete under cover of darkness when no one can see him or her. Each ceremony specifies the limited persons allowed to enter the house and see the secluded one. Informants are emphatic that gaze by others would harm the person in seclusion, causing bleeding, sickness, even death. This is most striking in the case of ceremonies for twins and breech-delivered children, because in other Bantu groups such as the Nyakyusa (Wilson 1957), their births are seen as a danger to the community, which seclusion guards against. For the Gusii, however, the primary danger of anomalous births is to the babies from the gaze of the community of neighboring kinsmen--represented in these beliefs abstractly and without specific identities or intentions. In seclusion, the individual is strengthened through feeding and

medicine, to make him less vulnerable to the life-threaten-
ing dangers in people's eyes.

I have shown, in briefest fashion here, that in the
ways contemporary Gusii represent themselves in routine
encounters, autobiographical narratives, and ceremonial
action, the idea that physical dangers to the self reside in
being looked at is the central one. The representations of
gaze and its dangers vary in abstractness from one arena to
another, but they are always poised against a highly vulnerable self. Seclusion—affording a temporary shelter from
the malevolence of vision, and a period of strengthening—is
a favored solution. I cannot prove that this imagined vulnerability has a source in the meanings acquired in early
mother-infant communication, but it is our working hypothesis as we analyze a large body of data.

Two tentative (and at this point, admittedly specula-
tive) conclusions from this ontogenetic perspective on the
meaning of being looked at among the Gusii seem worthy of
discussion: (1) As Kohut's theory might generally lead one
to expect, individuals who as children have not received
large doses of approving attention from their mothers, but
have been heavily exposed to maternal disapproval, tend to
respond to the thought of being looked at with a negative
rather than a positive affect. The result seems to be relatively low self-esteem, high anxiety about self-assertion,
and a heightened sense of vulnerability to the malevolence
of others. Perhaps there is a childhood schema equating
parental attention with disapproval or command that is symbolically elaborated in the course of cognitive development
and enculturation into metaphorical representations of the
dangers in social visibility—representations of varying
levels of abstraction but all leading to a fantasied disso-
lution of the self. (2) It would be wrong, even on the
basis of evidence presented so far, to assume an equivalence
between the Gusii and Western patients who have had deficits
in maternal approval during their early years. A major reason is that the Westerners are more likely to have developed
an elevated expectation of positive maternal attention during the first 18-24 months simply because of the powerful
cultural support for this kind of mother-infant interaction.
When the positive attention is withdrawn due to the birth of
a sibling or maternal emotional distress, the effect is dev-
astating to the child's established expectancies. The Gusii
child, as suggested by Table 1, may develop a low expecta-

tion of positive maternal attention between 6 and 24 months, which is likely to insulate him from the more pathological effects of further withdrawal later on. The Gusii may be better able to integrate a low level of self-esteem in subsequent development because of not being tormented by the sense of paradise lost (i.e., a once-accepted grandiose self now rejected by mother). If this analysis is correct, Kohut's view of normal development will have to be corrected to make room for non-Western data.

GUSII MOTHERS AND THE DEVELOPMENT OF SELF

Let us examine the Gusii situation from the side of the mother. The behavior of our Gusii mothers toward their infants and toddlers can be explained, and it is not due to their being "latent psychotics", depressed, or even unempathic. I see them as enacting normative scripts derived from the cultural ideals of Gusii society. The first and most general script applies to all interpersonal encounters: conversations between kinsmen or neighbors require neither a face-to-face position nor eye-contact (after the initial moment of greeting). Perhaps this is a function of the traditional kin-avoidance norms which tended to pervade social interaction; it may also reflect the desire for a protective social distance mentioned previously.

It is, in any event, a contextual factor of great importance in considering mother-infant interaction; for if the mother's ideal of communication between mature adults does not include eye-contact, then her "failure" to engage in eye-contact with her baby must be seen in that light.

The second script is specific to the maternal role in infant care, and emphasizes concern for the physical well-being of the child rather than communication or stimulation during the first year of life: mother should sleep with baby, permit breast-feeding on demand, respond rapidly to crying with feeding and shaking, keep the baby on or close to someone's body at all times, and act quickly to get medical care when baby is sick. If the child grows and develops normally, as measured by physical growth and motor skills, then maternal attention can be diverted to other tasks as the baby is increasingly taken care of by the child nurse. Walking (at about a year of age) and weaning (about four months later) are milestones indicating that the child needs

mother less. It is assumed that the baby and toddler will
be played with by older children in the family, especially
the child nurse; the mother does not see this as prescribed
for her by the norms of the maternal role.

Finally, there is the normative script for intergenerational relations in the Gusii kinship system, prescribing
hierarchy and avoidance or restraint between all "parents"
and their adult "children" (actual and classificatory).
Parents give commands to their children and avoid excessive
(i.e., incestuous) intimacy with them; children obey and
increasingly avoid intimate contact as they grow older.
While this script only reaches its final form in adulthood
(i.e., after the children have been initiated), it infil-
trates the mother-child relationship at least at 24
months--if not earlier. The child who can speak and
understand is said to be capable of learning obedience and
participating in the household economy. He is not to be
praised, for that would make him conceited, "spoiled," and
disobedient. He becomes part of a sibling group and,
particularly after the next baby is born, is outside the
focus of maternal attention.

All of these normative scripts militate against the
pattern of the mirroring, approving mother of Kohut's theory. In fact, they turn that pattern on its head, phasing
out maternal involvement and approval before the child
"needs" it to support his emerging capacities for self-
assertion and to enhance his incipient self-esteem. Does
this mean the average Gusii child should be seen as deprived
of the emotional resources necessary for normal development?

There are several reasons to answer in the negative.
First, although Gusii mothers may not engage in active and
prolonged mirroring and praise like Americans, this is not
to say they do not respond empathically to the baby. Their
empathic formula prescribes responsiveness to distress signals rather than other social interactions, and body contact
rather than eye-contact; furthermore, they adjust transi-
tions, like weaning, to the perceived size and health of the
baby. We do not understand this type of empathic mothering
adequately, and it is somewhat harder to study as a system
of communication; but we have to concede it the status of
adaptive infant care characteristic of many of the world's
peoples. Second, their mothering is clearly associated with
an attitude of concern for the growth and welfare of the

child, which they define in physical rather than emotional
(or communicative) terms. Since Kohut emphasizes the maternal attitude or feeling as the primary source of psychopathology for his patients, we are safer to assume that normal
Gusii mothers are more consistent and reponsive (though in a
style unfamiliar to us) than were the unempathic mothers of
his patients. Thirdly, the Gusii infant/toddler usually has
available for social interaction a group of older siblings
one of whom is specifically assigned responsibility for his
care. Mother diverts her attention from his daytime care
only as she delegates it to the child nurse and sees the
baby increasingly incorporated into the social life of the
sibling group—which generally contains children more
responsible at younger ages than their American counterparts. This socialization into a group of one's own generation compensates in part for the mother's relative lack of
attention and prepares the child for participation in same-
generation groups in maturity—a major feature of Gusii
adulthood. The question of whether, and in what sense,
infant-child social interaction replaces interaction with
the mother is one we shall be examining closely in our data.

Finally, it must be added that the traditional social
order of the Gusii was one which did not endorse self-assertion or even conspicuous self-esteem as positive qualities
for all individuals. Our "healthy self-esteem" is conceit
and selfishness by their standards. Individuals were being
deliberately shaped in their early years to be obedient
child laborers in the domestic work force, respectful subor-
dinates in an intergenerational hierarchy, and willing participants in a kinship system in which material giving and
sharing were obligatory. Thus, a person who might seem to
lack self-esteem by Western standards would be better prepared to adapt to the Gusii social order than an individualistic, assertive middle-class American child. In pre-
colonial days, the Gusii social system provided mature
adults with a heavily prescriptive structure in which individual initiative was regulated and contained. Western theories of the self usually assume that autonomy and self-suf-
ficiency are idealized as goals of development everywhere.
They incline one to think that persons not moving in that
direction with adequate amounts of self-esteem are psychologically defective. But the Gusii case, like that of many
other non-Western peoples, forces us toward a more variable
conception of self-development.

ENDNOTES

1. This study was supported by a Ford Foundation fellowship; its findings were reported in LeVine and LeVine
   (1966) and in articles listed in the bibliography of
   that monograph.

2. A two-month visit in 1964 (with Donald T. Campbell) and
   briefer trips in 1965 and 1967 were supported by the
   Carnegie Corporation of New York. The historical
   materials on pre-colonial Gusii life and inter-ethnic
   relations are available from the Human Relations Area
   Files. The demographic findings were published in
   Nerlove and LeVine (1972).

3. This study, carried out in collaboration with T. Berry
   Brazelton and P. Herbert Leiderman and their associates
   at Harvard Medical School (Constance Keefer and Suzanne
   Dixon) and Stanford University Medical School (David
   Feigal) was supported respectively by the National
   Science Foundation and National Institute of Mental
   Health (through a Research Scientist Award to the
   present author).

REFERENCES

Argyle, M. and Cook, M. 1976. Gaze and Mutual Gaze.
        Cambridge: Cambridge University Press.
Goffman, E. 1971. Relations in Public. Harmondsworth,
        U.K.: Penguin Books.
Hallowell, A.I. 1955. Culture and Experience.
        Philadelphia: University of Pennsylvania Press.
Kohut, H. 1971. The Analysis of the Self. New York:
        International Universities Press.
Kohut, H. 1977. The Restoration of the Self. New York:
        International Universities Press.
LeVine, R.A. 1980. "Adulthood Among the Gusii of Kenya."
        in Themes of Love and Work in Adulthood (ed. by
        N. Smelser and E. Erik), Cambridge: Harvard
        University Press.
LeVine, R.A. and LeVine, B. 1966. Nyansongo: A Gusii
        Community in Kenya. New York: Wiley. (Reprinted

1977, Huntington, New York:Robert Krieger)

LeVine, S. 1979. Mothers and Wives: Gusii Women of East Africa. Chicago: University of Chicago Press.

Nerlove, S. and LeVine, R. "Population Growth in a Kenya Community." American Anthropologist, 1972, 74:408-10.

Rapaport, D. 1967. "The Scientific Methodology of Psychoanalysis," orig. pub. 1944. In The Collected Papers of David Rapaport (ed. by M.M. Gill), New York Basic Books.

Stern, D. 1974. "Mother and Infant at Play: The Dyadic Interaction Involving Facial, Vocal and Gaze Behaviors." In The Effect of the Infant on Its Caregiver (ed. by M. Lewis and L. Rosenblum), New York Wiley-Interscience.

Tomkins, S. 1963. Affect, Imagery and Consciousness. New York: Springer.

Turner, V.W. 1967. The Forest of Symbols. Ithaca, New York: Cornell University Press.

Turner, V.W. 1969. The Ritual Process. Chicago: Aldine.

Whiting, B. & J. 1975. Children of Six Cultures: A Psycho-Cultural Analysis. Cambridge, Mass.: Harvard University Press.

Wilson, M. 1957. Rituals of Kinship Among the Nyakyusa. London: Oxford University Press.

PERSON, SELF, AND IDENTITY:

SOME ANTHROPOLOGICAL RETROSPECTS,

CIRCUMSPECTS, AND PROSPECTS

Raymond D. Fogelson

University of Chicago

All clowns are masked and all personae
Flow from choices; sad and gay, wise,
Moody and humorous are chosen faces,
And yet not so! For all circumstances,
Given, like a tendency
To colds or like blond hair and wealth
Or war and peace or gifts from the ground,
Stick to us in time, surround us:
Socrates is mortal.
"All Clowns are Masked"
Delmore Schwartz, 1938

Anthropology has important contributions to make in
extending the study of the self. An integrated and cumulative body of anthropological theory relevant to the self has
yet to be realized. Nevertheless, it is possible to connect
several lines of theory to suggest converging general orientations and research strategies bearing on the study of the
self and related ideas. In addition, the ever-expanding
comparative ethnographic record constitutes a valuable re-
source that can be exploited to examine the broader applica-
bility or inapplicability of Western conceptions of the
self--as well as to investigate, in their own right, self
concepts that have developed independent of Western influence.

Anthropologists have historically displayed both an explicit and an implicit concern with the self and related
concepts.[1] The late nineteenth-century British evolution-
ists focused primary attention on the idea of progress as it

was manifested in the cumulative accretions of generic cultural growth and in the orthogenic development of supposedly
universal institutions. They anchored their theories in a
conception of the human mind that operated under a self-evi-
dent, if not selfish, philosophy of utilitarianism and that
adopted an appropriate logic of self-conscious "rational"
choice. This self-fulfilling methodological individualism
viewed the human actor as operating, to some extent, inde-
pendently of social and cultural constraints. Contempora-
neous reactions to aspects of British evolutionism arose in
Germany and France.

Nascent German social science was strongly influenced
by idealistic philosophy. Völkerpsychologie (as elaborated
by Steinthal and Lazarus, Wundt, and others) stressed the
existence of the group mind or collective identity, a construct based in part on biology but more decisively shaped
by the cumulative effects of history and tradition. While
developmentalism and transformation were parts of the over-
arching schemes, there was recognition of varying Volk-
geisten (or ethé)--or to use Adolf Bastian's term, Völker-
gedenken, 'folk ideas'--produced by the different geograph-
ical situations (geographicische Provincen) and historical
experiences of human groups.[2] Methodological individualism, however, continued to prevail in the sense that group
psychology was conceived of as an individual psychology writ
large. Various cultural institutions were seen as differentially reflective of separate faculties of the individual
mind.[3]

Wilhelm Wundt rejected the simple Lockean tabula rasa/
cause-and-effect/stimulus-response psychology of British
associationism. Conation, or will, was coordinate with cognition; affects formed an important part of his system; and
processes of apperception could shape and transform sensory
perception. The individual mind--and by extension, the collective mind--was capable of creative synthesis based upon
particular past experiences, the momentary state of the
apperceiving mind, and a whole host of other contingent factors. Cause and effect, stimulus and response, could not be
understood without recourse to the intervening mediation of
the apperceptive mass. The Boasian notion of cultural integration and the particularistic resynthesis of diffused culture traits are direct analogues of the apperceiving individual mind.[4]

In France, with the ascendency of Durkheimian sociology
(circa the turn of the century), the individual self was
submerged into the collective conscience—only to surface
with the dispersion of social bonds attendant on increased
social density and the development of complex societies organized in terms of organic solidarity. For Durkheim and
his followers, the primacy of society was taken as a (god-)
given, and individual consciousness and sense of self were
products of society, rather than society being formed out of
a social contract consensually created by and voluntarily
entered into by autonomous individuals.

Despite his insistence that society was a _sui generis_
phenomenon, irreducible to the psychological motivations of
individuals, Durkheim does discuss the position of the self
or ego in his general system. These ideas are first set
forth in the Division of Labor (1893; 1933 ed., pp. 129-32),
are reiterated in The Elementary Forms of Religious Life
(1912; 1960 ed., pp. 387-90), and are most fully developed
in his late essay "The Duality of Human Existence" (1914;
1964 ed., pp. 325-40). Durkheim, in essence, argues for the
presence of two types of ego internalized within the individual. The first might be glossed as the psychobiological ego: that part of the self concerned with sensory processes, and given to self-interest and the satisfaction of
individual needs. The second may be rendered as the socio-
cultural ego: that portion of the self that originates from
outside the individual, and is involved with conceptual and
moral ideas. Durkheim sees this dualism echoed in well-nigh
universal notions of body and soul, to which his qualitative
distinctions of profane and sacred can be affixed [and to
which Lévi-Strauss might apply the nature/culture antithesis
(see, e.g., Totemism, 1963)]. These two egos coexist in a
state of chronic tension and opposition, a situation that
becomes increasingly aggravated with the advance of
civilization.

Durkheim's notion of the sociocultural ego is equivalent to the idea of a social person. The social person is,
paradoxically, an impersonal concept, almost a Kantian
abstraction defined in terms of suprapersonal reason and
morality. The social person refers neither to a specific
individual nor to a particular entity and can be compared,
in religious terms, to the evanescent soul with its divine
origin and continuous sacred connections, or can be thought
of, in social structural terms, as an intersect of social

relations (c.f. Krader 1966, p. 483 and Krader 1967). The
latter usage was introduced into social anthropology by A.R.
Radcliffe-Brown in the <u>Andaman Islanders</u> (1922), elaborated
by him in his 1940 essay "On Social Structure" (1953 ed.,
p. 193f.), and applied by other structural-functionalists as
an operational construct for the social analysis of jural,
moral, economic, and religious norms and relationships.

The Durkheimian image of primitive peoples emphasized
their supposed lack of individuality and consciousness of
self: the strong collective consciousness and correspond-
ingly uniform sociocultural ego overwhelmed the psychobiological ego, individual existence was inseparably tied to
the group, and individual representations were consonant
with collective representations. Individuation, egoism, and
true self-awareness, are possible, for Durkheim, only when
society begins to differentiate through increased social
density and expansion of the division of labor. When the
collective conscience begins to atrophy, a situation is produced in which meanings and emotions associated with collective representations rely less on principles of identity and
more on equivalence (c.f. Wallace 1961). Not only do individuals emerge in this social transformation; moral individualism—a cult or religion of the individual, in which the
individual is imbued with dignity and sacred qualities—also
arises.

The philosopher Lucien Levy-Bruhl shared many of the
presuppositions of the Durkheimian school. He made much use
of available ethnographic materials. Whereas Durkheim and
his followers tended to use data from particular primitive
cultures in intensive fashion, Levy-Bruhl's approach was
more extensive and encyclopedic (although he often displayed
the philosopher's uncanny knack of extracting plausible
meaning from small pieces of evidence). Levy-Bruhl's primary concern was the comparative analysis of thought. His
fundamental assumption—that the thought processes of primitive man were "pre-logical" (see 1910, e.g.)—has been much
maligned and misunderstood; before his death he repudiated
the term (1949; 1975 ed., pp. 47-49). The adjective
"pre-logical", as employed by Levy-Bruhl, referred less to
an evolutionarily anterior or inferior mode of thought than
to widely spread forms of thought that didn't recognize
certain canons of logic formalized in the post-Aristotelian
West. Levy-Bruhl overstated his contrast between prelogical
and logical thought by failing to sufficiently appreciate

the enormous differences existent among primitive cultures
and by neglecting the significance and incidence of prelogical thinking in modern society. Nevertheless, certain of his
ideas are germane to the present discussion.

One of Levy-Bruhl's more important ideas is what he
called the "Law of Participation" (in his later Notebooks,
he ceased referring to participation as a law; op.cit., p.
60f.). This "Law" refers to a suprasensible mental coinci-
dence between persons and things such that they form part of
one another, almost to the point of identity. Levy-Bruhl
brilliantly documents such phenomena in the mystical links
connecting a man to his name, his shadow, his totem, and his
clan. These participations, he maintains, must be judged
from the native point-of-view as parts of the self, components of identity, and extensions of ego. Any analysis that
limits consideration of self-related concepts to the boundaries of the skin must, by premature definition, be defective.

Although the connected volumes How Natives Think (1910;
Eng. trans. 1926) and Primitive Mentality (1922; Eng. trans.
1923) remain the most read and most cited of Levy-Bruhl's
works, his neglected volume on The "Soul" of the Primitive
(1927; Eng. trans. 1928) is a more refined and better-illus-
trated statement of his position. It is also more relevant
to our present concerns. The term "soul" (l'âme) is used,
with due qualifications, as an imperfect gloss for an inner
life essence and for the subjective (and sometimes objective) sense of self. Levy-Bruhl believed that notions such
as self, person, or "soul" were incapable of being conceptualized and articulated by primitive peoples. Thus, such
ideas could be studied only indirectly, through analysis of
their collective representations.

Durkheim's lineal intellectual heir, Marcel Mauss, also
provided some influential perspectives for understanding the
self. Two essays are of particular interest: "L'âme, le nom
et la personne" (1929) and "Une Categorie de l'esprit
humain: la notion de personne celle de 'moi" (1938). Like
Durkheim and Levy-Bruhl, Mauss sees the self as a social
product, which in primitive societies is relatively undifferentiated and intimately bound up with ideas of "soul",
appropriation of names, and roles in ritual performance.
Mauss's notion of "social person" (personne morale), however, differs in significant ways from Durkheim's formulation.

Mauss's "social person" is an empirical entity derived
directly from particular and variable cultural factors. A
concretized notion of "social person" is not necessarily
universally present in all societies. Mauss finds social
personality existing in rudimentary form among the Zuni,
Kwakiutl, and Aranda.

Although he shares with Durkheim and Levy-Bruhl the
belief that a developed conception of self and person tends
to emerge in more complex societies, Mauss does not view the
correlation as absolute. He has difficulty in discerning a
developed, objectified notion of the person in traditional
China and in Buddhist and Taoist philosophy. In a brilliant
excursion, Mauss accounts for the abstract, objectified category of social person in Western thought as eventuating
from a transformation of meaning attributed to the Greco-
Roman conception of persona or mask. Originally a mythic
representation (personnalité mythique), the mask in later
Roman drama comes to signify a social personality (personne
morale). The implication is that the mythic mask is a manifestation of a religiously based collective representation,
while the later use of masks has become desacralized and
represents a differentiated social status (for a more extended treatment of the concept of persona, see the discussion in Gordon Allport 1937, pp. 24-54).

Two repetitive assumptions run through the classic
French sociological interpretations of primitive man and his
society. First, because primitive society is seemingly undifferentiated, it is assumed that individual personality
and selfhood must be similarly undifferentiated. Indeed,
Durkheim was so taken by his metaphor of mechanical society,
replete with interchangeable parts, that he even briefly
suggests in The Division of Labor (1933 ed., pp. 133-35)
that all members of a primitive society tend to look alike!
The second assumption is that primitive peoples are
incapable of formulating an articulate philosophy of self or
individuality, since self-identity is so intimately tied to
the group that the very notion of individual selfhood is an
alien concept.

These assumptions were doubtless conditioned by the
fact that neither Durkheim, Levy-Bruhl, nor Mauss ever had
the opportunity to engage in first-hand fieldwork. It is
true that all three placed a high value on the fieldwork of
others and they steeped themselves in the available ethno-

graphic literature. However, their theoretical presuppositions that primitive societies and individuals were undifferentiated and lacking in a conscious philosophy of the
self led them into the logical trap of supporting their
assertions by recourse to a methodology that proceeded from,
and rarely went beyond, the analysis of collective representations. Had they paid more attention to individual representations—in the form of life histories, native testimo-
nies, and texts—their picture of primitive society, its
internal variability, and the capacity of its members for
self-expression might have been different. In brief, while
they were able to expose the flaws of vulgar forms of methodological individualism and simplistic psychological reduc-
tionism, their own methodology left them open to charges of
sociological reification that posed problems of equal magni-
tude.[5]

The French sociological tradition continues to be influential today. Fieldwork by French scholars has made a
difference. Thus, the works of Marcel Griaule and Germaine
Dieterlen have revealed sophisticated philosophical speculation among the Dogon of East Africa.[6] Maurice Leenhardt
(a Protestant missionary anthropologist with twenty-five
years of field experience in New Caledonia; and the successor to Mauss, and the predecessor of Lévi-Strauss, as occu-
pant of the chair in the History of Primitive Religions at
L'Ecole Pratique des Hautes Etudes) produced a major work
centrally concerned with conceptions of self and person.
This book, Do Kamo (1947), was recently translated (1979)
and is enjoying a born-again life in the English-speaking
world.

Leenhardt was much influenced by Mauss, and he carried
on a continuing dialogue with Levy-Bruhl (Crapanzano 1979);
in fact, some of Levy-Bruhl's retractions about the nature
of primitive mentality were inspired by problematic field
data presented by Leenhardt. Leenhardt's description of
self and person (or personage) are informed by a solid grasp
of the language and its nuances, and critical ethnographic
detail. His native New Caledonians are not partitive people
produced from the perspective of a Parisian armchair; they
are whole personages integrated into a phenomenologically
real, for them, behavioral environment. As Crapanzano notes
(1979:xxii–xxv), Leenhardt seems to view these native New
Caledonian conceptions from two perspectives: a relational
dimension and an existential one.

From a relational perspective, the personage is connected to other personages--human and non-human, material
and immaterial--through a variety of affective and suprasensible means. The distinction between self and other is
blurred; and the body is only a temporary locus, and not a
source of individual identity. As Levy-Bruhl and Mauss so
brilliantly anticipated, a man participates in his name or
names, and no simple name adequately sums up his being.
Reminiscent of the Platonic dialogue between Crotylus and
Hermogenes, the New Caledonians seem to feel, as does Crotylus, that names and nouns are indeed proper and are "wired
into"--by a binding law of causality--the nature of the
things they imitate; whereas Hermogenes would consider the
connection between nouns and names and the things they nom-
inate as arbitrary consequences of convention, treaty, contract, or covenant.

The implicit existential dimension of the New Caledonian concept of person comes out in Leenhardt's insistance
that these people are not individuated--that they are, in
essence, pre-persons or personages. Leenhardt's submerged
evolutionism surfaces in his consideration of the New Caledonian world as cosmomorphic, which is even anterior to an
anthropomorphic world-view and certainly far removed from
supposed Western analytic and positivistic perspectives
based ultimately on dualism and logical positivism (Crapanzano 1979:xxiv). Issues about individualism and personhood
will be considered further in subsequent sections of this
paper.

An interesting fusion of the Maussian approach to the
person and a traditional British social anthropological
perspective is represented in Meyer Fortes's insufficiently
appreciated article "On the Concept of the Person Among the
Tallensi" (1973). This many-layered and richly textured
ethnographic account provides an exemplary analysis of self
and person among this West African tribe, and resonates with
ethnopsychological understanding.

Theoretical interest in the self is deeply entrenched
in American social and behavioral science. A review of the
notable theoretical contributions by such early figures as
William James, George Horton Cooley, and James Baldwin will
not be attempted here.[7] However, the highly germinal formulations of George Herbert Mead deserve more than passing
mention, since the modern sociological and social psycholog-

ical symbolic-interactionist approach to the self can be
traced directly to him (1913, 1934). Mead provided a philosophical and behaviorist system that accounted for the onto-
genesis of the self through the emergence of symbolic capacities developed in interaction with others. The self was,
then, preeminently a social product. Partly out of Mead's
influence, models of social interaction were constructed in
dramaturgical terms. Thus sociologist Robert E. Park comments:

> It is probably no mere historical accident that the word
> person, in its first meaning, is a mask. It is rather a
> recognition of the fact that everyone is always and
> everywhere, more or less consciously, playing a role...
> It is in these roles that we know each other; it is in
> these roles that we know ourselves. (quoted in Goffman
> 1959, p. 19)

The view of social interaction as drama is highly elaborated
in Erving Goffman's work. Not only does social interaction
consist in masks and role-playing, but we can also analyze
the performance of actors in various defined scenes and
settings before an audience located both front-stage and
backstage. The gifted actor is a master at techniques of
impression management and face work, and is responsive to a
variety of promptings and cues. While the dramaturgical
model provides a powerful tool for analyzing not only ongo-
ing social interaction but also interaction preserved in
literature and in other expressive media, it does grow out
of Western dramatic conventions. Can the dramaturgical
model be productively applied in non-Western contexts where
different conventions and understandings, as well as different standards of dramatic performance, obtain?

As an opening wedge into this issue, let me suggest
some perspectives derived from the ethnographic study of
masking and ceremonial performance among the Indians of
Eastern North America.[8] Among some of these tribes the
terms for mask have some interesting cognates. Whereas some
experts derive the etymology of the Latin persona from per-
sonare, 'to sound through',[9] the Iroquois term is related
to the term for "face". With other Eastern Woodlands groups
we get cognates referring to "skin", "bark"--and for the
Creeks, a possible etymology relating the term for "mask" to
the word for "eye".[10] While most of the terms relate to
external image or outer covering (in fact, one type of Iroquois mask was fashioned out of plaited corn-husks), I think
we do not fully understand the meaning of masks in these

cultures if we treat their usage as analogous to our sense
of masks as disguise, as distortion or caricature that covers up a true reality hidden behind the mask.

The wooden Iroquois "False Face" masks were considered to possess vital properties. They were carved from a living
basswood tree (a type of wood known for its astringent and
absorptive qualities), and represented a primordial mythic
figure whose domain was the forest and who possessed curing
powers. Custodial care of the mask involved a social relationship in that the mask required periodic "feeding". It
is interesting to note that the "foods" craved by the False
Face were sunflower oil, old tobacco (<u>Nicotiana rustica</u>),
and corn mush—which were smeared on the protruding lips of
the mask. Since these plants represent the earliest horticultural horizons in the area, it seems that the ritual
feeding of the mask is an ancient practice extending back
into prehistory. In symbolic terms, the relationship can be
seen to represent a symbiosis whereby successful exploitation of the products of the forest (i.e., wild game) and
safe passage through this dangerous domain (nature) are
exchanged for the domesticated products (i.e., cultivated
plants) of human labor (culture). If the terms of this traditional form of reciprocity are not honored and the masks
are left unfed, nightmares, illness, and general misfortune
will result.

From what has been said, Iroquois masks can be considered social persons in the Maussian sense. However, it is
important to realize that the human being who dons the mask
does not impersonate the False Face spirit; rather he unites
with and becomes that spirit in a fashion consistent with
Levy-Bruhl's idea of participation. Another way of considering this phenomenon, then, is <u>not</u> to view it as role-playing or play-acting but to see it as a temporary incarnation
of cosmic reality: the False Face spirit, in effect, imper-
sonates the mask wearer.[11] To a large extent, what is
real and ultimately true for the Iroquois is what is outside
and "up front" in the faces and interfaces of these masked
personages. Perhaps a closer approximation of the Indian
reality can be gleaned from a quotation from Frank Speck
(1942) regarding the "stage" upon which Indian rituals are
"performed":

> Ceremonial grounds, whether in the open or enclosed, rep-
> resent a deeply significant allegory, a phase of the
> sky-world on earth within which human beings are carrying

on actions in ceremonial form, the counterpart of those
of the spirits above, the latter being invisibly present
during performances accompaning their living kinfolk.

Regretfully, I take leave of the living world of masks,
but I hope enough has been said to show the relevance of
this topic to studies of self and person, as well as to indicate some of the strengths and limitations of the Western
dramaturgical approach to performances.

The concept of identity, as employed by many contemporary social scientists, shows close connections to social-
interaction theories. The notion of identity first gained
currency through the work of Erik Erikson (1950, 1959).
Erikson's version of psychoanalytic ego psychology stressed
the enduring sense of self and self-continuity that he
labeled "identity". Identity was shaped by the historic un-
folding of this sense of self as it passed through specific
epigenetic phases. The course of movement through these
phases was conditioned by the residual effects of resolution
or non-resolution of phase-specific conflicts encountered at
previous stages in the epigenetic cycle. Despite developmental change, identity can be likened to, in Dylan Thomas's
words, a "green fuse" that provides a sense of continuity
and sameness through the individual life cycle.

Erikson boldly endeavored (1968) to use the concept of
ego identity as a bridge that would connect the psychobiological drives of man's inner nature with those influences
on the self originating from society and culture. Despite
his efforts to effect a psychosocial synthesis, Erikson's
model is ultimately powered by the ineluctable forces of the
Freudian Id. To his credit, Erikson did spend two brief
periods doing fieldwork among the Sioux and the Yurok. He
succeeded in making some acute observations regarding childhood and world-view; but in place of ethnopsychological insight, we get applied psychoanalysis. Thus, weaponless
Sioux warriors skewer their externalized feminine superegos
around a Sun Dance pole; and, alas, the poor Yurok find
themselves drifting up the alimentary canal without a pad-
dle.

Erikson became something of a godfather to troubled
youth of the 1960s, with his popular notions of identity
crises and psychological moratorium. He produced innovative
work in psychobiography; Young Man Luther (1958), in partic-

ular, must stand as a modern masterpiece of this genre.
However, I think it fair to conclude that Erikson's notion
of identity, with its universalist psychobiological grid and
residual influence of sociocultural factors, has only a limited utility for comparative studies of the self.

The term identity is used generally by many theorists
to denote an image of the self. Richard Robbins (1973a) has
produced a survey of the use of the identity concept within
anthropology. He isolates three basic approaches or models:
1) the identity-health model, which stresses processes of
adjustment and maladjustment—mostly from a clinical perspective (c.f. Kenneth Soddy 1961, for a review of some of
the relevant issues involved here); 2) the identity-interac-
tion model, which has been discussed above; and 3) the identity world-view model, which emphasizes culturally constituted meanings and values, and will be treated below.

For analytic purposes, most theorists have found it
necessary to divide the concept of identity into various
aspects, components, or dimensions. Thus Erikson felt the
need to separate ego identity from the more generic concept
of identity and to distinguish positive from negative identity. Daniel R. Miller (1963, p. 673) differentiates public
identity from self-identity. In other analytic models, the
structure of identity is seen as consisting of different
interacting regions or stratigraphic layers arranged hier-
archically or in terms of temporal priorities. A typical
example here would be Miller's tripartite scheme, which recognizes a core identity, various sub-identities, and a
peripheral personal identity (pp. 674-76).

Identity can also be broken down into components that
refer to evaluative or self-appraisal functions. For these
purposes, Miller proposed (pp. 679-83) analytic distinctions
between what he labels actual identity, potential identity,
and ideal identity. A somewhat more elaborated model of
this type was developed by Anthony F.C. Wallace and myself
(1965) to examine certain encounters that we termed identity
struggles. In this scheme, total identity is divided into
the following four components: a real identity, indicating a
self-report about where the individual "really" stands with
regard to particular dimensions of identity; an ideal identity, referring to the kind of positive identity the individual would like to emulate; a feared identity, a negatively
valued identity that the individual desires to avoid; and a

claimed identity, a set of images that the individual presents to others in order to influence their evaluation of
his identity.

Some illustrations may clarify the distinctions. Certain dimensions of identity may be ordered on a lineal
scale. Stature provides an obvious example: Thus I may have
a real identity of being 5' 6-3/4", an ideal identity of
6'2", a feared identity of being a four foot midget, and a
claimed identity--claimed on the basis of wearing platform
shoes, hot-air-fluffed hair, and an erect posture--of 5'8".
Other identity dimensions may not be ordinal. A college
freshman may have an ideal image of himself as a "Big Man on
Campus", a feared identity of being regarded as a "nerd", a
real identity as a pedestrian B-minus student from the middle-class suburbs, and a claimed identity--proclaimed by a
weather-beaten fringed leather jacket, a shoulder-length
haircut, and a crimson headband--as an Apache warrior.

In general, the individual strives to move the real
identity closer to the ideal identity and to maximize distance from the feared identity. This is attempted through
manipulation of the claimed identity in social interaction
by "identity work", a process similar to Goffman's notion of
"face work" (Wallace 1967). The model has proven useful in
analyzing the dynamics of family therapy sessions, as well
as for charting identity struggles occurring in certain
other cultural arenas (Wallace and Fogelson 1965, pp. 387-
98). Lawrence C. Watson (1970) has applied this framework
to study identity processes among the Guajiro Indians of
Venezuela. Robbins (1973b) has employed it in his investigation of drinking behavior among the Naskapi Indians of
Northeastern Canada, and John L. Caughey (1980) has adopted
the general model to help understand the relationship of
personal identity to social identity on Truk.

The concept of identity has been extended to the level
of groups. An enormously diverse literature has grown up
around such notions as "national identity" and the currently
fashionable concept of "ethnic identity" (e.g., DeVos &
Romanucci-Ross 1975). I have no desire to review this research here and shall restrict myself to two general comments. First, I do not feel that individual identity is a
microcosm of collective identity, as is too often assumed.
It is the very lack of isomorphism between these two levels
that seems to generate some of the most interesting problems

(e.g., Kevin Avruch's 1981 book on American immigrants to
Israel). Secondly, I think that certain analytic frameworks
developed for studying individual identity can be usefully
extended to the group level. However, I also believe that
data for constructing a collective identity should be sought
less from individuals and more from analyses of collective
cultural expressions. I have in mind here the interpretation of particular culture-heroes and their roles as group
imagos, the analysis of themes from literature and popular
media, and the study of cultural performances (at home or
abroad) wherein a group encapsulates selected aspects of its
identity that it wishes to present to others and to itself
(see Bell 1968, Singer 1977).

Having considered social-interactionist viewpoints on
the self, with special emphasis on the concept of identity,
I now turn to certain cultural perspectives on the self as
developed within American anthropology.

The modern pluralistic and relativistic concept of culture remains one of the hallmarks of Boasian and Boasian-
derived anthropology. While Boas himself retained a healthy
respect for the individual as the ultimate locus of culture,
some of his followers--most notably A.L. Kroeber (1917) and
Robert Lowie (1917)--conceived of culture as possessing its
own ontological reality, and argued for a sharp separation
between psychological and cultural levels of explanation.
This extreme form of cultural determinism, particularly as
manifested in Kroeber's superorganic view, precipitated a
reaction among certain Boasian anthropologists that ultimately led to the Culture and Personality movement. While
classic Culture and Personality studies drew heavily on psychological and psychoanalytic theory, it too remained at
base a form of cultural determinism (see Aberle 1957). It
was culture that determined personality and not vice versa;
the individual was lost in the aggregated picture of an
ideal type congruent with cultural premises: deviations from
the ideal type were considered to represent maladjustment
and pathology.

However, early attacks on the superorganic position,
particularly those launched by Edward Sapir (1917) and Alexander Goldenweiser (1917), led to a reaffirmation of the
significance of the individual--not only as a passive bearer
and transmitter of culture, but also as an active creator
and re-creator of culture. Sapir's (1938; 1949 ed., p.569f.)

rediscovery of missionary J. Owen Dorsey's notation on an Omaha text, "But Two Crows denies this", indicated that members of the same culture could disagree about fundamental parts of their cultural belief system. Culture was not an infallible multilith machine printing identical copies. Recognition of the existence of individuals within primitive societies pointed to the theoretical issues posed by intra-cultural variations. Some of these issues can, perhaps, best be highlighted by a brief consideration of the work of Paul Radin.

Perhaps more important to the present discussion is Radin's pioneering book, published in 1927, Primitive Man as Philosopher. In this work, Radin took aim on continental social philosophers and armchair anthropologists who denied the existence of elaborated philosophical systems among primitive peoples. Through a synoptic survey of native cosmologies, recorded informant testimony, and oral literature (including myths, proverbs and aphorisms) he demonstrated that primitive man does, indeed, ask questions about such ultimate epistemological concerns as the origin and meaning of life and death; about ethical concerns regarding human conduct, morality, and the good life; about logic and the nature of evidence. He also demonstrated that some members of primitive societies exercise a healthy skepticism about the supposedly prelogical beliefs and mystical participations attributed to them by Levy-Bruhl and others.

Radin is probably most remembered today for his introduction of the life history as a technique in fieldwork (1913, 1920). Such documents often offered an inside glimpse into the personal recall and experiencing of events. If nothing else, the material contained in life histories demonstrated that the individual did not always mechanically retrace the blueprints of his culture. Life histories have many limitations. Boas, in his austere search for scientific truth, distrusted the technique because he felt informants were wont to lie and exaggerate, and investigators could never control for their own bias (1938, pp. 680-82). A more serious consideration is that life history and autobiography are alien forms of expression that have no precedent in most native cultures. Indeed, personal history as a literary genre emerges in the Western World only in Renaissance times.[12]

Radin argued that all societies contained two intellectual classes or personality types: the philosophic type, who
is given to reflection; and the man of action, who unques-
tioningly follows the dictates of the culture and derives
his fulfillment through doing rather than thinking. If I can
abruptly transpose the antithesis to modern preferences in
Scotch whiskey; the man of action would prefer Dewar's White
Label, while the philosopher would settle for Teachers High-
land Cream. The philosophers are always outnumbered by the
men of action, but Radin maintained that both types—and
certain recurring dialectical relationships between them—
are necessary for a society to remain viable.

One chapter in Primitive Man as Philosopher is of particular concern here: "The Nature of the Ego and Human Personality" (1927, p. 257-74). In this chapter Radin summarizes data reported for the Maori, Oglala Sioux, and Batak
that indicate the presence of sophisticated notions of the
ego. The ego is regarded by these peoples as multiplex and
dynamic; it is composed of a substantive body and various
named insubstantive essences. Radin bewailed the fact that
too few of his fellow ethnologists had attempted to obtain
systematic accounts of the ego from informed natives (1927,
p. 260). Unfortunately, with few exceptions (e.g., Lee 1945
and Smith 1952), Radin's admonitions were not heeded for
another quarter-century.[13]

A major stimulus for renewed interest in the self within American anthropology was a series of brilliant papers by
A. Irving Hallowell. A programatic essay, "The Self and Its
Behavioral Environment", appeared in 1954; a related group
of papers on behavioral evolution, which paid special attention to the evolutionary significance of the self, culmi-
nated in "Personality, Culture, and Society in Behavioral
Evolution" (1963a); several other papers provided in-depth
analyses of the conceptions of self and person among the
Ojibwa Indians (1955, 1960, 1963b, and 1966).

Hallowell regarded self-awareness, with the implicit
corollary assumption of subject/object distinction, as a
generic prerequisite for and universal feature of all human
culture. The notion of the self as an object that could be
differentiated from other objects that were non-self developed ontogenetically as a product of social interaction.
However, self concepts were also seen to be culturally constituted and thus variable in different human groups. Hal-

lowell situated the self in what he termed the behavioral environment—a culturally constituted field that is meaningful, perceptible, and phenomenologically real for participants in a particular culture. Hallowell felt that the self and the behavioral environment, so delineated, were subjects amenable to empirical research. To facilitate such study, he outlined a set of five basic orientations—provided by every culture—that function instrumentally in the individual's psychological adjustment to his world. These orientations are: a self orientation, an object-orientation, a spatio-temporal orientation, a motivational orientation, and a normative orientation.

In his related article on "The Ojibwa Self and Its Behavioral Environment" (1955), Hallowell makes an initial foray into this newly charted territory. He utilizes a synthetic first-person autobiographical statement to elucidate some dimensions of the Ojibwa self, but he doesn't formally analyze the five orientations listed above.

The article "Ojibwa Ontology, Behavior, and World View" (1960), originally published in a _festschrift_ for Paul Radin, has probably had the greatest impact of all of Hallowell's writings on the self and related concepts. In this brilliant exploration of ethnometaphysics, Hallowell concentrates on the Ojibwa view of the person. Culturally recognized classes of beings are delineated, and the concept of "person" is shown to be not coterminous with human beings. The category of person can include certain culturally postulated other-than-human beings who play a significant role in the Ojibwa's adjustment to their behavioral environment. The notion of person serves as an important tool for bringing to the surface many deeply embedded aspects of Ojibwa world-view: seemingly inconsistent features of Algonkian grammatical categories, name usage, ideas about power, mythologic beliefs, conceptions of dreams, metamorphoses, and "souls" are unified into a coherent moral universe.

Hallowell's richly detailed (1960) account does offer some startling insights into Ojibwa ethnometaphysics, but certain conceptual and methodological questions remain: how is the concept of the person related to the notion of the self that Hallowell discussed so cogently in previous programatic statements? How are data relevant to notions of the self and person collected? Let us consider some of these issues in some of the work that attempts to follow Hallowell's lead.

Mary Black, in her unpublished doctoral dissertation
(1967) and in several important papers (1969a, 1969b, 1976,
1977a, and 1977b), has attempted to test Hallowell's infor-
mally derived classification of Ojibwa ontology with more
formal ethnosemantic eliciting procedures. She has paid
particular attention to a taxonomy encompassing "persons".

In general, Black's findings tend to validate the
general classification of "persons" advanced by Hallowell.
Black shows that agreement as to what is included in the
category of non-human persons is not altogether consistent
for her Ojibwa informants. Hallowell had anticipated some
of these difficulties by recognizing that outward appearance
of form--the basis of most classification--might obscure a
common inner essence; he also noted that certain Ojibwa
"persons" were capable of metamorphosis and thus couldn't be
constrained to a single taxonomic category. Black extends
the explanation of categorical ambiguity to include situa-
tional variables (1977a) and native notions of inherent and
transitory power (1977b). She also argues that a certain
degree of percept ambiguity and categorical indeterminancy
may be an important (and necessary?) feature of Ojibwa (and
all?) cognitive orientations.

One interesting feature of Black's (and Hallowell's)
analysis is that by making an initial distinction between
self and objects-other-than-self, the category of persons
(both human and other-than-human) is subsumed under the category of living things, which in turn becomes a sub-category
of objects-other-than-self. The unexamined implication of
all this hierarchical taxonomy is that the self cannot be
considered a person, either as a human being or as an object
possessing other-than-human attributes (e.g., degrees of
power). Such a conclusion seems incongruous in the face of
Ojibwa ethnographic data, and calls for a more detailed and
inclusive treatment of the taxonomic features defining the
Ojibwa self (a topic that Hallowell leaves incompletely analyzed in his article "The Ojibwa Self and Its Behavioral
Environment").

Black's reanalysis of Hallowell's Northern Ojibwa data,
plus her own focused fieldwork among related Minnesota
Chippewa, invite consideration of appropriate methodological
approaches to studying such complex matters as the self and

<u>person</u>. Hallowell's insights·into the significance of the self and person came only late in his career--after extended ethnographic field research, control of the documentary record, acquisition of linguistic proficiency, and experience derived from administering projective tests. He did not set out explicitly to study the self and person; the significance of these concepts for understanding Ojibwa phenomenological realities arose gradually. Evidence for the structure of Ojibwa ethnometaphysics was based on linguistic clues, critical anecdotes, and apparent relations between different ranges and levels of ethnographic data. Only in his later papers did he attempt to construct a taxonomic model that unintentionally resembled the paradigms of the ethnoscientists.

Black's work decisively builds on the foundation provided by Hallowell and goes directly to the problem of the Ojibwa classification of things, or ontology. Rather than a distillation of implicit emic categories derived from what Geertz (1973) would label "thick description", Black utilizes formal eliciting procedures from her informants ("teachers") to generate ethnosemantic distinctions. Ethnographic grounding and salience are clearly of secondary concern, although certain suggestive insights into matters such as Ojibwa ideas of "power-control" and medicine (1977b) do emerge from her continuing research.

However, the degree of linguistic determination inherent in Black's approach may preclude deeper understanding of the notions of self and person. Black is not so naive as to fall victim to the nominalistic fallacy, "If the natives do not have a term for something, then it doesn't exist." Like Hallowell, she recognizes that the fact that the Ojibwa do not have a term for "person" does not deny its reality as a "covert category" occupying demarcatable semantic space in the Ojibwa classification of living things. Nevertheless, Black's adherence to formal eliciting procedures conducted in artificial settings makes one wonder if perhaps she is tapping only verbal behavior (and artifical behavior, at that, since it is divorced from everyday discourse).

I do not mean to dismiss the significance of formal ethnosemantic inquiry. Obviously the preponderance of information that an anthropologist obtains in the field comes from interviews and conversations. The more stuctured and controlled these interactions are, the more reliable these

data tend to be. But I do feel that ungrounded ethnoseman-
tics will lead us only part-way toward understanding ideas
such as self and person.[14]

Another approach to the study of self and person, which
also utilizes Ojibwa data and builds upon some of Hallowell's ideas, is represented in the work of Thomas Hay
(1968, 1973, 1977). Hay distinguishes between a conscious
self-concept (which is relatively easily verbalizable) and
an unconscious self-concept (usually out of awareness; when
raised to consciousness, subject to vigorous denial). These
two self-concepts, thus, can be inconsistent.

To illustrate, Hay points out that the conscious Ojibwa
self-concept emphasizes a lack of "powers," either natural
or magical, and denial of capacity for anger. However,
according to Hay, they unconsciously attribute to themselves
great magical power, especially when angry; they further
assume that this anger can be easily triggered and can have
dangerous consequences for the object of their anger. Hay
interprets this inconsistency between the conscious and
unconscious self-concepts as psychodynamically premised on
repression of these powerful capacities to harm others and
projection of these impulses onto other-than-human or <u>pawág-
anak</u> persons. The conscious self of the Ojibwa avoids expression of anger and behavior toward others that might be
considered demanding; they picture themselves as helpless
and powerless, petitioning the powerful <u>pawáganak</u> for
assistance in times of need. By analyzing over 600 observed
adult responses to annoying behavior by children, Hay
supports his hypothesis that the unconscious self-concept
accounts for the observed behavior better than the conscious
self-concept does. He goes on to argue that the genesis of
the Ojibwa unconscious self-concept results from characteristic adult noncontrol of aggressive behavior in children.

While some of Hay's assumptions may be questioned and
alternate interpretations of his data could be advanced, I
think his work is important in demonstrating the salience of
unconscious and non-verbalizable aspects of the self that
would be missed in the type of analysis pursued by Black.
Hay's approach also shows how systematic and statistical use
can be made of naturally occurring observed behavior. However, it is important to recognize that the emic level of
interpretation, the Ojibwa's <u>own</u> conscious theories about
their self-concept and motivational dispositions, loses out

to Hay's psychoanalytic-based interpretations. In short, Hay provides a sufficient but not a necessary explanation of certain aspects of the Ojibwa self.

Anne Straus's ethnopsychological research among the Northern Cheyenne (1976, 1977) also clearly grows out of the pioneering studies of Hallowell. Since Dr. Straus is a contributor to this volume and is more than capable of speaking for herself, I won't presume to summarize her contributions. However, I will take the opportunity to comment briefly on some aspects of her work that strike me as relevant to the present discussion. Unlike the fragmentary description of the Ojibwa self presented by Hallowell, Black, and Hay, Straus provides a comprehensive account of the Cheyenne conception of self, including its component parts and their integration. She also offers a native model of the normal development of the self through the procreative-life-death cycle, a course marked with interlocking sets of Cheyenne symbols that sum up to an enclosed total system.

Finally, she offers an extended description and analysis of the Cheyenne concept of person. Unlike the Ojibwa case, person is a named concept among the Cheyenne. The Cheyenne notion of person also extends beyond human beings to encompass various other-than-human persons. However, not all human beings are persons. Personhood is a status that must be attained through participation in the Cheyenne moral community of persons. Children lack knowledge and responsibility for their own actions, and thus are considered only potential persons. Deaf-mutes lacking powers of Cheyenne speech are non-persons, as are the insane and the celebrated Cheyenne "contraries".

Personhood is regarded as a status that can be lost. Depersonalization can eventuate from serious transgressions against the tribal norms, such as murder or violations of sacred taboos. My own research among the Cherokees also indicates that not all human beings are persons. Witches, for example can assume a human appearance and thereby be classified as human beings; but they are not persons, since they operate outside the constraints of the moral community. Personhood is just one of their guises; they are considered to be counterfeit persons. They subsist only by capturing the life essence of others. In fact, some Cherokees do not even consider witches to be living beings. For all intents and purposes, witches are "dead" vis-à-vis the human commu-

nity; and once exposed, given the right time and opportunity, they <u>are</u> killed (Fogelson 1975).

The Cheyenne self attains individuation through different admixtures of qualities arranged along two polar
continua: a good/crazy axis and a wisdom/energy axis.
Differentially accented combinations are characteristic of
different stages of the life cycle and appropriate to complementary sex-role patterning. Thus, while personhood em-
bodies a minimal set of shared qualities necessary for participation and functioning within the Cheyenne moral universe, Cheyenne persons possess distinctive individual
selves.

Straus's orientation and methodology in obtaining this
extraordinary rich corpus of material deserve comment. Like
Mary Black, she clearly set out to study aspects of ethnopsychology: her project was not a serendipitous spin-off of
more general ethnographic concerns; from the outset, she had
misgivings about the dominant thrust of psychological anthropology in which the major effort is to apply Western
theories of psychological processes and Western conceptions
of personality to understand, or translate, the beliefs and
behaviors of non-Western peoples. While in the field, she
consciously kept Western theories and models at arm's length
and attempted, as much as possible, to gain an emic reading
of Cheyenne psychology and personality (or conversely, to
obtain the Cheyenne's own etic categories in these areas).
In order to accomplish this, she acquired a working knowledge of the Cheyenne language, she engaged in intensive par-
ticipant-observation, and she developed some close friend-
ships with her Cheyenne colleagues. Much of her data derive
from the close questioning and counter-questioning of her
Cheyenne friends. The results from sporadic attempts to use
formal testing and eliciting techniques were disappointing.
As in most successful fieldwork, the ultimate instrument
proved to be a sensitive and responsive investigator.

Perhaps the next step is to relax the arm-length hold
on folk and formal Western psychological theories. Maybe
these theories can now be brought into closer proximity to
Cheyenne formulations, in an effort to discern significant
similarities and differences. Another future strategy might
be to attempt a more fine-grained comparison between Cheyenne and Ojibwa concepts of self and person. The Cheyenne
and Ojibwa languages both belong to the Macro-Algonkian

family. If I am correct in assuming that a proper understanding of concepts like the self and person involves much
more than linguistic labeling and taxonomic classification,
then critical differences between Cheyenne and Ojibwa ethnopsychology demand historical, sociological, and cultural explanations.   In short, there are possibilities here for at
least partially controlled comparisons and the raising of
questions that could stimulate reanalysis of existing materials and the collection of critical new data.

     I want to reemphasize here my conviction that the prop-
er study of ethnopsychology and ethnopersonality requires
more than fragmentary ethnographic observations supposedly
reflective of primitive, or qualitatively different, mental-
ities; more than a collection of linguistic terms imprecise-
ly translated into approximate English equivalents, without
consideration of the connotative and etymological meanings
of these terms or their sociolinguistic usage; more than the
construction of a taxonomy (taxonomy is, after all, only a
tool for understanding and should not be an end in itself).
Rather, ethnopsychological and ethnopersonality data must be
integrated into the larger structures of meaning inherent in
any cultural system. Perhaps my plea will ring less hollow
if I provide a truncated example of the kind of understanding that I am advocating.

     Levy-Bruhl, in The "Soul" of the Primitive (1927; 1928
ed., p. 134f.), cites the following quotation from the early
government ethnologist James Mooney as testimony for the
Cherokee belief in the existence of an "external soul":
     Some war-captains knew how to put their lives up in the
     tree-tops during a fight, so that even if they were
     struck by the enemy they could not be killed. Once in a
     battle with the Shawano [Shawnee], the Cherokee leader
     stood directly in front of the enemy and let the whole
     party shoot at him, but was not hurt until the Shawano
     captain, who knew this war medicine himself, ordered his
     men to shoot into the branches above the head of the
     other. They did this and the Cherokee leader fell dead.
Levy-Bruhl perceptively notes that the term "life", rather
than the much-abused term "soul", is used in this account to
refer to "vital principle". He poses the seeming paradox of
how an individual can gain security by removing "life" or
"vital essence" from his corporeal body and answers that the
prelogical mind sees nothing extraordinary about bi-presence
in which a being can coexist in two places at once.

I have collected several Cherokee sacred formulas, written in the Sequoyah syllabary, dealing with war and ballgame "medicine". In these documents, the "life essence" (which my informant did, indeed, translate as 'soul') is frequently elevated to the safety of the "tree-top trail", whereas the 'soul' of the enemy is conversely mired in the ground, where it is exposed and can be trod upon. Displacement of "vital essences", or of life-sustaining organs, within the body is also characteristic of certain Cherokee mythological figures whose "hearts" may be located in their fingers or some other unnatural locus.

Levy-Bruhl would probably be amused, if not startled, to learn that Cherokee metaphysics posits the existence of four separate vital essences or souls. The first soul, which can be glossed as the 'soul of consciousness', is located in the head or throat and is associated with saliva. The second soul is centered in the liver, is related to black and yellow bile, and can be termed the 'hepatic soul'. The third soul can be translated as the 'visceral soul', is located in the flesh, and is associated with blood. The fourth and final soul is the 'osseous soul' that resides in the bones and is associated with sperm.

These four souls normally coexist within the body; but one or several can depart during sleep or by means of certain ritual actions, as in the war medicine cited by Levy-Bruhl. These souls can be affected by or be captured by the machinations of a sorcerer or witch and result in illness or death. The specific bodily fluids, or humours, mentioned above contain vital properties and provide contiguous connection between the internal bodily soul and its external manifestation. Care must be exercised in disposing of these substances.

Cherokee beliefs about death are associated with this quadripartite-soul theory. Death is less of an event and more of a process, in the Cherokee belief system. What we would regard as physical or clinical death is marked for the Cherokees by the loss and permanent departure of the soul of consciousness. One week later, often after primary burial, the hepatic soul takes its leave of the body. The visceral soul departs a month (or 28 days, to use the multiple of the two sacred Cherokee numbers: four and seven) after physical death; this timing may once have coincided with secondary interment, reburial after the flesh was freed from the bone.

The osseous soul separates from the skeleton one year after physical death, and this final juncture in the life-death cycle was commemorated among some Southeastern tribes by a feast of the dead.

As implied earlier, this normal sequence of soul departure can be inverted by sorcery and witchcraft. Thus, a man whose liver soul has been stolen and destroyed is already dead—though he, and any one else, may not know it until he expires within the span of seven days.

Many Cherokee disease categories also have reference to soul disturbances. Thus one class of disease literally translates as "my saliva is spoiled"; a variety of liver malfunctions are diagnosed as the "Yellow", the "Black", or in combination as the "Black Yellowness having Spots"; blood disorders, including one that resembles our commercial syndrome of "tired blood", are recognized, as are various diseases of the bone that tend to afflict older people.

The Cherokee notion of progressive soul departure is recapitulated in reverse order in their theory of procreation. The soul of consciousness is bestowed by the ultimate creator-being on high, who probably can be identified with the Sun (the 'apportioner', in the sense of the one who divides night and day). I have been unable to derive the source of the hepatic soul, but I suspect it may originate from an underworld power who stands in opposition to the sun. Flesh and blood are contributed by the mother, while the father provides bone, which in its uncongealed state exists as sperm. The frequent metaphoric relationship between blood and descent thus takes a more substantive turn among the matrilineal Cherokee.

I could go on to document the linkage of soul concepts to Cherokee taboos, burial customs, directional symbols, calendrics, and color categories; but I hope I have said enough to convince the skeptic that these components of the Cherokee self, these life-essences or souls, are linked to other domains of Cherokee culture by a ramifying system of ethno-logic. The structure of the Cherokee self possesses a systemic coherence that demands attention in its own terms. This structure organizes, makes meaningful, and almost seems to generate superficially disparate ranges of Cherokee belief, behavior, and experience. The Cherokee self system outlined here cannot be properly understood without some

comprehension of the larger culture of which it is part.
The life essence in the tree-tops represents more than an
example of the prelogical mind violating our law of contradiction with vouchsafed impunity.

Our ultimate purpose in the comparative study of the
self and related concepts should be to develop analytic
frameworks, methodological procedures, and theoretical explanations that can not only accommodate diverse data from
non-Western societies, but can also preserve and capitalize
on the distinctive features and embedded meanings inherent
in these materials. To approach these distant and possibly
unattainable goals, let me suggest some more proximal
research priorities and strategies.

First, we need more systematic examination of our own
folk and scientific theories of the self. In studying our
folk conceptions, a possible first step might be to look at
semantic usage. What are the assumptions underlying such
commonplace expressions as: "It was a self-less act.", "I
was beside myself.", "He has an inflated ego.", "She
attended in-person.", "He has a lot of personality.", "New
Jersey suffers an identity crisis in being located between
Philadelphia and New York.", "The Russians saved face by
rejecting the Salt Treaty.". Examples of such statements
from everyday speech are not hard to come by; but the question to be asked is how such utterances can be decoded and
combined to produce coherent systems of meaning, and how
these revealed systems relate to other aspects of culture.
The example of New Jersey's identity crisis, attributed to
former Governor Hughes, was purposely included to demonstrate that social scientific terminology (frequently
scorned as jargon) is not always insulated from popular
usage. And indeed, as has been long recognized, folk
cultural assumptions permeate scientific conceptions.

If this paper has demonstrated nothing else, it has
shown how muddled our own scholarly and scientific conceptions about the self have become. What would a Cherokee
philosopher be able to make of our overlapping--and often
contradictory--conceptions of self ego, person, identity,
individuality, persona, personality...? Sometimes these
conceptions are used as synonyms; at other times, to stress
different dimensions or shades of meaning. A comprehensive
and consistent semantic and pragmatic systematization of
these concepts is probably too much to envision.

More intensive and coordinated work on non-Western concepts of the self and person are needed.[15] The available
literature, deficient as it frequently is, should be reex-
amined with an eye to clarifying and synthesizing what is
already known and to discover problems that might yield to
fresh research.   I have in mind here a review not only of
published material directly dealing with the self and related concerns, but the excavation of usable data buried in
ethnographic writings. My exploration into Cherokee soul
concepts suggests that a reinterpretation of other theories
of the soul might be a productive endeavor. The soul fig-
ured prominently in early disputes about primitive religion
that were initiated by E.B. Tylor's Primitive Culture (1871)
and continued by his critics and followers. Much recyclable
material probably exists in monographic treatments of the
soul, such as those produced by A.E. Crawley (1909), Sir
James Frazer (1911), Levy-Bruhl (1927), and Ake Hultkrantz
(1953).

More important, certainly, will be new field investigations in which systematic study of self and person concepts
becomes a central rather than a peripheral concern.   The
primitive world was fast disappearing when anthropology
first became a scholarly discipline. The situation is even
more urgent today.   It is important that evidence of the
thought-ways of non-Western peoples be recorded before such
material becomes permanently erased from the human record.
All three Cherokee instructors who taught me about Cherokee
notions of the self are now dead.

Prospective investigators of ethnopersonality should
have a grasp of the native language and sensitivity to linguistic nuance. They should be skilled ethnographers capable of collecting behavioral and social interactional data
relevant to the expression of the self. Knowledge of the
general culture is also essential because, as my Cherokee
example tried to indicate, pursuit of ideas about the self
can lead in unforeseen directions.

The acquisition of self-conceptions through socialization and enculturation is an obviously important topic that
has been neglected in this presentation. The application of
Piagetian and other developmental schemes to non-Western
peoples should continue to prove useful in studying processes leading to self-awareness and subsequent capacities.
My only caution is that such schemes be juxtaposed with im-

plicit and explicit native models of human development, the
existence of which is well illustrated by Straus (1977) and
Robin and Tonia Ridington (1970).

The immediate results of following through on the kinds
of research priorities and strategies proposed here will be
the discovery of a plurality of theories and conceptions
regarding the self. In time, however, the seemingly chaotic
multiplicity may be reduced through careful comparative
analysis. General principles and dimensions may be adduced
that will approach universal validity.

The anthropology of the self is in its infancy, and it
awaits self-awareness of its own significance.

ENDNOTES

1. This historical section has been informed by numerous
   secondary, as well as primary, sources. Among the more
   useful secondary sources that have influenced the present discussion are Alexander Goldenweiser (1933), Fay
   B. Karpf (1932), A. Irving Hallowell (1954a), E.E.
   Evans-Pritchard (1965) and David Bidney (1967).

2. These German concepts defy precise translation into
   English. Völkerpsychologie can be, and has been, rendered 'group psychology', 'social psychology', and 'the
   psychology of peoples'. The literal translation 'folk
   psychology' is perhaps misleading, as it might suggest
   the particular people's own psychological conceptions.
   Therefore, it is probably wisest to retain the original
   German term. H. Steinthal and M. Lazarus, in a pragmatic article in the first issue (1860) of their journal, Zeitschrift fur Völkerpsychologie und Sprachwis-
   senshaft (perhaps the first journal devoted to what we
   would now call Psychological Anthropology and Language
   and Culture), envisioned two approaches to the study of
   Völkerpsychologie: first, a general völkerpsychologie
   that would encompass processes of generic human mental
   evolution; and secondly, a specific völkerpsychologie
   that would be concerned with the psychology of particular peoples.

The term Völkgeist ('folk spirit') again is difficult
to translate. In the hands of nineteenth- and early
twentieth-century German social philosophers, it took
on varying shades of meaning ranging from a disembodied
spiritual quality, to a collective sense of the French
le moral as "mind" or "being", to the modern use of the
term "ethos" as denoting the emotional tone associated
with a collectivity. Gregory Bateson, in Naven (1936)
is usually credited with establishing the modern usage
of the concept of "ethos". However, it is interesting
to note that John Stuart Mill uses this Greek term in
its approximate modern usage, in his conception of
"ethology".

3. Thus, for example, it was argued that a people's
    imagination could be discovered in their literature,
    their moral sense in their laws and customs, their
    emotions in their religious rituals, etc.

4. The implicit use of the notion of apperception can be
    traced back in Boas's work to his doctoral disserta-
    tion, which was a psychophysical experiment on differ-
    ent reports of the color of sea water. The notion of
    apperception was taken up and elaborated in America by
    William James (Principles of Psychology, 1890), and
    formed an important part of his psychological system.

5. It is worth emphasizing that the legitimate criticism
    of early culture-and-personality theory, to the effect
    that culture cannot be deduced from the personality of
    its individual members, finds an equally egregious par-
    allel in the efforts of social-and-cultural determin-
    ists to derive the personalities from social structures
    or cultural systems.

6. For major implications of Dogon philosophy, see espe-
    cially Griaule (1948) and Griaule & Dieterlen (1954).
    These scholars also explored Dogon concepts of "soul"
    and "person" (e.g., Griaule 1940, 1947; Dieterlen 1941,
    1973).

7. Reasonable starting points for surveying psychological
    understandings of the self concept can be found in All-
    port (1943) and Sherif (1968).

8. This account draws heavily on the typological work of Frank G. Speck (1950) and that of William N. Fenton (1940), as well as interpretative leads provided by John Witthoft (1967). An exploration into the deeply embedded meanings of Eastern Woodland masking will be found in R.D. Fogelson and A.B. Walker (1980 and in press).

9. According to the Oxford English Dictionary, this popular etymology is made dubious by the long o in persona. Others have suggested other roots for the word, including an Etruscan form with a quite different meaning. (Robert Elliot, personal communication)

10. I am indebted to Amelia B. Walker for tracing the semantics of some of this lexical material.

11. Many of the Iroquois False Faces have twisted visages, supposedly resulting from an usuccessful power struggle in which the prototypical False Face was defeated by the Great Spirit or Sapling. William Sturtevant, in a paper presented to the 1979 International Congress of Americanists, related an instance in which one of these masks slipped off a dancer during a ceremony, and the face of the man behind the mask mirrored the distorted physiognomy represented by the mask.

12. Thus we read in Paul Murray Kendall's fascinating entry, "Biographical Literature", in the New Encyclopaedia Britannica (Macropaedia, II:1010):

>   Speaking generally, then, it can be said that autobiography begins with the Renaissance in the 15th century; and, surprisingly enough, the first example was written not in Italy but in England by a woman entirely untouched by the "new learning" or literature. In her old age Margery Kempe, the sobbing mystic, or hysteric, of Lynn in Norfolk, dictated an account of her bustling, far-faring life, which, however concerned with religious experience, racily reveals her somewhat abrasive personality and the impact she made on her fellows. This is done in a series of scenes, mainly developed by dialogue. Though calling herself, in abject humility, "the creature," Margery knew, and has effectively transmitted the proof, that she was a remarkable person.

The questions of why the genre of autobiography emerges
in the West only in the 15th century, in England, with
an unstable woman, and why the major form is
dialogic--these are indeed matters for the sociology
(or anthropology) of knowledge to ponder.

13. Discussion of conceptual issues concerning "the individual" and "individualism" continue to generate much
heat, but little light, in the recent literature. It
seems to me that three separable issues have become
hopelessly confused in these recent discussions: 1) the
"reality" of the individual in society and culture; 2)
the analytic utility of such a concept for comparative
research; and 3) the nature of individualism as an ide-
ological doctrine or value emphasis in different cultures.

   With regard to the first issue, the "reality" of
individuals seems undeniable. Culture, language, mind,
and thought seem premised on the existence of a reflexive, self-monitoring, individual self. What seems at
issue is culture variation and differential degrees of
articulateness and elaboration of this individual self.
Thus the boundaries of the individual vary enormously,
as do body-image conceptions and the components of the
individual self--the latter frequently phrased as material entities or immaterial essences that approximate
the notion of "soul". The reality of the individual
self or ego can be vouchsafed by the observation made
long ago by Franz Boas in The Mind of Primitive Man
(1911) that no known language lacked personal pronouns
to indicate "I, thou, and he" (1938 ed.:165).

   The utility of a concept of the individual in historical and cross-cultural work has been questioned by
many. Perhaps most visible in this debate has been
Louis Dumont, who considers the notion of the individual an obstacle to understanding Indian society and
history (1965a, 1965b, 1967). Dumont's more encompassing concern has been to contrast basic orientations in
Western and Indian civilizations. While one can concede that Hindu society is less "individualistic" than
Western society in terms of value emphases and styles
of thought, it would be harder to concede that Indians
lack a vocabulary for expressing notions of an indivi-

dual self, do not have a system of names that help
label and differentiate an "individual," or that Indians are incapable of internal dialogues, self-reflection, and distinctions between self and other(s), all
of which imply an individual self.

The second issue, as represented by Dumont, is
obviously related to the third: individualism as ideology. Individualism has long been pointed out as an
abiding value and mode of thought in Western society.
Steven Lukes (1973) offers a useful survey of the history and components of the Western idea of individualism as expressed in philosophy and social science. (It
is interesting to note here that Western intellectuals
have so internalized the notion of individualism as
dominant in Western world-view that they tend to ignore
or deemphasize the presence of such competing ideas as
the development of socialism as a particularly Western
notion, or the wisdom of the collective voice as embodied in the idea of vox populi (see G. Boas 1969.).

Kenelm Burridge's recent book Someone, No One
(1979) is an ambitious effort to clarify the understanding of individuality. I cannot here do justice to
the subtlety of his argument, which involves cross-cultural as well as Western historical data, Burridge
poses an analytic opposition between a person—defined
as someone with a social and moral identity—and an
individual, who lacks such an identity and therefore is
capable of a conscious perception of morality and society and thus can act as an independent commentator and
innovator. Burridge questions the simplistic association of individualism with greed, selfishness, and
exploitation of others and discerns a positive value in
individualistic moral responsibility that he traces
back to the New Testament and Early Christianity. Nevertheless, his distinction seems almost a modern reit-
eration of classical evolutionary and French sociological theories, since individualism is viewed as a Western development historically precipitated from a more
general matrix of undifferentiated personalism. While
Burridge's scheme bears superficial resemblance to
Radin's distinction between men of thought ("individuals") and men of action ("social persons"), Radin would
be more prone to recognize the existence of primitive
philosophers.

Another trend in recent considerations of the individual self is to see the construction (and deconstruction) of the self as a dynamic process mediated by symbols. Such a viewpoint is implicit in "The Invention of the Self" (a chapter in Roy Wagner's The Invention of Culture, 1975), explicit in Abner Cohen's "Symbolic Action and the Structure of the Self" (1977) and in Bruce Kapferer's essay "Mind, Self, and Other in Demonic Illness: The Negation and Reconstruction of Self" (1979). While less dynamic, Milton Singer's attempt to establish a semiotic anthropology of the self (1980), based upon Peirce's theory of signs, represents a notable effort to incorporate the self into mainstream symbolic anthropology.

In partial opposition, perhaps, to symbolic studies of the individual or self, which are premised on an essential dualism between self as subject and self as object, are various recent pleas for a more holistic and phenomenologically informed understanding of the self. These would include T.M.S. Evens' essay on "The Predication of the Individual in Anthropological Interactionism" (1977); Lawrence Watson's attempt to distinguish the study of personality from the study of I ndividuals more or less on the basis of nomothetic versus ideographic emphases (1978); and Gelya Frank's eloquent plea for a phenomenological perspective that will emphasize the experiencing self in life-history research (1979).

14. I do not mean to disparage the quality and significance of Mary Black's work, for which I have considerable respect; for her, ethnoscientific analysis is a means to an end of deeper understanding of native conceptions, rather than an end in itself. Rather, I think, the barreness of the ethnoscientific approach to ethnopersonality study is most clearly revealed in recent work with the Melanesian A'ara by Geoffrey White (1978, 1980) and similar research in Africa among the Masai by Kirk & Burton (1977), Burton & Kirk (1979). In these methodologically sophisticated studies, formally elicited "personality descriptors" are mapped and statistically analyzed with regard to particular individuals and situations. This meticulous work comes close to a revival of a discredited trait-psychology in exotic dress. The "personality descriptors" themselves do not

seem to form part of a natural system recognized or
recognizable by the A'ara or Masai, and the lateral and
deeper semantic associations of those decontextualized
lexemes are inadequately explored. We end up with
admirably "clean" studies that possess undoubted reli-
ability, but the validity is limited to such an artificial and restricted domain--so abstracted from real
people, real behavior, and real situations--that we
learn very little about A'ara or Masai ethnopersonality.

15. The focus in this text has been on the ethnopersonality
of Algonkian-speaking Indians mainly because a certain
continuity in research has been achieved here, and various approaches to the study of ethnopersonality can be
illustrated and evaluated. Important ethnopersonality
work has been reported in other parts of the world and
seems to be increasing: e.g., Read did pioneering work
on the person concept among the Gahuku—Gama of New
Guinea (1954/1955); Valentine produced an interesting
analysis of Lakalai (New Britain) ethnopsychology
(1963); Geertz's extended essay on "Person, Time and
Conduct in Bali" (1966) follows an interesting perspective; Fred Myers has described the self and personhood
for the Pintupi Aborigines of Australia (1979); Mary
Druke has demonstrated the possibilities for deriving
ethnopersonality from ethnohistoric documents concerning the Iroquois (1980); Christopher Boehm has examined
the moral self among Montenegrens (1980); and J. Christopher Crocker has published two papers on self concepts among the Bororo of South America (1977, 1979);
Michelle Rosaldo's monograph (1980) on the Ilongot of
the Philippines contains rich ethnopersonality data
(although it is not always informed by a consistent
analytic or theoretical scheme). Finally, several man-
uscripts by McKim Marriott should soon see the light of
published day and illuminate the complexities of Hindu
ethnopsychology.

REFERENCES

Aberle, D. 1957. "The Influence of Linguistics on Early
   Culture and Personality Theory". In Essays in
   the Science of Culture (ed. by G. Dole & R.
   Caneiro, New York: T.Y. Crowell), pp. 1-29.
Allport, G.W. 1937. Personality: A Psychological Inter-
   pretation. New York: Henry Holt.
Allport, G.W. 1943. "The Ego in Contemporary Psychology",
   Psychological Review, L:451-78.
Avruch, K. 1981. American Immigrants in Israel: Social
   Identities and Change. Chicago: University of
   Chicago Press.
Bateson, G. 1965. Naven: A Survey of the Problems
   Suggested by a Composite Picture of a New Guinea
   Tribe Drawn from Three Points of View. 2nd ed.
   Stanford: Stanford University Press.
Bell, D. 1968. "National Character Revisited: A Proposal
   for Renegotiating the Concept". In The Study of
   Personality: An Interdisciplinary Appraisal (ed.
   by E. Norbeck, D. Price-Williams, & E. McCord;
   New York: Holt, Reinhart and Winston), pp.103-20.
Bidney, D. 1953. Theoretical Anthropology. 1967, aug-
   mented ed., New York: Schocken.
Black, M.B. 1967. "An Ethnoscience Investigation of Ojibwa
   Ontology and World View". Ph.D. Dissertation,
   Stanford University.
Black, M.B. 1969a. "Eliciting Folk Taxonomy in Ojibwa".
   In Cognitive Anthropology (ed. by S.A. Tyler, New
   York: Holt, Reinhart and Winston), pp. 165-89.
Black, M.B. 1969b. "A Note on Gender in Eliciting Ojibwa
   Semantic Structures". Anthropological Linguis-
   tics, XI:177-86.
Black, M.B. 1976. "Semantic Variability in a Northern
   Ojibwa Community". Papers in Linguistics,
   (special issue: Language Use in Canada, ed. by
   R. Darnell, Edmonton: Linguistic Research, Inc),
   IX:129-57.
Black, M.B. 1977a. "Ojibwa Taxonomy and Percept Ambigu-
   ity". Ethos, V:90-118.
Black, M.B. 1977b. "Ojibwa Power Belief System". In The
   Anthropology of Power (ed. by R.D. Fogelson &
   R.N. Adams, New York: Academic Press), pp. 141-
   51.

Boas, F.   1911.   The Mind of Primitive Man.   1938 rev. ed.,
New York: Macmillan.

Boas, F.   1938.   "Methods of Research".   In General Anthropology, (ed   by F. Boas, Boston: D.C. Heath), pp.
666-86.

Boas, G.   1969.   Vox Populi: Essays in the History of an
Idea.   Baltimore: Johns Hopkins Press.

Boehm, C.   1980.   "Exposing the Moral Self in Montenegro:
The Use of Natural Definitions to Keep Ethnography Descriptive".   American Ethnologist, VII:
1-26.

Burridge, K.   1979.   Someone, No One: An Essay on Individuality.   Princeton, N.J.: Princeton University
Press.

Burton, M. & L. Kirk.   1979.   "Sex Differences in Masai
Cognition of Personality and Social Identity".
American Anthropologist, LXXXI:841-73.

Caughey, J.L.   1980.   "Personal Identity and Social Organization".   Ethos, VIII:173-203.

Cohen, A.   1977.   "Symbolic Action and the Structure of the
Self".   In Symbols and Sentiments (ed. by I.
Lewis, New York: Academic Press), pp. 117-28.

Crapanzano, V.   1979.   Preface to Do Kamo (see Leenhardt
1947).

Crawley, A.E.   1909.   The Idea of the Soul.   London:
Methuen.

Crocker, J.C.   1977.   "The Mirrored Self: Identity and Ritual Inversion Among Eastern Bororo".   Ethnology,
XVI:129-45.

Crocker, J.C.   1979.   "Selves and Alters Among the Eastern
Bororo".   In Dialectical Societies (ed. by D.
Maybury-Lewis, Cambridge: Harvard University
Press), pp. 249-300.

DeVos, G. & L. Romanucci-Ross.   1975.   Ethnic Identity:
Cultural Continuities and Change.   Palo Alto:
Mayfield Publishing Co.

Dieterlen, G.   1941.   Les Âmes des Dogon.   Paris: Institut
d'Ethnologie (Travaux et memoires, 40).

Dieterlen, G. (ed.).   1973.   Colloque international sur la
notion de personne en Afrique.   Paris: Centre
National de la Recherche Scientifique.

Druke, M.A.   1980.   "The Concept of Personhood in Seven-
teenth and Eighteenth Century Iroquois Ethnopersonality".   In Studies on Iroquoian Culture (ed.
by N. Bonvillain, Occasional Papers in Northeastern Anthropology, No. 6), pp. 59-70.

Dumont, L. 1965a. "The 'Individual' in Two Types of Soci-
     ety". Contributions to Indian Sociology, 8:8-61.
Dumont, L. 1965b. "The Functional Equivalents of the Indi-
     vidual in Caste Society". Contributions to
     Indian Sociology, 8:85-99.
Dumont, L. 1967. "The Individual as an Impediment to Soci-
     ological Comparison and Indian History". In
     Social and Economic Change (ed. by V.B. Singh &
     B. Singh, Bombay: Allied Publishers), pp. 226-48.
Dumont, L. 1977. From Mandeville to Marx. Chicago: Uni-
     versity of Chicago Press.
Durkheim, E. (1893). The Division of Labor in Society.
     1933 ed. trans. by G.E. Simpson, New York:
     Macmillan.
Durkheim, E. (1912). The Elementary Forms of Religious
     Life. 1915 ed., trans. by J.W. Swain, 1960
     repr., New York: the Free Press.
Durkheim, E. (1914). "The Duality of Human Existence".
     1964 repr. in Essays in Sociology and Philosophy,
     ed. by K. Wolff, trans. by C. Blend, New York:
     Harper and Row, pp. 325-40.
Erikson, E.H. 1950. Childhood and Society. New York:
     Norton.
Erikson, E.H. 1958. Young Man Luther. New York: Norton.
Erikson, E.H. 1959. "Identity and the Life Cycle: Selected
     Papers". Psychological Issues, New York Inter-
     national Universities Press, I, 1.
Erikson, E.H. 1968. "Identity, Psychosocial". In Interna-
     tional Encyclopedia of the Social Sciences (New
     York: Macmillan and Free Press), VII:61-5.
Evans-Pritchard, E.E. 1965. Theories of Primitive Reli-
     gion. London: Oxford University Press.
Evens, T.M.S. 1977. "The Predication of the Individual in
     Anthropological Interactionism". American
     Anthropologist, LXXIX:579-97.
Fenton, W.N. 1940. "Masked Medicine Societies of the Iro-
     quois". Smithsonian Annual Report, Publication
     3624:397-430.
Fogelson, R.D. 1975. "An Analysis of Cherokee Sorcery and
     Witchcraft Beliefs and Practices". In Four Cen-
     turies of Southern Indians (ed. by C. Hudson,
     Athens, Ga.: University of Georgia Press), pp.
     113-31.
Fogelson, R.D. & A.B. Walker. 1980. "Self and Other in
     Cherokee Booger Masks". Journal of Cherokee
     Studies, V:88-102.

Fogelson, R.D. & A.B. Walker. In press. "The Cherokee
    Booger Mask Tradition". In Masks and Masquerades
    in the Americas (ed. by N.R. Crumrine, Vancouver,
    B.C: University of British Columbia Press).
Fortes, M. 1973. "On the Concept of the Person among the
    Tallensi". In Colloque international sur le
    notion de personne en Afrique (see Dieterlen
    1973), pp. 283-319.
Frank, G. 1979. "Finding the Common Denominator: A Phe-
    nomological Critique of Life History Method".
    Ethos, VII:68-94.
Frazer, J. 1911. Taboo and the Perils of the Soul. Lon-
    don: Macmillan.
Geertz, C. 1966. "Person, Time and Conduct in Bali: An
    Essay in Cultural Analysis". 1973 repr. in The
    Interpretation of Culture (see above), pp. 360-
    411.
Geertz, C. 1973. "Thick Description". In The Interpre-
    tation of Cultures (New York: Basic Books), pp.
    3-30.
Goffman, E. 1959. The Presentation of the Self in Everyday
    Life. Garden City, N.Y.: Doubleday.
Goldenweiser, A. 1917. "The Autonomy of the Social",
    American Anthropologist, XIX:447-49.
Goldenweiser, A. 1933. History, Psychology and Culture.
    New York: Knopf.
Griaule, M. 1940. "La Personnalité chez les Dogons (Soudan
    Francais)". Journal de Psychologie Normale et
    Pathologique, XXXVII:468-75.
Griaule, M. 1947. "Nouvelles recherches sur la notion de
    Personne chez les Dogon (Soudan Francais)".
    Journal Psychologie de Normale et Pathologique,
    XL:425-31.
Griaule, M. (1948). Conversations with Ogotemmeli. 1965
    ed., trans. by R. Butler, A.I. Richards, & B.
    Hooke; London: Oxford University Press.
Griaule, M. 1965. Le Renard pâle. Paris: Institut d'Eth-
    nologie (Travaux et memoires, 72).
Griaule, M. & G. Dieterlen. 1954. "The Dogon of the French
    Sudan". In African Worlds (ed. by D. Forde, Lon-
    don: Oxford University Press), pp. 83-110.
Hallowell, A.I. 1954a. "The Self and Its Behavioral Envi-
    ronment." 1955 repr. in Culture and Experience
    (Philadelphia: University of Pennsylvania Press),
    pp. 75-110.

Hallowell, A.I. 1954b. "Psychology and Anthropology".
       1976 repr. in Contributions to Anthropology (Chi-
       cago: University of Chicago Press), pp. 163–209.
Hallowell, A.I. 1955. "The Ojibwa Self and Its Behavioral
       Environment". In Culture and Experience (see
       above), pp. 172–82.
Hallowell, A.I. 1960. "Ojibwa Ontology, Behavior, and
       World View". 1976 repr. in Contributions to
       Anthropology (see above), pp. 357–90.
Hallowell, A.I. 1963a. "Personality, Culture, and Society
       in Behavioral Evolution". 1976 repr. in Contri-
       butions to Anthropology (see above), pp. 230–310.
Hallowell, A.I. 1963b. "The Ojibwa World View and Dis-
       ease". 1976 repr. in Contributions to Anthro-
       pology (see above), pp. 381–448.
Hallowell, A.I. 1966. "The Role of Dreams in Ojibwa Cul-
       ture". 1976 repr. in Contributions to Anthro-
       pology (see above), pp. 449–74.
Hay, T. 1968. "Ojibwa Restraint and the Socialization
       Process". Ph.D. dissertation, Michigan State
       University.
Hay, T. 1973. "A Technique of Formalizing and Testing
       Models of Behavior: Two Models of Ojibwa Re-
       straint". American Anthropologist, LXXV:708–30.
Hay, T. 1977. "The Development of Some Aspects of the
       Ojibwa Self and Its Behavioral Environment".
       Ethos, V:71–89.
Hultkrantz, A. 1953. Conceptions of the Soul Among North
       American Indians: A Study in Religious Ethnology.
       Stockholm: The Ethnographical Museum of Sweden,
       Monograph Series, 1.
James, W. 1890. Principles of Psychology. 2 vols. New
       York: Henry Holt.
Kapferer, B. 1979. "Mind, Self, and Other in Demonic Ill-
       ness: The Negation and Reconstruction of Self".
       American Ethnologist, VI:110–33.
Karpf, F.B. 1932. American Social Psychology: Its Ori-
       gins, Development and European Background. New
       York: McGraw-Hill.
Kendall, P.M. 1975. "Biographical Literature". In Macro-
       paidia, II, (The New Encyclopaedia Britannica,
       15th ed., Chicago: Encyclopaedia Britannica,
       Inc.)
Kirk, L. & M.L. Burton. 1977. "Meaning and Context: A
       Study of Contextual Shifts in the Meaning of

Masai Personality Descriptors". American
Ethnologist, IV:734-61.
Krader, L. 1966. "Person, Ego, Human Spirit in Marcel
Mauss: Comments". Psychoanalytic Review, LIII:
481-90.
Krader, L. 1967. "Persona et Culture". Les Etudes philo-
sophiques, November.
Kroeber, A.L. 1917. "The Superorganic". American Anthro-
pologist, XIX:163-213.
Lee, D. 1945. "Notes on the Conception of Self Among the
Wintu Indians". 1959 repr. in Freedom and Cul-
ture (Englewood Cliffs, N.J.: Prentice-Hall), pp.
131-40.
Leenhardt, M. (1947). Do Kamo: Person and Myth in the
Melanesian World. 1979 ed., trans. by B.M.
Gulati, Chicago: University of Chicago Press.
Lévi-Straus, C. 1963. Totemism. Trans. by R. Needham,
Boston: Beacon Press.
Levy-Bruhl, L. (1910). How Natives Think. 1962 ed.,
trans. by L.A. Clare, London: George Allen and
Unwin, Ltd.
Levy-Bruhl, L. (1922). Primitive Mentality. 1923 ed.,
trans. by L.A. Clare, London: George Allen and
Unwin, Ltd.
Levy-Bruhl, L. (1927). The "Soul" of the Primitive. 1928
ed., trans. by L.A. Clare, London: George Allen
and Unwin, Ltd.
Levy-Bruhl, L. (1949). The Notebooks on Primitive Men-
tality. 1975 ed., trans. by P. Riviere, New
York: Harper and Row.
Lowie, R.H. 1917. Culture and Ethnology. New York: Doug-
las C. McMurtrie.
Lukes, S. 1973. Individualism. New York: Harper and Row.
Mauss, M. 1929. "L'âme, le nom, la personne". 1968 repr.
in Oeuvres, (Paris: Les Editions de Minuit), II:
131-35.
Mauss, M. 1938. "Une Categorie de l'esprit humain: la
notion de personne celle de 'moi'". Journal of
the Royal Anthropological Institute, LVIII:263-
81. 1979 Eng. trans. by B. Brewster, in Sociology and Psychology (London: Routledge & Kegan
Paul), pp. 57-94.
Mead, G.H. 1913. "The Social Self". Journal of Philosophy, X:374-80.
Mead, G.H. 1934. Mind, Self and Society. Chicago: University of Chicago Press.

Miller, D.R. 1963. "The Study of Social Relationships:
     Situation, Identity, and Social Interaction". In
     Psychology: A Study of a Science (ed. by S. Koch,
     New York: McGraw-Hill), V:639-738.
Myers, F.R. 1979. "Emotions and the Self: A Theory of
     Personhood and Political Order Among Pintupi
     Aborigines". Ethos, VII:343-70.
Radcliffe-Brown, A.R. 1922. The Andamen Islanders. 1948
     ed., Glencoe, Ill.: The Free Press.
Radcliffe-Brown, A.R. 1940. "On Social Structure". 1952
     repr. in Structure and Function in Primitive
     Society (New York: The Free Press), pp. 108-204.
Radin, P. 1913. "Personal Reminiscences of a Winnebago
     Indian". Journal of American Folklore, XXVI:
     293-318.
Radin, P. 1920. "The Autobiography of a Winnebago Indian".
     University of California Publications in American
     Archaeology and Ethnology, XVI:381-473.
Radin, P. 1927. Primitive Man as Philosopher. New York:
     Appleton and Co.
Read, K.E. 1954/55. "Morality and the Concept of the Per-
     son Among the Gabuku Gama, Eastern Highland, New
     Guinea". Oceania, XXV:233-82.
Ridington, R. & T. 1970. "The Inner Eye of Shamanism and
     Totemism". History of Religions, X:49-61.
Robbins, R.H. 1973a. "Identity, Culture and Behavior". In
     Handbook of Social and Cultural Anthropology (ed.
     by J.J. Honigmann, Chicago: Rand McNally), pp.
     1199-1222.
Robbins, R.H. 1973b. "Alcohol and the Identity Struggle:
     Some Effects of Economic Change on Interpersonal
     Relations". American Anthropologist, LXXV:99-
     122.
Rosaldo, M.Z. 1980. Knowledge and Passion: Ilongot Notions
     of Self and Social Life. Cambridge: Cambridge
     University Press.
Sapir, E. 1917. "Do We Need a 'Superorganic'?". American
     Anthropologist, XIX:441-47.
Sapir, E. 1938. "Why Cultural Anthropology Needs the Psy-
     chiatrist". 1949 repr. in Selected Writings of
     Edward Sapir in Language, Culture and Personality
     (ed. by D.G. Mandelbaum, Berkeley: University of
     California Press), pp. 569-77.
Sherif, M. 1968. "Self Concept". In International Ency-
     clopedia of the Social Sciences (New York: Mac-
     millan and Free Press), XIV:150-59.

Singer, M. 1977. "On the Symbolic and Historic Structure
    of an American Identity". Ethos, V: 431-54.
Singer, M. 1980. "Signs of the Self: An Exploration in
    Semantic Anthropology". American Anthropologist,
    LXXXII:485-507.
Smith, M.W. 1952. "Different Cultural Concepts of Past,
    Present and Future: A Study of Ego Extension".
    Psychiatry, XV:395-400.
Soddy, K. (ed.). 1961. Identity: Mental Health and Value
    Systems. London: World Health Organization.
Speck, F.G. 1942. The Tutelo Spirit Adoption Ceremony,
    Reclothing the Living in the Name of the Dead.
    Harrisburg: Publication of the Pennsylvania
    Historical Commission.
Speck, F.G. 1950. "Concerning Iconology and the Masking
    Complex in Eastern North America". Philadelphia:
    University [of Pennsylvania] Museum Bulletin,
    XV:6-57.
Straus, A.S. 1976. "Being Human in the Cheyenne Way."
    Ph.D. dissertation, University of Chicago.
Straus, A.S. 1977. "Northern Cheyenne Ethnopsychology".
    Ethos, V:326-57.
Tylor, E.B. 1871. Primitive Culture (2 vols.). London:
    John Murray.
Valentine, C. 1963. "Man of Anger and Man of Shame: Laka-
    lai Ethnopsychology and Its Implications for So-
    ciopsychological Theory". Ethnology, II:441-77.
Wagner, R. 1975. The Invention of Culture. Englewood
    Cliffs, N.J.: Prentice-Hall.
Wallace, A.F.C. 1961. Culture and Personality. 1970 rev.
    ed., New York: Random House.
Wallace, A.F.C. 1967. "Identity Processes in Personality
    and in Culture". In Cognition, Personality and
    Clinical Psychology (ed. by R. Jessor & S. Fesh-
    bach, San Francisco: Jossey Bass), pp. 62-89.
Wallace, A.F.C. & R.D. Fogelson. 1965. "The Identity
    Struggle". In Intensive Family Therapy (ed. by
    I. Boszormeny-Nagy & J.L. Framo, New York: Harper
    and Row), pp. 365-406.
Watson, L.C. 1970. "Self and Ideal in a Guajiro Life His-
    tory". Acta Ethnologica et Linguistics, Series
    Americana 5, Vienna.
Watson, L.C. 1978. "The Study of Personality and the Study
    of Individuals: Two Approaches, Two Types of
    Explanation". Ethos, VI:3-21.

White, G.M. 1978. "Ambiguity and Ambivalence in A'ara
          Personality Descriptors". American Ethnologist,
          V:334-60.
White, G.M. 1980. "Social Images and Social Change in a
          Melanasian Society". American Ethnologist, VII:
          352-70.
Witthoft, J. 1967. The American Indian as Hunter. Harris-
          burg: Pennsylvania Historical and Museum Commis-
          sion.

THE STRUCTURE OF THE SELF IN NORTHERN CHEYENNE CULTURE

Anne S. Straus

Concepts of the self--its structure, development, and variability--vary cross-culturally and bear a significant relationship to the kinds of selves and self-pathologies that develop in a particular community. Such concepts are pervasive, incorporated in the actors' representations of every social interaction: they are fundamental to the meaning of social action within the community. The pervasiveness of these concepts in all cultures, and their unconscious status, accounts for the tenacity of cultural blinders in the cross-cultural study of the self.

Anthropologists, whose special training should best equip them to minimize such blinders, have commonly failed to recognize the importance of ethnopsychology in the analysis of behavior and the interpretation of cultures. There has been little change since 1923, when Radin lamented (1957 ed., p. 260) that "Few ethnologists have ever attempted to obtain from a native any systematized account of their own theory (of the Ego). It has, in fact, been generally contended that they have none." Anthropologists especially interested in American Indian personality have concentrated on analyzing native behavior in terms of Western psychological theory. Projective tests (Rorschach, Draw-a-Man, T.A.T.) have been popular methods; and the emphasis has been on the study of child development, adult development being denied or disregarded. If native concepts are noted at all, they are likely to be remarked as interesting esoterica unrelated to behavior.

An alternative to cross-cultural comparison of results from individual psychological tests has been to look at whole cultures in terms of their generic "psychological" characteristics--in short, to interpret cultures as though they were dreams. Such studies label whole cultures as being, for example, "paranoid, megalomaniac" (Benedict--e.g., 1934; 1959 ed., p. 222--on the Kwakiutl), or "inhibited", "atomistic" (Hallowell--e.g., 1946; 1974 ed., p. 147)--on

the Ojibwa), applying concepts from individual psychopathology to characterize other cultures in Western terms.
These efforts are both presumptuous and misguided. Culture
is not personality writ large, nor is personality culture
writ small: our own theories are not the only reality, other
theories cannot adequately be viewed as dreams.

Insisting upon the importance of native concepts to understanding native behavior invokes two important issues
relevant to Spiro's inquiry "Whatever Happened to the Id?"
(American Anthropologist, 1979, LXXXI, pp. 5-13). His query
underlines the problem of overemphasizing cognitive/concep-
tual material. Native concepts of the self are critical to
but not exhaustive of individual experience: the study of
ethnopsychology does not obliterate the Id. The Id, more-
over, belongs to a particular theory of personality itself
culturally constituted. There are some cross-cultural psychologists who claim that our own theories (including that
of the Id) have a greater truth value than others, and thus
hold a privileged status in the explanation of all behavior.
But this misses the very point which makes social science
"soft" and other sciences "hard". In the analysis of human
social behavior, meaning is critical. The most valuable insights into native behavior in any culture will come from
analyses which reflect an understanding of native meaning
systems—and in particular, native concepts of the self.

This paper focuses on Northern Cheyenne conceptualizations of the self. The material included here is illustra-
tive rather than exhaustive of Northern Cheyenne ethnopsychology: native definition of the life cycle will receive
scant attention, and there is no discussion of native categories of emotional experience. The structure of the self
is selected to demonstrate the relevance of such concepts to
understanding Northern Cheyenne behavior and the self which
organizes it.

The classic Cheyennes of the 19th century were typical
nomads of the western Great Plains. Newly equipped with
guns and horses, they hunted the buffalo in small bands during most of the year, coming together in the summer months
to celebrate major tribal rituals and meet in tribal council. Competition for resources and for status led them into
repeated military encounters with other tribes, as well as
with federal troops. The Northern Cheyennes engaged the

special interest of ethnographers for their exemplary political organization, the Council of Forty-Four, held to be a
representative body akin to our own Congress. Also intrigu-
ing to ethnographers was the apparent resilience of the
tribe in the face of cataclysmic social change.

Northern and Southern Cheyennes drifted apart in the
early 19th century. The Southern Cheyennes were confined to
Indian Territory many years before the Northern Cheyennes
consented to join them there (1877). Suffering the heat,
disease, and inadequate rations of the south, however, and
certain that their agreement included the right to return
north, the Northern Cheyennes made an heroic march back to
their homeland (1878)--preferring to die honorably in the
effort rather than to despair in the Indian Territory. The
few who survived disease, starvation, and federal troops
were ultimately rewarded with a small reservation in southeastern Montana. Tribal population has increased steadily
since the establishment of the reservation; it includes some
3000 enrolled members at present.

The fieldwork for this paper was conducted on that reservation, the Tongue River Reservation, 1972-1974. While I
participated in and observed a wide range of activities and
situations, my primary informants were "fullbloods"--and
specifically those who were recommended by tribal members as
people who might know about and/or be interested in the
kinds of questions I was asking.[1] The majority of Cheyennes, like the majority in any society, are not interested
in developing or discussing theories of the self. Only a
few "thinkers" (see Radin 1923) concern themselves with examining cultural postulates, though their number may be expanded by conscious efforts at revitalization of traditional
culture. The knowledge itself is not, however, pure intellectual fluff unrelated to the substance of mundane existence. Certain fundamental assumptions concerning the self,
articulated and examined by these "thinkers", are widespread
and have an obvious and significant influence on behavior.

The human self as constituted in Northern Cheyenne
culture has four basic parts: ametane ('having physical
life', 'living'); omotome (sometimes translated 'soul');
mahta?sooma (typically glossed as 'spirit'); and mahtsehestah ('heart', the 'center' of the individual). These
four may be represented as:

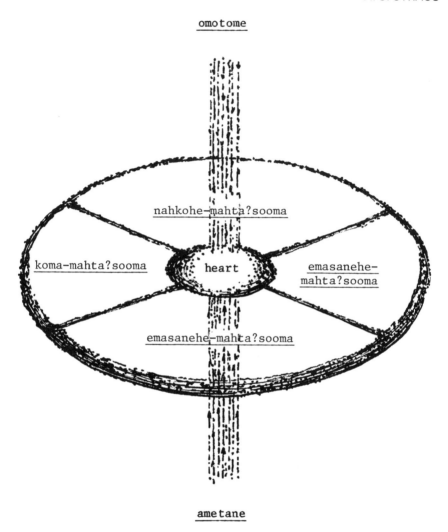

Ametane is associated with the earth: human beings are traditionally understood to have emerged from their animal-like
existence inside the earth to a second birth, delivered onto
the surface of the earth. There Man received his omotome,
his special blessing/breath from the Above. Inherent but
undeveloped in the omotome is the mahta?sooma, which differentiates into four parts only in the course of experiences
and relationships on the surface of the Earth. Mahtsehestah

(the heart; the seat of tribal relationships and of personal
identity) is understood as both the physical and spiritual
"center" of the individual--that which summarizes and epito-
mizes his personality.

AMETANE

Physical life is the first of man's blessings from the
"Great Spirit" (Ma?heo?o). It is a blessing he shares with
all living things. For hovahne (four-legged mammals) and
man, conception combines physical substances (variously understood) from the male and the female with Ma?heo?o's
blessing to produce a viable fetus. The life-soul of the
body, first recognized in the growth and movement of the fetus, is not localized in a particular organ but is diffused
throughout the body. The blessing of physical life is tenuous: it may be withdrawn at any time during the growth of an
infant into full personhood. During this time, the child is
described as "close to the spirit"; and his continued health
and proper development depend primarily upon his parents.

Physical life is understood as essential to human existence and to the development of the human self: realization
of the omotome and differentiation of the mahta?sooma occur
only in association with a particular human body. The human
body is understood to be influenced by conditions of the
non-physical self, and that self can be attacked through
bodily parts. Violations of spiritual taboo may cause physical injury or illness. "Accidents" do not happen here: if
a young man falls from his horse and breaks his arm, he
will--in thinking back over the incident--recall some previous transgression, some powerful person he offended, some
taboo he violated. With an isolated part of the human body,
on the other hand (notably the hair) another individual can
"work on" the person of its owner. In one such case, "love
magic" (which, surprisingly, is "black") was worked on a
woman by her first husband such that she could not resist
leaving her current family for him whenever he so wished.

Physical illness and spiritual imbalance are closely
associated in etiology, symptoms, and treatment. Na-hao-
motah ("I don't feel good") means both "I feel sick" and "I
feel unhappy, upset". The same herbal remedy was traditionally used for paralysis and for irrationality (Grinnell
1972,II, p. 185), and most common therapies (sucking cures,

purification in the sweat lodge, the burning of cedar, and peyote) treat both physical and psychic ills. More intensive therapy may require a full reorientation or centering of the individual through developmental recapitulation and analysis which helps the individual to find his place in the tribe and the world (a native practice long before Freud argued for the value of the "talking cure" for certain somatic symptoms).

The physical life and the self are closely associated for human beings, but that association is impermanent. The self, once fully developed in the course of human life, is no longer dependent upon it. The Western view in which a physical body is essential to all "real", functioning selves has been described by one Cheyenne as exemplifying "narrow vision", narrowly limiting the range of selves within our community. In the Cheyenne view, bodies identify and house human selves, but those selves are not ultimately bound to those bodies: that which defines the self is the "spirit" or non-physical self.

Reports of out-of-body experiences are common. In dreams, the self may wander from the body—though the self of dreams and the waking self are considered to be the same. In other circumstances the self may briefly depart the body, leaving it senseless, unconscious (naa?e); prolonged separation results in death (also naa?e!). In major illness or trauma, the spirit may wander for several days—visiting the Land of the Departed—and still return. There are even accounts of skeletons (seo?otse) that come back to life. Complete separation of body and self is neither simple nor immediate: death is a process, not an event.

An individual is said to experience his own death, to separate from his body and follow the path of the Milky Way to seana (Land of the Departed). There he will be reunited with other departed Cheyennes (called heama-vo?estaneo?o; 'Above People') and live very much the way he did on the surface of the earth. He continues to participate in the tribal community—aware of himself and of the moral order, the Way. He has a name and is a relative: his place in the tribe is secure. He can communicate verbally with living Cheyennes in sleeping dreams, and he usually chooses to associate with close relatives. From his new perspective and in his new liberation from physical constraint, he is more powerful than he was on earth and is able to warn and advise

his living relatives. The heama-vo?estane (disembodied human self) does not leave the tribal community: rather, he
extends that community in space and time.

OMOTOME

Physical life is man's first blessing—one which he
shares with all living things. Distinguishing him from animals, though, is his second blessing, omotome ('breath',
'air', 'word', 'consciousness'). Generically achieved after
the Emergence, the second blessing is recapitulated in the
first breath of every child. Man's individuation, his
self-awareness, and his capacity for verbal communication
depend upon this blessing.

Of all living things, only human beings are recognized
as individuals. A well-known sacred story points to the
folly of behaving as though animals were individuals.
Eheovestea (Yellow-Hair Woman), knowing that she should not
single out an animal, was once moved to pity an orphan buffalo calf. "Poor calf", she thoughtlessly exclaimed of its
particular plight, and thus caused the disappearance of the
buffalo from the area (Erect Horns eventually reintroduced
the buffalo, leading them out of the sacred mountain). Four
years ago, I was driving with a close friend to visit Noaho-
vosa (the sacred mountain in South Dakota); we passed a
feedlot jammed with domestic beef cattle and, without thinking, I remarked, "Poor cows". I was severely reprimanded.
"Never say 'poor cows'", I was told, "There is always another cow, but there is only one Terry [my nickname]." That
incident clearly recalled the lesson of Eheovestea, and demonstrated that the principle still holds among contemporary
Cheyennes.

Animals breathe and have souls, but their souls are generic. The death of a wild animal is precisely recouped in
the birth of a new one; it is as though they were continu-
ously reincarnated. Each new human,[?] however, despite in-
herited traits, is regarded as a new entity: he must develop
his own individual direction within the Way. This distinction between humans and other living things is evident in
naming procedures. Each human receives an "Indian name"
which is used by only one individual at a time, while wild
animals are unnamed, unidentifiable as individuals.   Domestic animals (horses and dogs) occupy a kind of middle ground

here; with unsocialized children, they are known by what are called "pet names".

As 'word', omotome is the capacity for verbal communication—one which is distinctive of humans among living things, and of persons among all things. In mythic times, the animals could talk and held councils; they had social organization and social relationships. But the Great Race ended that. In his victory over the animals, Man established the exclusivity of his verbal ability and personhood, as well as his right to kill and eat the buffalo. The Way is known through words; without them Man would be incapable of moral distinctions.

Infants, obviously, do not talk. The capacity for speech cannot be demonstrated for 1-2 years after birth. During this early time, the child is unnamed and not completely differentiated from animals; the human self has not yet been established. Parents and others talk a lot to infants, and make a great effort to encourage them to speak. In the old days, the eggs of the meadowlark (a bird whose call is said to repeat the Cheyenne words vetanove-o?he?e, 'Tongue River') were fed to the infant for the same purpose. Until recently, an ear-piercing ceremony celebrated the "opening up" of verbal communication as the infant became a child and learned to speak Cheyenne. The "opening" of the ears symbolically validated the child's human status, and prepared him for instruction and for the development of a moral sense. Today a public "give-away" (of valued items) for the child replaces that ceremony.

As the capacity for speech, omotome is also man's access to power in a world in which he is born otherwise weak, ignorant, and unendowed. Power and knowledge are closely associated here: being powerful means having many "medicines", and having medicines means knowing how to use and to respect them. Medicines earned through participation in tribal ceremonies require a recognized ceremonial instructor, and repeated instruction in four separate ceremonies, to secure the knowledge. Medicines gained in vision-experiences or given by powerful human beings also necessitate instruction of the recipient. Man acquires power through verbal instruction: power is transferred, not created.

Power is ranked among living human beings and among all persons, and the norms of social interaction adhere to relative rank in the hierarchy. Infant humans are the least of powerful things, unable to survive alone. Each gains access to power and personhood through verbal communication, and each is ranked according to the power/respect he develops. In order to know how to behave towards each other, any two individuals must assess their relationship within the hierarchy. Where rank is unknown or unsure, the conservative course should be followed: those more powerful than you are dangerous to you, and your protection lies in part in treating them properly. A man's peculiar powers/medicines identify him: they determine behavior, fortune, and status. They are integral to his own sense of self and to others' assessment of him. But they are not static: power can be gained or lost, and change is expected. The self thus viewed is a dynamic entity, the content of which defies definition, specification.[3]

Verbal communication, individuation, power acquisition--all are distinctive features of persons or selves in the Cheyenne view. Omotome--received in the first breath and liberated in the last as heamavo?estane ('Above Person') is fundamental to selfhood in the Cheyenne view, whereas the body is not.

The omotome is closely associated with the "four spirits" (mahta?sooma), which are dependent on it. In fact, the two are often referred to together as mahta?sooma.

Mahta?sooma

The mahta?sooma is implied in the first breath (omotome), but develops only in the course of social interaction in the living Cheyenne community. Whereas omotome is specifically associated with the consciousness of self, mahta?sooma is the moral potential, the consciousness of moral order, the Way. It also is prerequisite to a functioning self in Cheyenne definition: omotome and mahta?sooma are the distinctive features of the self here. Human selves have bodies and a substantive tribal link in the heart; they are described as HAVING mahta?sooma. Other, non-human persons, such as the heama-vo?estaneo?o, ARE mahta?sooma.

Originally the four spirits are undifferentiated. The process of differentiation is gradual but is presumed completed by around the onset of puberty, the final instructions traditionally coming during isolation at menarche for girls and during the first hunt and/or first war party for boys. Children are considered to have no real moral sense: they "do not know the difference", as is commonly remarked. They are qualitatively different from adults, then. They are not yet persons—and indeed, if improperly raised, may never become persons. The selves of children are rudimentary, inadequate as constituted in Cheyenne culture; their parents are held in large part responsible for their behavior.

Two of the four spirits are called emasanehe-mahta?sooma, 'crazy spirits'; two are epeva?e-mahta?sooma, 'good spirits'. "Crazy", the Cheyenne-English translation, means poorly directed, off-center, confused, uncontrolled. Control is especially focused around anger and sexuality, since both are perceived as threatening to the tribe and to the Way. The crazy spirits in human beings are the result of their animal heritage, their unemerged phylogeny, that part of all men that is ignorant of the Way. "Crazy" is clearly distinguished from "evil" (haveseva?e; also 'dirty'), which signifies a failure of human relatedness. All men have crazy spirits, yet all men are presumed to be either neutral or predisposed to good: there is no original sin in the Northern Cheyenne view of the world.

In Northern Cheyenne culture, then, 'good' indicates controlled, modulated, centered; but the meaning of the term varies contextually. There are two modalities of "good": one summarized as "energy", the other as "wisdom". The young men ideally exemplify "energy", the old men, "wisdom": between them, mature men combine both modalities.[4] Traditionally, young men were the hunters and the warriors, the "braves"; their best efforts were directed towards using their physical energies in positive, courageous—even glorious—ways. The more they came to know, the more "medicines" they had, the more successful they were in these enterprises. The old men used their wealth of accumulated knowledge/power to support these endeavors and, more generally, to sustain tribal and world order. They were namseme, "grandfathers", to the nexah, "grandchildren" or younger ones in the tribe, instructing and thus transferring power to them. In return they received offerings (food and other goods) and respect. Every such exchange of offering and blessing echoes the original instruction of the culture-heroes in the sacred mountain, and contributes to the perpetuation of the Way.

In addition to being distinguished as "good" and "crazy", the four spirits also are distinguished according to the two modalities of "good". Hence, they may be represented as:

	Good	Crazy
Energy	nahkohe-mahta?sooma	emasanehe-mahta?sooma
Wisdom	koma-mahta?sooma	emasanehe-mahta?sooma

The two good spirits are named nahkohe-mahta?oooma ('bear spirit', after the strength and physical prowess of the bear) and koma-mahta?sooma ('straight spirit'; fully knowledgable, well-directed one). These names reflect the two modalities described above. Since there are also two crazy spirits, the same energy-wisdom construct is presumed to apply to crazy spirits as well. The crazy spirits, however, do not have names (as far as anyone was willing/able to remember).

The four spirits are believed to be related to individual behavior, as is implied in the discussion above—although the nature of that relationship is by no means clear. People who consistently behave in ways assessed as "crazy" are believed to have a spiritual balance that stresses the crazy spirits. Similarly, people whose behavior is described as "good" are presumed to have strong good spirits. Behavioral aberrations may be attributed to spirit loss (most commonly following the violation of taboo); the spirits lost are presumably good spirits, thus shifting the balance towards the crazy.

Personal descriptions in Cheyenne are almost always behavioral descriptions. Where we might say of someone, for example, "he's a real fighter", implying some persistent internal trait or quality, a Cheyenne will remark "ehkema-taaeo?otse", 'he fights a lot'. There are very few qualitative descriptors in Cheyenne, 'good' and 'crazy' being the basic categories by means of which behavior is sorted. Even these terms must be understood as more active than their ad-

jectival English gloss suggests: the proper translation of
emasanehe is 'he crazies', "crazy" being an active verb sum-
marizing patterns of manifest behavior. But there is the
implication, in the use of the personal descriptors, of some
association with "personal" spiritual balance. The mahta?sooma is associated with the head, the mind; and it depends for its energy and its meaning on the heart, mahtsehestah.

MAHTSEHESTAH

The heart, mahtsehestah, is the personal core of the
individual: it is his ethnic identity and the seat of his
"deep" motivations. It is the symbolic center of the individual, and reveals his basic nature. Those who are "good"
are also described as "strong-", "large-", or "open-heart-
ed", while those few whose behavior is assessed as truly
bad/sinful (haveseva?e) are understood to be excessively
"weak-", "small-", or "closed-hearted".[5]

Tsetsehestahase, the Northern Cheyenne word for "themselves", means "those who are hearted alike". The heart is
the central container of blood and thus of blood relationships, blood being an explicit symbol of consanguinity here.
To be Cheyenne, one must have Cheyenne blood; and non-Chey-
enne are viewed as persons apart, not as significant in the
social environment as the "real/native" people. Each Cheyenne is inextricably linked to every other Cheyenne through
the blood which pulses through him, encapsulated and symbolized in the heart. He is part of an interdependent tribal
system, sensitive to and open to influence by any tribal
member—especially those who are "close", who share the most
blood.

Thus enmeshed, the Cheyenne understands his behavior to
be ever dependent upon others. He shares a part of himself
with every other Cheyenne, and is invariably influenced in
his own behavior by their actions. If asked for an autobiographical statement, he will typically begin "My grandfa-
ther..."; if attending a meeting or social event, he may arrive at the appointed hour but does not expect it to begin
until everyone else is ready; if questioned about his absence from work, he will respond (in what often appears to
white employers as a lame excuse) by describing the behavior

of some third party (e.g., "I didn't get to work this morning because my brother went to town.").

The condition of interpersonal interdependence enjoined upon those of same blood, those who are "like-hearted", renders the future particularly uncertain: individual plans are dreams rather than programs. One cannot really anticipate one's own action, since the actions of others have a continual and unspecified influence upon it: "We shall see" is a much more appropriate attitude towards the future. Even the personal descriptors discussed above are summaries of manifest behavior more than expectations of future behavior, since future behavior cannot be known. Linguistic structure is consistent here, supporting a radical split between the future and all manifest/known times. Cheyenne tenses do not initially distinguish past from present, but do distinguish future/unknown from present-past/manifest.

A similar pattern of "expectation of change" is noted by E. Friedl (1956) among the Ojibwa Indians (a related, Algonquian-speaking tribe); and the Spindlers (1971), recognizing it among the Menomini (another related, Algonquian-speaking group), describe it as "latescence", the attitude of "waiting expectantly" and "depending on outside agents for realization".

Because the Cheyennes are tsetsehestahase ("hearted-alike; see above discussion), motivation is understood to depend more on external demands than on internal needs. The future is uncertain; and one must learn to react, to adapt to change. Perhaps Friedl was right: it may well be that the resilience of the tribe throughout radical changes in lifeway (from their horticultural villages in Minnesota to their nomadic life on the high plains, and finally their lot as wards of the federal government) is due at least in part to a preadaptation in the expectation of change. It is doubtless equally due to the continuing recognition of what one Cheyenne called "the Cheyenne connection" in the heart/blood which they alone share.

Four fundamental aspects of the self have been considered above. Some relationships among them have been suggested, but such considerations are of little concern to native "thinkers" in the Northern Cheyenne community. A dynamic interdependence and intermingling of parts is assumed for the individual as it is for the family, the tribe, and

the life-system. Systematic definition of those relationships is inappropriate and impossible, since the system is
understood to be in constant flux.

The relevance of ethnopsychology to native behavior
should already be clear. Some implications of the ethnographic example for the special concerns of this symposium
must still be remarked.

First, a major consequence of the Cheyenne view of the
relationship between body and self is the relevance of relationships with other-than-human persons to the developing
self. As Hallowell has pointed out,
    In Western culture, as in others, 'supernatural' beings
    are recognized as persons, although belonging, at the
    same time, to an other-than-human category. But in the
    social sciences and psychology, persons and human beings
    are categorically identified. (1960; 1975 ed., p. 143)
Perhaps in other terms this might be described as the recognition of the full range of self-objects available to the
individual in a particular culture. The Cheyenne lives in a
"great society" peopled both by human and by other-than-human selves. The traditional Cheyenne learns that <u>heama-
vo?estaneo?o</u> and other spirit beings are valid objects in
his behavioral environment--every bit as much "selves" or
"persons" as living human beings: the word for the category
"all persons", living or otherwise (<u>vo?estaneo?o</u>) has the
same root as the word for my-self (<u>na-vo?estane</u>). The Cheyenne thus knows to interact with, listen to the advice of,
and heed the warnings from spirit-persons; this interaction
is regulated by the same norms which govern human interaction and is presumed to have similar consequences.

The Cheyenne view is clearly different from that of
Western social science. One reponse to this difference
might be to dismiss Cheyenne culture as "delusional" and
attempt to analyze the origins of the particular pathology
which leads to such projections. But such an approach ac-
complishes little, as was suggested above. Alternatively,
we can proceed without a classification system--to recognize
that prerequisite to understanding the meaningful constitution of Cheyenne social interaction, and the selves which
emerge within it, is the ability to distinguish person from
not-person, selves from not-selves, according to an informed
native perspective.

Individuality and power associated with the omotome have certain further and obvious implications for the kinds of selves which emerge in Cheyenne culture. Individuation and consciousness of self are said to bring with them what Cheyennes consider to be the universal human condition-- loneliness.[6] Cheyennes fear loneliness and isolation per- haps more than anything else. The individual--fearful of malevolence at the hands of those more powerful than him- self--does his best to avoid offending others and lives defensively, continually thrown back on his own resources. The result is the "atomism" pattern commonly described from Rorschach responses for Cheyennes and other Algonquian speaking peoples. But in Cheyenne culture, self-reliance implies intense involvement with those who are "close", and entails a personal strategy for increasing the network of "close" ones. (There is, of course, an ordered segmentation in the identification of those who are "close" and those who are not, which itself contributes to the insecurity of social interaction.)

Individuality is by no means peculiar to modern Western society. That theory, popular among French sociologists and their converts, must be laid to rest. But the meaning of individuality differs in different cultural contexts. In Western society the valued self is independent, internally driven, "self-actualizing"; the dependent, other-directed person is defined as having an unhealthy self. In Northern Cheyenne culture, individuality does occur and is respected unquestioned, but (as one woman stated it) "the individuals are like the poles of a tipi--each has his own attitude and appearance but all look to the same center [heart] and sup- port the same cover". For Cheyennes, individuality supports a tribal purpose, a tribal identity. Individual freedom does not consist in distinguishing oneself from the group. Indeed, without the tribe there is no freedom; there is only being lost.

Intrapsychic and interpsychic processes are not distin- guished in Cheyenne perspective. The Cheyenne self partici- pates in, and cannot be defined by contrast with, other Cheyenne selves. Motivation is understood to be seated in the heart, symbol of social relationship, and is presumed to be inherently social. Cheyennes learn all this in the course of the socialization process, and reflect it in their own behavior and their interpretation of the behavior of others.

An analysis, then, which assumes a priori a self distinguished from--though emerging out of--a social environment, and/or accepts a theory of motivation based primarily
on the energies of an independent Id, cannot adequately account for Cheyenne behavior. Such an analysis ignores that
which is central to motivation and to the interpretation of
behavior, namely meaning. Cultural postulates must be examined, and Cheyenne culture in particular must surely remind
us that

> the Western conception of the person as a bounded,
> unique, more or less integrated motivational and cogni-
> tive universe, a dynamic center of awareness, emotion,
> judgment, and action organized into a distinctive whole
> and set contrastively both against other such wholes and
> against its social and natural background, is, however
> incorrigible it may seem to us, a rather peculiar idea
> within the context of the world's cultures. (Geertz
> 1974, p. 31)

Personal constructs (cf. Kelly 1955), the categories in
terms of which social interaction and self-image are structured, are also culturally constituted. The personal descriptors available to an individual as a part of his cultural repertoire are of great importance in the study of the
personal characteristics of those individuals. The developing self learns to identify both itself and others by means
of such categories, and this importantly affects its reactions both to others and to itself. The polar categories
"good"-"crazy" and "energy"-"wisdom" are such categories in
Cheyenne culture. While these categories seem to echo other
classification systems (cf. Valentine 1963), they are culturally specific. The association of the categories with
particular life-stages exemplifies the specificity of their
cultural content: a succession of adult personalities is defined, expected, and thus generally confirmed in native interpretation of behavior--'men of energy' becoming 'men of
wisdom', and the "craziness" expected of youth becoming entirely inappropriate to old age.

While few Cheyenne may ever contemplate the stucture of
the self, the implications of their unexamined assumptions
for their behavior--and for understanding their behavior--
should now be clear. Culturally constituted conceptualizations of the self are "essential to the operation of all
human societies" (Hallowell 1960; 1975 ed., p. 142) and are
implied in the representation of every social interaction.

Such conceptualizations, often unelaborated, often unarticulated, are essential to the analysis of the self in any culture. They are pervasive, relevant to every interactional situation—and thus have a certain claim to analytical priority over other cultural domains.

And so we return to the beginning: the kinds of selves which develop in any social group are critically informed by the ways in which the self is conceptualized within that group. This seems both simple and obvious.

But if it is so obvious, why is it so often ignored? Perhaps our "narrow vision" needs expanding.

ENDNOTES

1. A full discussion of methods and involvement in the reservation community appears in Straus 1976.

2. Twins differ from single-born humans in this respect: they are more animal-like. Twins are continually reincarnated, and thus all recognize and know each other— as most tribal members will tell you.

3. "It may at once be said that one thing he [primitive man] has never done: he has never fallen into the error of thinking of it (the Ego) as a unified whole or of regarding it as static. For him it has always been a dynamic entity, possessed of so many constituents that even the thinker has been unable to fuse them into one unit." (Radin, 1957 ed., p. 259)

4. I focus on men here because the data is clearest. For a discussion of women, see Straus 1976, 1977.

5. An extreme expression of this is found in the mythical "no-hearts" who maimed and killed Cheyenne, demonstrating a complete lack of tribal connection, sinning against the Way and against the blood.

6. Comparison with animals (hovahne) is again instructive. For animals and humans, a central vehicle and symbol of connection is the umbilical cord. The word for the cord, hesta?e (the same word as "twin"—the first twin

being formed, according to legend, from the thrown-away
cord of a single-born child), shares the same root as
"heart" (hestah); and some believe that the cord is a
direct connection between maternal and fetal hearts.
Animals, mindless of and therefore essentially without
separation, consume and destroy the cord, while humans
preserve and respect it, wearing it in a beaded pouch
to remind them of their special blessing and of their
particular condition.

REFERENCES

Benedict, R. 1934. Patterns of Culture. 1959 ed., Boston:
        Houghton Mifflin.
Friedl, E. 1956. "Persistence in Chippewa Culture and Per-
        sonality", American Anthropologist, LVIII: 814-25.
Geertz, C. 1974. "From the Natives' Point of View", Bulle-
        tin, American Academy of Arts and Sciences,
        XXVIII, 1:26-43.
Grinnell, G.B. (1923). The Cheyenne Indians, 2 vols. 1972
        repr., New Haven: Yale University Press.
Hallowell, A.I. 1946. "Characteristics of the Northeastern
        Indians". 1974 repr. in Culture and Experience
        (Philadelphia: University of Pennsylvania Press),
        pp. 125-51.
Hallowell, A.I. 1960. "Ojibwa Ontology, Behavior, and
        World View", 1975 repr. in Teachings from the
        American Earth (ed. by Tedlock, New York:
        Liverright), pp. 141-79.
Kelly, G. 1955. The Psychology of Personal Constructs, 2
        vols. New York: W.W. Norton.
Radin, P. 1923. Primitive Man as Philosopher. 1957 ed.,
        New York: Dover Publications.
Spindler, G. & L. 1971. Dreamers Without Power. New York:
        Holt, Rinehart, and Winston.
Straus, A.S. 1976. Being Human in the Cheyenne Way. Ph.D.
        dissertation, University of Chicago.
Straus, A.S. 1977. "Northern Cheyenne Ethnopsychology".
        Ethos, V:326-57.
Valentine, C. 1963. "Men of Anger and Men of Shame:
        Lakalai Ethnopsychology and Its Implications for
        Sociopsychological Theory". Ethnology, II:
        441-78.

PERSONAL AND SOCIAL IDENTITY IN DIALOGUE

Milton Singer

University of Chicago

> We must not begin by talking of pure ideas—
> vagabond thoughts that tramp on the public roads
> without any human habitation,—but must begin with
> men and their conversation. (Charles S. Peirce,
> Collected Papers [hereafter referred to as CP],
> vol. VIII: section 12.)

PROLOGUE

About two years ago at a birthday party for an eight-year-old boy named Simon, I was surprised to hear him sing, as the birthday cake was brought in, first with the rest of the company "Happy birthday to you. Happy birthday to you. Happy birthday, dear Simon. Happy birthday, to you." and then by himself "Happy birthday to me. Happy birthday to me. Happy birthday, dear Simon. Happy birthday to me." The party was a small family affair; besides Simon's mother and grandmother, an aunt and uncle, several older cousins, my wife, and I joined in what has become an annual affair.

A day or two later when I described to some colleagues Simon's shift from "you" to "me" in the song and commented that this was a way of accenting the self-reference, a senior anthropological linguist challenged my interpretation and suggested that one couldn't be sure that there was any self-reference in the boy's words, that he may have been only joining in a kind of ceremonial chant.

My first inclination was to insist that I had directly "observed" the self-reference, that everyone else also "observed" it, and that the words themselves obviously indicated the self-reference. However, as other colleagues (several of them also anthropological linguists) took a skepti-

cal approach and cited the problematic character of the limited technical literature on the use of pronouns and deictic
expressions, I began to have second thoughts and started to
do a little research on psychological observation and the
relation of the use of personal pronouns to personal and social identity. The present paper represents the outcome of
that research.

Since the paper was stimulated by several events as
serendipitous as Simon's birthday party, I shall mention
briefly the circumstances of their occurrence:
   1) In a paper on Peirce's anti-Cartesian and semiotic
theory of the self (see Singer 1980), I had already included
a section on personal identity; the discussion with my colleagues reopened the question for me, and led me, to reread
what Peirce and some, of his commentators (especially Murphey and Goudge) had to say. I was surprised to find that
in his "cosmological" papers of the early 1890s, which I had
used for the section on personal identity in "Signs of the
Self", Peirce had tried to construct a theory of collective
as well as individual personality on the basis of a physio-
logically based psychology with practically no explicit reference to his semiotic or to pragmatism. This discovery
posed the question of how Peirce integrated his personality
theory with his semiotic and with his pragmatic theory of
the self to produce a social psychology that does not pre-
suppose physics and physiology. The discussion, in my 1980
paper, of the dialogue of the interpreters-and-utterers of
signs was a major clue to the answer, but the details and
the role of pronouns as indexical signs had to be worked
out.
   2) A preliminary portion of the present paper was presented and discussed at the conference on New Approaches to
the Development of the Self (Center for Psychosocial Studies, Chicago, 29 March-1 April 1979). Following the conference, I discussed with the research staff at the Center the
relationship of Peirce's theory of personal identity to the
later theories of James, Baldwin, Cooley, and Mead.[1]
   3) Writing to me in August 1979 about my "Signs of the
Self" paper, Max Fisch, the general editor of the new critical edition of Peirce's papers (Writings of Charles S.
Peirce), called my attention to Peirce's undergraduate writings on "I", "It", and "Thou" and to his 1863 essay on "The
Place of Our Age in the History of Civilization" (in Peirce
SW), with the paragraph on the egotistical, idistical, and
tuistical stages.

Later Fisch sent me a few pages from Peirce's early formulations on the three pronouns as names for his three categories, and a draft of his Introduction (1979b) to Volume I (1857–1866) of the above-mentioned new edition of Peirce papers.

When Fisch came to speak in Chicago at the Center for Psychosocial Studies on November 6, 1979, he used as a basis for his talk his presidential address to the Semiotic Society of America (1979). Upon reading in Fisch's address that "Peirce began where most of us begin, with a model which, taken by itself, would suggest too narrow a definition; the model, namely, of conversation between two competent speakers of the same natural language", I was encouraged to think that the dialogical interpretation of sign-process was the pathway to the social psychology of personal identity. While the paper may not faithfully reflect all the dialogues that stimulated it, this prologue may help explain its development.

TOWARD A SOCIAL AND SEMIOTIC PSYCHOLOGY
OF PERSONAL IDENTITY

In my earlier paper (1980, pp. 494-96), I suggested that Peirce's conception of personality and personal identity was both social and semiotic. This interpretation, however, was based on combining several different sources: some of Peirce's "cosmological papers" published in The Monist in 1891 to 1893 ("The Architecture of Theories", The Monist, I (1891), pp. 161-76; reprinted CP VI:7-34. "The Doctrine of Necessity Examined", The Monist, II (1892), pp. 321-37; CP VI:35- 65. "The Law of Mind", II (1892), pp. 533-59; CP VI: 102-63. "Man's Glassy Essence", III (1892), pp. 1-22; CP VI:238-270. "Evolutionary Love", III (1893), pp. 176-200; CP 287-317.), his paper "What Pragmatism Is" (CP V:421), and his correspondence with Lady Welby (see Semiotics and Significs, hereafter referred to as (SS)). If we consider only his views in the "cosmological papers" we find a much narrower conception of personality and personal identity as some kind of coordination of feelings and ideas within the individual organism, and some kind of connection between these feelings and ideas in different organisms. Murphey (1961, p. 347) has suggested that Peirce uses two languages in his "cosmological papers": the language of psychology and the language of physics, representing the inside and the

outside views of the mind. In spite of recognizing a parallelism between the terms of the two languages (feeling,
will, habit; chance, haecceity, love), Murphey thinks that
Peirce regarded the psychological language as more fundamental than the physical.

If Murphey's interpretations are correct, they would
imply that Peirce's conception of personal identity in the
cosmological papers rests on a psychophysical parallelism or
on a physiological psychology, but not on a semiotic and a
social psychology. Murphey avoids this conclusion by arguing
(1961, p. 344) that Peirce reaffirms in the cosmological
papers his earlier theory that man is a sign. The evidence
for this interpretation is inconclusive. There is only one
reference to the earlier semiotic theory in the cosmological
papers, and it is ambiguous:

> Long ago, in the Journal of Speculative Philosophy, I
> pointed out that a person is nothing but a symbol involv-
> ing a general idea; but my views were, then, too nominal-
> istic to enable me to see that every general idea has the
> unified living feeling of a person. (CP VI:270)

In this same passage, Peirce also asserts the converse: that
"a person is only a particular kind of general idea".

This passage is hardly a sufficient ground for conclud-
ing that Peirce abandoned his semiotic theory in the early
1890s. It is not inconsistent, however, with the impression
that Peirce's conception of personality and personal identity in the cosmological papers had not yet freed itself from
psychophysics and physiological psychology to become the
genuinely semiotic and social psychological conception of
the later papers. In a letter to William James (circa 1909),
Peirce contrasts the physiological approach of Psychology
Proper to the phenomenological approach, or Phaneroscopy, as
he calls it (CP VIII:303-05):

> On the one hand "a sort of physiology of the mind"--
> An account of how the mind functions, develops, and de-
> cays, together with the explanation of all this by mo-
> tions and changes of the brain, or in default of this
> kind of explanation, by generalizations of psychical phe-
> nomena, so as to account for all the workings of the soul
> in the sense of reducing them to combinations of a few
> typical workings...
> On the other hand "phaneroscopy"--or a description of
> what is before the mind or in consciousness,as it appears

in the different kinds of consciousness, which I rank
under three headings. [emphasis in original]

The three headings are Peirce's three categories considered as kinds of consciousness: First, "Qualisense"
("consciousness of the quality of feeling", "the sort of
consciousness of any whole regardless of anything else, and
therefore regardless of the parts of that whole"); Second:
"Molitions" ("a double consciousness of exertion and resistance"); and Third, "Recognition of Habit" ("a consciousness
at once of the substance of the habit, the special case of
application, and the union of the two").

In view of Peirce's preference for a phenomenological
to a physiological description, it seems justified to interpret his statements about personal identity and personality
especially in the coomological paporu--in phunomunological
terms without seeking direct parallels in physiology, physics, or chemistry. If personal identity is primarily defined in terms of consistency and continuity of feelings,
actions, and ideas (as Peirce defines it in the cosmological
papers), we can accept this definition without necessarily
accepting Peirce's definitions of physiological and physico-
chemical analogues. In this manner, the question of how
much (if any) of the physical organism enters into personal
identity can be left open as we explore the semiotic and social aspects of consistency and continuity in personal identity.

ON THE SEMIOTICS OF DIALOGUE

Levi-Strauss (1976:11) has defined anthropology as a
"conversation of man with man", and has also proposed that
a study of the exchange of words be joined to the study of
the exchange of women and goods and services--to bring linguistics, social anthropology, and economics into a unified
science of communication. This conception is not identical
with the inclusive view of symbolic interaction that Firth
(1973, p. 196f.) attributes to Parsons, G.H. Mead, and
Schneider, according to which "all relations of people to
one another are mediated and defined by systems of culturally structured symbols". Levi-Strauss's unified science of
communication would restrict itself to a structural analysis
of the relations abstracted from the specific conversations
of specific people in specific social contexts. As Jakobson

(1973, p. 36) has said of Levi-Strauss's aspiration, a unified science of communication would have to incorporate
"semiotic proper", "that is the study of sheer messages and
their underlying codes, plus those disciplines wherein messages play a relevant yet solely accessory role". Margaret
Mead's suggestion (see Sebeok et al. 1964, p. 275) that
"semiotics" be used to designate the study of patterned communication in all modalities comes closer in spirit and
scope to the more inclusive view and to symbolic interactionism than to Levi-Strauss's unified science of communication (see Singer 1978, p. 212f.).

Most of the symbolic interactionists have a good deal
to say about conversation—as a distinctive form of human
symbolic interaction, and as both the nursery of human personality and the forum for its expression. Before discussing the relation of personality and personal identity to
conversation, I should like to briefly discuss the semiotics
of conversation as it has been developed within the symbolic
interactionist tradition. While several different contributions need to be distinguished and different theoretical
positions recognized, the most comprehensive and general
semiotic theory of conversation as a form of symbolic interaction was formulated in the writings of Charles S. Peirce.
Not only are those writings sprinkled with fragments of colloquial conversation to illustrate his abstract and sometimes abstruse analyses, but as Fisch (1979c) has observed,
Peirce took the model of conversation as a starting point
for his general theory of signs In this model, at least
two competent speakers of the same natural language (for example, English) interpret one another's sounds with some
assistance from lip movements and gestures.

As Royce, who was significantly influenced by Peirce's
theory of signs, pointed out, "The objects of knowledge are
public and therefore interpretation is social. The metaphor
of conversation appropriately suggests the manner in which
interpretative processes are generated and developed" (as
quoted in Fuss 1965, p. 106; see also Royce 1913, II, p.
159).[2] For Peirce the appropriate suggestion was that of a
dialogue between the utterers-and-interpreters of signs.
Fisch (1979a) believes that Peirce's emphasis on the dialogical nature of conversation and of thought was probably suggested to him by some of Plato's Dialogues.

Fisch is probably right about Peirce's source of suggestion, but it is relevant to point out that modern linguistics and information-theory also use the dialogical model of communication. For example, Lyons, a linguist, specifies (1977, II, p. 637) "the canonical situation of utterance" in terms which, while not identical with Peirce's semiotic, in effect describe a colloquial conversation between two interlocutors which "involves one-one, or one-many, signalling in the phonic medium along the vocal auditory channel, with all the participants present in the same actual situation able to see one another and to perceive the associated non-vocal paralinguistic features of their utterances, and each assuming the role of sender and receiver in turn". Writing as a communications engineer, Cherry (1966, pp. 89, 110) not only constructs a similar dialogical paradigm for human communication but also points out the parallels with Peirce's semiotic analysis.

Peirce's semiotic analysis of conversation is based on a concept of sign-action or sign-process which is irreducibly triadic: a sign is determined by an object, and in turn determines an interpretation or interpretant in the mind of a person. An essential feature of Peirce's theory is that the interpretation of the sign assumes the same relation to the object as the sign itself has.

That Peirce's conception of the sign-process ("semiosis", as he called it) is essentially dialogical has not been sufficiently recognized because his most general definitions of "sign" and sign-process tend to omit mention of persons and their interaction (SS, pp. 192-95). In these formulations, he defines a sign as something (a First) which is determined by an object (a Second) to determine an interpretant (a Third) to assume the same relation to the object which the sign has. There are at least three reasons why Peirce omitted reference to persons in such abstract definitions: 1) He wanted to demonstrate that it is possible to give a mathematically formal definition of "sign" (and of "mind"), just as mathematicians were beginning to define "number" and "line" formally without explicit reference to the usual interpretations of these concepts; 2) he wanted to distinguish a semiotic analysis in terms of signs from a psychological analysis in terms of persons and personality; and 3) he wanted to leave open the possibility that there might be nonhuman intelligences capable of triadic sign-action.

Peirce never denied, however, that sign processes in the case of __human__ minds are mediated by the interpersonal interactions between the utterers-and-interpreters of the signs. The fact that some "natural signs" (as in meteorology or in medicine) might not have been produced by utterers did not alter his conception of human semiosis as a social and dialogical process. And even his most formal and abstract definitions and classifications of signs were usually accompanied by informal comments, in the English metalanguage, about the personal utterers-and-interpreters of the signs (cf. Singer 1980, p. 497f.; Fisch 1978, p. 55f.).

For Peirce, not only are human sign-processes essentially dialogical and social, but many of the ingredients of the processes also are dialogical. As he often writes, "a sign addresses somebody" (__Philosophical Writings__ [hereafter __PW__], p. 99). Indexical signs, particularly, direct someone's attention to some thing or to some person. The use of __selectives__, as Peirce calls them ("some", "any", etc.) usually occasions a question-and-answer dialogue: "Man is mortal." "What man?" "Any man you like." (__CP__:505).

Symbolic signs are implicated in the dialogues of verbal discourse. Peirce's emphasis on the systemic and endless nature of such discourse should not obscure the fact that for him language is part of a vast semiotic system and is intrinsically social and dialogical. Individual signs should be interpreted as items in such sign-systems and not in isolation, and every interpretation will generate further interpretations indefinitely. Peirce, however, is neither a formalist nor a linguistic solipsist; the human sign-processes are limited at any given time by the utterers-and-interpreters' sensory experience and by their habits of action. While he envisions an enlargement of experience and the growth of new habits, Peirce also envisages (__CP__ VIII: 45-46) the possibility of a complete destruction of the species and an end to human semiosis.[3] In the meantime, the criteria for the meaning and truth of signs, and for the reality of the objects designated by them, will depend on the eventual consensus arrived at by the community of all investigators. Such a consensus will be the result of the continuing dialogues between the utterers-and-interpreters as they bring their respective interpretations and previous experience into a shared understanding:
      There is the __Intentional__ Interpretant, which is a deter-
      mination of the mind of the utterer; the __Effectual__ Inter-

pretant, which is a determination of the mind of the interpreter; and the Communicational Interpretant, or say
the Cominterpretant, which is a determination of that
mind into which the minds of utterer and interpreter have
to be fused in order that any communication should take
place. This mind may be called the commens. It consists
of all that is, and must be, well understood between utterer and interpreter at the outset, in order that the
sign in question should fulfill its function.
...It is out of the nature of things for an object to be
signified (and remember that the most solitary meditation
is dialogue) otherwise than in relation to some actuality
or existent in the commens. (SS, p. 196f.).

INNER DIALOGUE AND OUTER DIALOGUE

     The dialogues between the utterers-and-interpreters of
signs, their objects and interpretants, characterize human
conversation and human communication generally in Peirce's
conception of sign-process. He also extends this kind of
semiotic analysis to thinking, which he sees as "talking to
oneself". Fisch cites Peirce's use of the colloquial "I
says to myself, says I" as a confirmation for this interpretation; but even when he addresses others, Peirce's conversation is often imaginary:
     I say to people,--imaginary interlocutors, for I have no-
     body to talk to,--you think that the proposition that
     truth and justice are the greatest powers in this world
     is metaphorical. Well, I, for my part, hold it to be
     true. (in a 1902 letter to James, CP VIII:272)

     All thinking, according to Peirce, takes the form of an
inner dialogue: "Your self of one instant appeals to your
deeper self for his assent" (1909; CP VI:338).   The inner
dialogue is "conducted in signs that are mainly of the same
general structure as words"--but not only words, or linguistic symbols, for "the substance of thoughts" also includes
icons (which "chiefly illustrate the significations of predicate thoughts") and indices, ("the denotations of subject-
thoughts") (ibid.). The subject is singular, and is known
by the compulsion and insistency that characterize experience; the matter of the predicate is known by the senses and
feeling, and its structure by reason (CP VI:340).

Peirce's analysis of thought as an inner dialogue between an old self and a new self just coming into being—in
which indexical signs denote subjects; iconic signs signify
predicates or "forms of fact"; and the two are brought together by verbal symbols—seems to be a consistent extension
of his semiotic analysis into the subjective inner world of
the self. But is this extension consistent with his anti-
Cartesianism, declared in the 1860s, to the effect that all
knowledge of mind and the self is based on the observation
of external facts and not on intuition and introspection?
(See Singer 1980:486-89.)

Peirce's lectures on pragmatism in 1903 (CP V:14-212)
and his correspondence with Lady Welby (SS) indicate that he
remained consistently anti-Cartesian to the end. His distinction between an inner world of "thought" and an outer
world of external facts was not ontological but phenomenological, and depends ultimately on the degree of muscular
effort that is required to overcome the resistance of external facts (PW, pp. 86, 276, 283). The similarity of the inner dialogue of thought to the semiotic structure of conversation is not the result of a preestablished harmony between the inner and outer worlds but simply the result of
the fact that the interlocutors (or "selves") are products
of, as well as agents in, both inner and outer dialogues.
They are the objects designated by, as well as the subjects
creating, the semiotic systems constituting the dialogues
(see Singer 1980, pp. 489-493).

PERSONAL IDENTITY: PRIVATE AND PUBLIC

Just how the intrapersonal dialogue (self-consciousness
and thought) comes to have a semiotic structure similar to
that of interpersonal dialogue (consciousness of, and communication with, others) is for Peirce—as it is for most
other symbolic interactionists—not a question that can be
answered by introspection but only by empirical observation
and inference.
    Introspection is wholly a matter of inference. One is
    immediately conscious of his feelings, no doubt; but not
    that they are feelings of an ego. The self is only in-
    ferred. (1905; CP V:462).

If immediate consciousness (of feelings, powers and
capacities, actions) precedes consciousness of self, then

selves must appear relatively late in individual experience.
Peirce accepted this implication and cited an observation by
Kant in support:

> There is no known self-consciousness to be accounted for
> in extremely young children. It has already been pointed
> out by Kant that the late use of the very common word "I"
> with children indicates an imperfect self-consciousness
> in them. (1868; CP V:227)

But, Peirce added, children manifest powers of thought before they are self-conscious (op. cit.:228).

Peirce then went on to describe, in the same paper, a
plausible course of experience in a child's encounter with
others and the world that leads it to develop the consciousness of a private self to which all sorts of qualities are
attributed. Essential to Peirce's explanation of the rise
of selves in individual experience is the notion that the
child discovers in his interactions with others that his
perceptions, actions, and judgments are often the result of
ignorance and error (for example that fire does not burn),
and therefore he must suppose a private self which is fal-
lible (op. cit.:234). The discovery assumes that the child
already understands verbal commands and testmony such as
"Don't touch the hot stove; it will burn you" (op. cit.:
227-37).

In the child's experience of surprise when he fails to
heed commands, there is a discovery of the external non-ego
as well as of the inner ego. Peirce speaks of a "double
consciousness" of an ego and a non-ego "directly acting upon
each other" at the instant of surprise (CP V:52).   The ego
represents "the expected idea suddenly broken off"; the
non-ego, "the strange intruder in his abrupt entrance"
(op. cit.:53).

In the first instance, [Peirce's emphasis], we attribute a quality of feeling to a Non-Ego and "only come to
attribute it to ourselves when irrefragable reasons compel
us to do so" (CP V:57). The interplay between ego, and
non-ego, in the experience of interaction and surprise, becomes—for the mature, reflective adult—analogous to the
inner dialogue of the old self and new self coming into being in the flow of time:

> The perceptual judgment, then, can only be that it is the
> Non-Ego, something over against the Ego and bearing it
> down, is what surprised him. But if that be so, this

direct perception presents an <u>Ego</u> to which the smashed
expectation belonged, and the <u>Non-Ego</u>, the sadder and
wiser man, to which the new phenomenon belongs.
(op. cit.:58)

   The ever-widening circles of interaction and surprise,
which correct and revise the ego's familiar expectations
with the non-ego's novelties, are circles of society and of
social relations and imply a personal identity that is social in form if not in content.
   Two things here are all-important to assure oneself of
and to remember. The first is that a person is not absolutely an individual. His thoughts are what he is "saying to himself", that is, is saying to that other self
that is just coming into life in the flow of time. When
one reasons, it is that critical self that one is trying
to persuade; and all thought whatsoever is a sign, and is
mostly of the nature of language. The second thing to
remember is that the man's circle of society (however
widely or narrowly this phrase may be understood), is a
sort of loosely compacted person, in some respects of
higher rank than the person of an individual organism.
(<u>PW</u>, p. 258; <u>CP</u> V, p. 421)

   If self-consciousness and the consciousness of others
emerge from the child's interactions with others, then the
individual's sense of personal identity is social in origin.
That an individual's personal identity may consist of <u>pri-
vate</u> feelings, thoughts, and actions is admitted by Peirce
in his his early as well as in his later papers. For example:
   By self-consciousness is meant a knowledge of ourselves.
   ...The self-consciousness here meant is the recognition
   of my <u>private</u> self. I know that <u>I</u> (not merely <u>the</u> I)
   exist. (1868; <u>CP</u> V:225)
   It is plain that intelligence does not consist in feeling
   in a certain way but in acting in a certain way. Only
   we must acknowledge that there are inward actions--what
   might be called potential actions, that is actions which
   do not take place, but which somehow influence the formation of habits. (1893; <u>CP</u> V:286)

   Here Peirce anticipates the concept of "incipient response" that was to play so important a part in Mead's and
in Morris's (e.g., <u>Signs, Language and Behavior</u>, 1946) behavioristic analyses of symbolic interactions mediated by

gestures. Peirce emphasized, however, the role of imagination and phantasy:
  The whole business of ratiocination, and all that makes
  us intellectual beings, is performed in imagination
  ...Mere imagination would indeed be mere trifling; only
  no imagination is mere.
  "More than all that is in thy custody, watch over thy
  phantasy", said Solomon, "for out of it are the issues of
  life".

  The apparent paradox of a personal identity private in
content, and public and social in origin did not compel
Peirce to retreat to a Cartesian intuition and introspection. By maintaining that all thinking is by mans of
signs, that it takes the form of an inner dialogue struc-
turally similar to and continuous with the outer dialogue of
conversation with others, Peirce was able to develop a concept of personal identity that is not confined to the individual organism but that extends as far as his social and
cultural consciousness and his circle of society (see Singer
1980, pp. 494-96). The individual's consciousness of self
and of others is a "double consciousness", in which the consciousness of others may precede the consciousness of self,
and, in any case, develops with the individual's interactions with others and with the world as selves emerge from
these interactions.

                   THE DRAMA OF FIRST, SECOND,
                      AND THIRD PERSONS

  A crucial link in Peirce's social theory of personal
identity is the assumption that there are signs symptomatic
or indicative of self-consciousness that are observable to
others. In his early papers Peirce takes this assumption
for granted, when for example he accepts Kant's observation
of the child's late use of the pronoun "I" as evidence for
the relatively late appearance of a self. His whole theory
of indexical signs and of pronouns as a kind of indexical
sign was developed, in his later papers on semiotics, to
deal with this problem now known to linguists as "person
deixis".

  Lyons's explanation of "deixis" (1977, II, p. 637) is
probably widely accepted by linguists:

The location and identification of persons, objects,
events, processes and activities talked about, or referred to, in relation to the spatiotemporal context
created and sustained by the act of utterance and the
participation in it, typically, of a single speaker and
at least one addressee.

The application of this concept of deixis to expressions referring to persons—for example, to pronouns, proper
names, and definite noun phrases—has become known through
the work of Benveniste and other linguists (e.g., Silverstein 1976). Such applications depend on interpreting
first- and second-person pronouns as indexical signs that
refer to the speaker and hearer, respectively, in the situation of utterance. It is probable that these interpretations of "person deixis" were influenced, at least indirectly, by Peirce's theory of indexical signs: "Thus a token of
'I' means the person uttering that token: in other words, it
is part of the symbolic meaning of 'I' that one finds the
object indicated by a token of this type by proceeding from
the token to the speaker". (Burks 1949, p. 686; Italics in
original). (See also discussion in Singer 1980, p. 493.)

Burks's formulation is fairly close to Benveniste's,
although it does not refer explicitly to the situation of
utterance. Peirce himself, however, does this in several
passages on pronouns and proper names:
The pronoun, which may be defined as a part of speech
intended to fulfill the function of an index, is never
intelligible taken by itself apart from the circumstances
of its utterance. (1903; CP V:153) When we express a
proposition in words we leave most of its singular subjects unexpressed, for the circumstances of the enun-
ciation sufficiently show what subject is intended.
(ibid.)
A proper name has a certain denotative function peculiar,
in each case, to that name and its equivalents; every
assertion contains such a denotative or pointing-out
function. (1905; CP V:429)

The interpretation of pronouns such as "I", "me", and
"mine" as deictic and indexical signs identifies the utterer
of the expression as their object, but does not necessarily
identify the expressive and social functions of the signs.
Peirce specified three criteria for any indexical sign: that
it not resemble its object, that it direct attention to its

object, and that it refer to individual objects or individual collections of objects (PW:108). The use of personal
pronouns and other signs of person meets these three criteria, but that is not sufficient to determine which personal
pronouns will be used by a particular speaker on a particular occasion. Nor will the use of a particular pronoun tell
us whether the speaker is following a customary rule of
usage or is also intending an application to himself. Pronouns, in other words, cannot be interpreted as "indicators"
and "symptoms" of personal or subjective conscious meanings
without making additional theoretical assumptions.

One common assumption is that of egocentricity. Lyons,
who adopts this assumption quite explicitly, explains it
(1977, II, p. 638) as follows:
The speaker, by virtue of being the speaker, casts himself in the role of ego and relates everything to his
viewpoint....Egocentricity is temporal as well as spatial, since the role of the speaker is being transferred
from one participant to the other as the conversation
proceeds, and the participants may move around as they
are conversing.

The debatable status of this assumption becomes apparent if we ask whether it is based on an empirical survey of
conversations, a hypothesis, or a normative rule. Suppose
some speakers cast themselves in the role of the second person, or the third person: What happens to the doctrine of
egocentricity--in honorific terms of address, for example?[4]

The context of Lyons's discussion clearly indicates
that his assumption of egocentricity derives from a broader
theory that correlates the grammatical categories of personal pronouns with the social roles of a drama:
The grammatical category of person depends upon the
notion of participant roles and upon their grammaticali-
zation in particular languages....The Latin word "person-
a" (meaning "mask") was used to translate the Greek word
for "dramatic character" or "role", and the use of this
term by grammarians derives from their metaphorical conception of a language event as a drama in which the prin-
cipal role is played by the first person, the role sub-
sidiary to his by the second person, and all other roles
by the third person. It is important to note, however,
that only the speaker and addressee are actually parti-

cipating in the drama. The term "third person"...does
not correlate with any positive participant role.
(ibid.)

Given this dramatic theory of language and the personal pronouns, it is easier to understand the assumption of
egocentricity, although the question can still be raised: Do
all languages and all speakers grammaticalize the speaker's
reference to himself in the first person?[5]

There is some evidence that Peirce answered this question in the negative, at least in his earliest papers. Accepting the social drama of the three personal pronouns, he
regarded the second person—not the first person—as the
most important social role, and defined "Tuism" as the doctrine that "all thought is adresssed to a second person, or
to one's future self as a second person", a definition he
wrote for the Century Dictionary of 1891 (Fisch 1979b).

In a paper he wrote as a sophomore at Harvard, Peirce
connected the I, the It, and the Thou with Schiller's three
drives or impulses, respectively: the formal I-impulse
toward the infinite, the sensuous It-impulse toward the
particular, and the harmonizing Thou-impulse toward others
(Fisch, personal communication). Peirce also used these
three pronouns to designate three historical eras: the "primitive" egotistical age, his own "idistical" age, and a coming "tuistical" age (SW, p. 1966; Fisch 1979b).

Peirce's use (1966) of the three pronouns to name the
ethos of an age, and individual personality types, seems to
have anticipated the psychoanalytic typology of Id, Ego, and
Superego later developed by Freud (1927, 1930), Groddeck
(1923), and other analysts. This parallel is especially
striking in Peirce's interpretation of the trinity in terms
of the three persons: Father, Mother, and Son (Peirce in
Fisch Introduction, p. 15f.).[6]

Peirce's chief interest in the three pronouns I, It,
and Thou, however, was in their use as names for his three
phenomenological categories—names that he eventually replaced by the designations Firstness, Secondness, and Thirdness. After he introduced the latter names, he seems to
have lost interest in the drama of the pronouns and their
family romance. Perhaps he felt that the pronouns were sufficiently provided for by being analyzed as indexical signs.

PRONOUNS OF PERSONAL AND INTERPERSONAL IDENTITY

Despite his assumption of egocentricity in person deixis, Lyons asserts (1977, I, p. 52) that "every utterance is,
in general and regardless of its more specific function,   an
expressive symptom of what is in the speaker's mind, a symbol descriptive of what is signified and a   vocative   signal
that is addresssed to the receiver".

Lyons sees an "obvious connection" between Bühler's and
Jakobson's analysis of an utterance's descriptive, expressive, and vocative functions, and the analysis of the typical situation of utterance as a drama in which three roles
are given grammatical recognition by means of the category
of person (ibid.).   If this connection is valid, can the
particular social role be inferred from the particular personal pronoun used? Although Lyons summarizes the Bühler-
Jakobson theory of functions in neutral terms,   in   fact he
collapses   the   social and expressive functions into a joint
function, that of establishing and maintaining a social   relationship and expressing a symptom that "covaries with the
characteristics of the speaker". In effect, this means that
personal pronouns that   express   a   personal   identity   also
serve to establish interpersonal relations, and conversely.
"For it is only by virtue of our membership in social groups
that we are able to interact with others, and in doing so,
to establish our individual identity and personality" (Lyons
1977, I, p. 51).

This conclusion is remarkably similar to Peirce's
position on pronouns and proper names   as   indexical   signs.
Peirce may have lost interest in the social and family drama
of I, It, and Thou; but he did not lose interest in his
doctrine of "Tuism". On the contrary he expanded "Tuism",
from a doctrine about the dialogical nature of thought and
"inner" speech, to embrace the dialogical nature of all
signs, conversation, and all triadic social relations such
as giving and exchange.[7] Such an expansion and generalization of his tuistic doctrine was a relatively easy step
for Peirce--in view of his analysis of all sign-action as a
triadic relation of sign, object, and interpretant, and his
conception of an indexical sign in dynamical connection with
the utterer-and-interpreter of the sign as well as with the
sign's object.   Following such an analysis of sign action,
it is plausible to assume that thinking (which for Peirce is

carried on by means of signs) and significant social communication are similar in semiotic structure.

Peirce did not live to test and develop his indexical
theory of personal pronouns. Beyond the incidental illustrations and his suggestions of how indexical signs combine
with iconic and symbolic signs to form statements (for indices are expressive and do not assert anything), the development and application of the theory is now on the agenda of
literary scholars, linguists, anthropologists, and social
psychologists.[8] As this development proceeds it will undoubtedly continue to draw inspiration from Peirce's pioneer
contributions and also from the symbolic interactionists who
followed him. That personal identity should still be so
strongly associated with the relationship between the pronouns "I" and "Me", and interpersonal identity with the relationship of "I" and "You", is a legacy not only from
Peirce but also from James, Royce, Baldwin, Cooley, and Mead
--all of whom accepted Peirce's anti-Cartesian approach to
the self. For all of them, the inner dialogue of the self
was a dialogue between an immediately experienced "I" and a
remembered social "me", just as the outer dialogue was a
public conversation between an "I" and a "You", a conversation in which "I" and "You" express alternating social roles
in symbolic, face-to-face interaction. (Cf. Wiley 1979.)

Both dialogues are social in origin, and to some extent
in content, because the boundary between "I" and "Me" is
relative, as is that between "I" and "You". Having rejected, with Peirce, both a Cartesian self and a Kantian transcendental ego, the symbolic interactionists turned to empirical distinctions and observable processes. James, who was
probably the first to distinguish the I and the Me as the
subject-self and the object-self, was quick to add (1961
ed.:43) that "the identity of the I with Me, even in the
very act of their discrimination, is perhaps the most in-
eradicable dictum of common-sense".

His famous description of the social self as a man's Me
(op. cit., p. 44) extends the boundaries of that self "to
all that he can call his"—
     not only his body and his psychic powers, but his
     clothes, and his house, his wife and children, his
     ancestors and his friends, his reputation and works, his
     lands and horses, and yacht and bank-account.

Despite James's well-known individualism and pluralism, he was apparently not quite the nominalist about the self that Peirce accused him of being—particularly if we take seriously his practical identification of the I and the Me, and of Me and Mine:

Between what a man calls Me and what he simply calls Mine the line is difficult to draw. We feel and act about certain things that are ours very much as we feel about ourselves. (op. cit., p. 43)

A somewhat similar emphasis on the social nature of "I" was expressed by Cooley, who based his opinion (1908, p.342) on close and systematic observation of his own children's use of "self-words":

"I" is social in that the very essence of it is the assertion of self-will in a social medium of which the speaker is conscious...."I" is addressed to an audience —usually with some emphasis—and its purpose is to impress upon the audience the power ("I make go"), the wish ("I go play sand-pile"), the claim ("my Mama"), the service ("I get it for you") of the speaker. Its use in solitude would be inconceivable (though the audience may, of course, be imaginary).

To put it otherwise, "I" is a differentiation in a vague body of personal ideas which is either self-consciousness or social consciousness, as you please to look at it. In the use of "I" and of names for other people, the ego and alter phases of this consciousness become explicit.

Mead said (1930a) that his account of the "I" and "You" dialogue was more objective than Cooley's subjective and ethnocentric account. Mead claimed to analyze the development of mind and self from early conditions shared with animal behavior: a "conversation of gestures", the matrix for significant communication. But Mead also used introspective and phenomenological descriptions in his concept of role-playing.[10] Cooley on the other hand makes room for historical studies of preconditions, "primary groups" (family play groups, neighborhood) in face-to-face interaction.

In retrospect, Peirce's semiotic analysis of the inner and outer dialogues, and of their interconnection through an indexical theory of pronouns, bypasses the controversy between mentalism and behaviorism. Personal pronouns act by "blind compulsion" on the human nervous system, as indexical signs; but they also signify properties when joined to icons

by verbal symbols such as "Happy Birthday". Cooley observed
(1908, p. 354, e.g.) that "You" was often used for "I" in
early childhood. If a two-year-old can redirect the self
reference from "You" to "I", it should not surprise us that
an eight-year-old redirects it from "You" to "Me"!

CORPORATE PERSONALITY AND COLLECTIVE IDENTITY

In one of his cosmological papers, "Man's Glassy Essence" (1892), Peirce introduced a concept of corporate personality that he drew as a consequence from his theory that
the necessary condition for the existence of a person is
that his feelings "should be in close enough connection to
influence one another" (CP VI:271). That something like a
personal consciousness, and a corporate personality, should
emerge "in bodies of men who are in intimate and intensely
sympathetic communion" seemed to Peirce a logical consequence of his theory that could be tested by observation and
experiment. He cited (loc. cit.) "ordinary observations" of
esprit de corps, national sentiment, sympathy, and the mind
of corporations, as giving evidence—at first appearance—of
"the influence of such greater persons upon individuals".
The gathering of thirty thousand young people of the Society
for Christian Endeavor seemed to him to generate "some mys-
terious diffusion of sweetness and light". Further evidence
of such corporate personality, he suggested, should be
looked for in the Christian Church, where Christians "have
always been ready to risk their lives for the sake of having
prayers in common, of getting together and praying simultaneously with great energy, and especially for their common
body".

In making these suggestions, Peirce was aware of the
commonsense belief that personality and personal consciousness do not extend beyond the individual's body; and he
seems to have anticipated and replied to that view when he
writes in the same paper (loc. cit.):
It is true that when the generalization of feeling has
been carried so far as to include all within a person, a
stopping-place, in a certain sense, has been attained;
and further generalization will have a less lively character.

Peirce gave a more explicit reply to the commonsense
point of view in his notes on William James's 1890 work,

Principles of Psychology: quoting selected passages from the
latter, he asked James critical questions about them. The
confrontation between Peirce and James is particularly dramatic on the issue of "personality" and personal identity
and the communication of thought between individuals. James
was emphatic that "no thought even comes into direct sight
of a thought in another personal consciousness than its own.
Absolute insulation, irreducible pluralism, is the law"
(quoted in CP VIII:81). To this Peirce asks (loc. cit.):
   Is not the direct contrary nearer the observed facts? Is
   not this pure metaphysical speculation? You think there
   must be such isolation, because you confound thoughts
   with feeling-qualities; but all observation is against
   you. There are some small particulars that a man can
   keep to himself. He exaggerates them and his personality
   sadly.

   James strongly insisted that the "breaches" between the
thoughts belonging to different personal minds are "the most
absolute breaches in nature", that "neither contemporaneity
nor proximity in space nor similarity of quality and content
are able to fuse thoughts together which are sundered by
this barrier of belonging to different personal minds....The
personal self rather than the thought might be treated as
the Immediate datum in psychology" (quoted in CP VIII:82).

   To this direct challenge to his own concept of a corporate personality formed from the connection of feelings
and thoughts between different individuals, Peirce replied
(op. cit.:82-85) in a half-ironic tone, calling the tongue
the "very organ of personality":
   Everybody will admit a personal self exists in the same
   sense in which a snark exists; that is, there is a phenomenon to which that name is given. It is an illusory
   phenomenon; but still it is a phenomenon.   It is not
   quite purely illusory, but only mainly so. It is true,
   for instance, that men are selfish, that is, that they
   are really deluded into supposing themselves to have some
   isolated existence; and in so far, they have it. To deny
   the reality of personality is not antispiritualistic; it
   is only anti-nominalistic. It is true that there are
   certain phenomena, really quite slight and insignificant,
   but exaggerated, because they are connected with the
   tongue which may be described as personality. The agili-
   ty of the tongue is shown in its insisting that the world
   depends upon it. The phenomena of personality consist

mainly in ability to hold the tongue. This is what the
tongue brags so about.
Meantime, physicians are highly privileged that they can
ask to see people's tongues; for this is inspecting the
very organ of personality. It is largely because this
organ is so sensitive that personality is so vivid. But
it is more because it is so agile and complex a muscle.

James was not the only psychologist to express scepti-
cism about the existence of a corporate personality. Baldwin's Dictionary of Philosophy and Psychology, defined a
"Tribal Self" (1957 ed., p. 714f.) in terms of "the psychological factors involved in the organization of a social
group (tribe), when conceived after the analogy with the individual's mental organization in the form of a personal
self", but then added that "the conception is often vague
and stands upon much the same plane as that of general (or
social) will".

In a more general definition of Social Unit, Baldwin
adopts (p. 541) a relational point of view—anticipating
Radcliffe-Brown, and the later sociological and anthropological theories:
It is true that the individual is the unit of the social
group....But he is not the social unit, since the social
is a relation of individuals....There is no general social unit, and it is doubtful whether in the social sciences any final unit of analogy will ever be discovered
in terms of which all the phenomena of the class can be
quantitatively increased....The phrase "fundamental social fact"...better expresses the scope of this field.

Contrary to Peirce (who himself contributed to it some
articles on logic and signs), Baldwin's Dictionary seemed to
restrict the definitions of Personality and Personal Identity to the individual—even when considering the essentially
legal Roman conception of the person as the subject of
rights, and the Christian conception of the absolute moral
worth of personality (pp. 282ff.). Baldwin's own theory emphasized the role of social factors in personality formation.

In the context of the cosmological papers, Peirce often
formulated his concept of corporate personality in psychological terms and not semiotically, analogously to the practice he followed in his formulation of an individual person-

ality concept. For the latter, I have suggested that semiotic formulations were later developed for an inner dialogue
of "I" and "Me" and an outer dialogue of "I" and "You".
Peirce himself suggested these formulations, although they
were discussed more explicitly by James, Baldwin, Cooley,
and Mead. Is there an analogous discussion of dialogues
between corporate personalities?

Peirce occasionally refers to the use of "we" and "our"
as indicating evidence for the existence of corporate personality. For example (CP V:355):
  The constant use of the word "we"--as when we speak of
  our possessions in the Pacific--our destiny as a repub-
  lic--in cases in which no personal interests at all are
  involved, show conclusively that men do not make their
  personal interests their only ones, and therefore may, at
  least, subordinate them to the interests of the community.

This is reminiscent of his assumption in the early papers that the use of "I" is a symptom of self-consciousness,
and implies that the use of "we" and "our" are to be interpreted as symptoms of a collective consciousness or a collective identity. There is not much along these lines in
the cosmological papers and not a great deal more in his
later papers. The symbolic interactionists who came after
Peirce were more explicit about the formation of a corporate
personality. Cooley, for example, wrote (1909) about the
"we" ideal in terms that would have pleased Peirce:
  I am aware of the social group in which I live as immediately and authentically as I am aware of myself; and Descartes might have said "we think", cogitamus, on as good
  grounds as he said cogito. (p. 9)
  Children and savages...see themselves and their fellows
  as an indivisible, though various, "we", and desire this
  "we" to be harmonious, happy, and successful. [(pp.
  33f.).

Cooley's theory (1909, 1922) of how the individual is
moulded by the primary group of face-to-face associations in
family, play-group, and neighborhood to develop a social
self and to bring under the discipline of sympathy the
"passions of lust, greed, revenge, the pride of power" is
too well known to require elaboration here. So is Mead's
equally familiar behavioristic variant of the theory (1922,
1925), which sees a socialized self emerge from a "conver-

sation of gestures", play, and organized games, taking the
role of a "generalized other".

The controversy between the followers of Cooley and of
Mead, over the issue of introspective mentalism and scienti-
fic behaviorism, can be resolved by recalling Peirce's non-
Cartesian approach to the relation of mind and matter (CP
VI:268):

> Viewing a thing from the outside, considering its rela-
> tions of action and reaction with other things, it
> appears as matter. Viewing it from the inside, looking
> at its immediate character of feeling, it appears as con-
> sciousness.

Applying Peirce's approach to a semiotic analysis of
corporate personality, I would suggest that the appropriate
dialogue is a "we/they" dialogue and that it is both inner
and outer. It is an inner dialogue insofar as it is viewed
from the inside, as feeling and immediate consciousness, and
an outer dialogue insofar as it is viewed from the outside
as a social interaction. Following the analogy with Peirce's
analysis of the ego/non-ego (or "I and You") dialogue, we
can construct the hypothesis that in the "we/they" dialogue,
"we" and "they" are experienced practically simultaneously
as a contrast--that "we" appears as familiar, and "they" as
strange and surprising. The element of surprise introduced
by "they" gives the dialogue the quality of a physical encounter; but as "they" become familiar, the dialogue is
raised to a level of feeling and consciousness.

The alternating reversal of "I" and "You", in conversation with others, does not seem to have an exact analogue
in the "we/they" dialogue for two reasons. It is much more
difficult to shift from a "we" to a "they" than from an "I"
to a "You" in a conversation. A particular "we/they" contrast is usually correlated with a heavy load of associated
contrasts: for example, "natives/foreigners", "old timers/
newcomers", "Northerners/Southerners", and all sorts of religious, racial, national, and class contrasts. Where these
contrasts are intensely and emotionally felt, they are not
quickly picked up or dropped; it is therefore difficult for
"us" to take "their" point of view or to see "ourselves" as
"others" see "us". (See Kipling's 1926 poem "We and They").
Analogous resistances may occur in an "I/ You" dialogue, but
it is not usually as heavily loaded or as highly charged.

The difficulty (or ease) with which a "we" can shift to "they" and back to "we" depends not only on the felt emotional intensity of a particular "we/they" contrast but on the legal and customary constraints surrounding distinctions of race, religion, ethnicity, social class, and sex. Where the constraints are rigorous, and conversion (even at an individual level) is followed by severe penalties, intergroup dialogues of "we/they" will be slow to start and intermittent in their course.

The other obstacle to a smooth-flowing "we/they" dialogue is an "I/we" dialogue. This is especially so in a highly individualistic society, where individual self-interest and independence are major social values. The conflict between individual and society then becomes a major preoccupation. In the second half of the nineteenth century, Peirce saw the United States dominated by a "gospel of greed" that exaggerated the beneficial effects of selfishness and needed to be replaced by a "gospel of love". As early as 1863, he prophesied in his essay "On the Place of Our Age in the History of Civilization" as follows:

First there was the egotistical stage when man arbitrarily imagined perfection, now is the idistical stage when he observes it. Hereafter must be the more glorious tuistical stage when he shall be in communion with her and this is exactly what, step by step we are coming to. (SW; Fisch 1979b).

This sentiment was to blossom in Peirce's cosmological papers of the 1890s into a doctrine of "evolutionary love" (agapastic evolution--as distinct from tychastic evolution by chance, and from anancastic evolution by necessity). It was also expressed in his doctrine of tuism (that all thought and conversation is addressed to a second person) and was embodied in his social theory of logic, which held that an identification with the interests of the unlimited community is an indispensable condition for the validity of all reasoning.

Each of us is an insurance company....But, now, suppose that an insurance company, among its risks, should take one exceeding in amount the sum of all the others. Plainly, it would then have no security whatever....If a man has a transcendent personal interest infinitely outweighing all others, then upon the theory of validity of inference just developed, he is devoid of all security, and can make no valid inference whatever. What follows?

That logic rigidly requires, before all else, that no de-
terminate fact, nothing which can happen to a man's self,
should be of more consequence to him than everything
else. He who would not sacrifice his own soul to save
the whole world is illogical in all his inferences, collectively. So the social principle is intrinsically
rooted in logic. (CP V:354)

In his social sentiments and interpretation of "evolutionary love", Peirce was out of step with the individualism
and Social Darwinism of his times. His position did however
find some support in Cooley, as already indicated, and in
Josiah Royce. A contemporary of Peirce's who heard his
lectures and corresponded with him, Royce restated many of
Peirce's arguments in more popular language and based them,
as Peirce did, on modern logic and a semiotic doctrine of
interpretation (see especially Royce's Problem of Christianity). As for corporate personality, Royce was even more
confident of its existence and its influence on the individual person than was Peirce:

For me, at present, a genuinely and loyally united community, which lives a coherent life, is in a perfectly
(literal) sense a person....On the other hand, any human
individual person, in a perfectly literal sense, is a
community. The coherent life which includes past, present and future and holds them reasonably together, is the
life of what I have also called...a Community of Interpretation, in which the present, with an endless fecund-
ity of invention, interprets the past to the future.
(letter to Mary W. Calkins, 20 March 1916; in Royce 1970,
pp. 644-46)

Royce gave this position a theological application and
identified it with Pauline Christianity and the Christian
view of a community as a Person—"and at the same time, to
enrich its ideal memory of a person, until he became transformed into a community". The process in question was not,
for Royce

merely theological, and is not merely mystical, less
merely mythical. Nor is it a process invented merely by
abstract metaphysicians. It is the process which Victor
Hugo expressed in Les Miserables when he put into the
mouth of Enjolras the words: "Ma mère, c'est la répub-
lique". As I write you these words, Frenchmen are writing the meaning of these words in their blood, about Ver-
dun. The mother which is a republic, is a community,

which is also a person--and not merely an aggregate, and
not merely by metaphor a person. (op. cit., p. 647)

The individual's sacrifice to a nation in time of war
represented for Royce during the First World War, as it did
for Peirce during the Civil War and the Spanish-American
War, compelling testimony to the existence of corporate personality and a collective identity. That national loyalty
and patriotism could and should be generalized to the
interests of an unlimited World Community was a matter of
faith for both Royce and Peirce. In a post-World War I
article on "National-Mindedness and International-Mindedness," (published in 1929), Mead took a more realistic view
of the problem of reconciling the diversity of interests in
a modern community with national unity and international
peace. He saw nothing in an industrial civilization "to
sweep the individual into emotional realization of his identity with the community....Loyalties to the family, business, or schools, the more intense they are, the more exclusive they are" (p. 388). Applying his social psychological
theory of how selves are formed Mead found that a self is
an interaction between two parts of our nature: the fundamental impulses (i.e., "the primitive, sexual, parental,
hostile, and cooperative impulses out of which our social
selves are built up"), and the power we get from language to
control our thinking and our conduct through talking to ourselves and taking the role of the generalized other (p.396):
We import the conventions of the group into our inner
sessions and debate with ourselves. But the concatenated
concepts which we use are ours because we are speaking in
the language of the outer universe of discourse, the organized human world to which we belong. (p. 395)

The unity of society, and of the self, Mead believed,
derived from two sources: the identity of fundamental emotional and hostile impulses ("a unity from below"), and the
"sophisticated self-consciousness" of a unity-in-diversity
among the members of a highly organized industrial society
(1929, p. 396).
[Because] every war will now become a world war and will
take as its objective not the destruction of hostile
forces but of enemy nations in their entirety..., it has
become unthinkable as a policy for adjudicating national
differences. It has become logically impossible.
(p. 400)

Recognizing that wars may still arise, Mead concludes
that we cannot any longer think our international life in
terms of warfare and appeals to the unity from below, to
"our diaphragms and the visceral responses which a fight
sets in operation" (p. 402).   Instead,

> We are compelled to reach a sense of being a nation by
> means of rational self-consciousness. We must think our-
> selves in terms of the great community to which we be-
> long. We cannot depend upon feeling ourselves at one
> with our compatriots, because the only effective feeling
> of unity springs from our common response against the
> common enemy. No other social emotion will melt us into
> one.   Instead of depending upon a national soul we must
> achieve national mindedness. (p. 401; emphasis in orig-
> inal)

The kind of corporate personality and collective identity discussed by Peirce, Royce and Mead is essentially a
phenomenon of wartime and shows two characteristic features:
it grows and declines as a war-fever waxes and wanes; and it
involves not only a conflict between a nation and its ene-
mies ("we/they") but also a conflict between the national
interest and the interests of its citizens and diverse constituent groups ("I and we"), particularly when sacrifices
are called for. Semiotically, the conflict gets expressed
in an "I/we" dialogue as well as in a "we/they" dialogue.
Pericles's Funeral Oration and Lincoln's Gettysburg Address
are classic and eloquent rhetorical expressions of such dialogues. They are not, of course, restricted to wartime conditions but may also be expressed during periods of religious and patriotic enthusiasm, political reform, and national memorials and celebrations--as Peirce, Royce, and
Mead suggest.   (For Durkheim's and Warner's analogies with
totemic rituals see Singer 1981a.)

Durkheim's distinction between mechanical and organic
solidarity--and the related social theories of Maine, Mor-
gan, Tönnies, Weber, and Redfield, among others--indicate
that a corporate personality and collective identity change
with the forms and foundations of political, social, and
economic organization and are not independent and unchanging
biological and psychological "givens" of social and cultural
structure and organization   (See Singer 1961.)

It may well be that the grammatical distinction between
the exclusive "we" ("I and they") and the inclusive "we" ("I

and you"), which occurs in many languages, represents a linguistic expression of fluctuating "I/we" and "we/they" dialogues that are associated with social and cultural changes.
Benveniste, who does not necessarily share this interpretation, points out (1971, p. 203):
  "We" is not a quantified or multiplied "I"; it is an "I"
  expanded beyond the strict limits of the person, enlarged
  and at the same time amorphous. As a result there are two
  opposed but not contradictory uses--outside of the ordinary plural. On the one hand the "I" is amplified by "we"
  into a person that is more massive, more solemn, and less
  defined; it is the royal "we". On the other hand, the
  use of "we" blurs the too sharp assertion of "I" into a
  broader and more diffuse expression: it is the "we" of
  the author or orator.

     A recent study of the rhetoric of autocracy and democ-
racy in Nepal illustrates how, under changing social conditions, these conflicting tendencies in the "I/we" dialogue
are reflected in the King's speeches:
  The ambiguity characterizing the King's position is also
  mirrored in the philosophy that is the vehicle through
  which he puts forth his political strategy. Panchayat
  Democracy is a vague concept blending traditional authority and power politics....The greater specificity in King
  Birendra's speeches (when compared to those of his father) does not reflect a fundamental change in the King's
  position, but rather the King's stronger control of the
  country. But this has been achieved without abolishing
  the ambiguous nature of his rule, and can be seen in his
  use of the word "we", for instance. Just as Mahendra did,
  Birendra uses "we" in reference to himself as the exalted
  ruler--the traditional ruler--and as the ruler merging
  with his people--the politician who promises to do his
  share of the work in cooperation with his electorate.
  (Borgstrom 1980, p. 49. For another, more personal, interpretation of the use of the royal "we", see footnote 5
  of the present paper.)

            TOWARDS A CONVERSATION OF CULTURES AND
                A CIVILIZATION OF THE DIALOGUE

     Writing in the frigid Cold War atmosphere of 1953, Rob-
ert Redfield asked whether it would be untactful to suggest

that America needs a hearing aid. He acknowledged that   "we
Americans have long been known as a talkative people".
    While the strong silent man is one recognized type among
us, visitors find most of us very ready with our tongues.
Mrs. Trollope wrote in 1828 that "Americans love talking", and she recorded some of the abundant talk that she
heard--and did not admire.   A little later Alexis de
Tocqueville characterized us as "garrulous" and repo=ted
that the American "speaks to you as if he were addressing
a meeting". The French observer was also impressed with
the fact that what the American talked about   was often
himself.   He recognized that those Americans were proud,
with reason, of their achievement in building a new and
democratic nation. It was our patriotism that Tocqueville
found garrulous.   He found us unsatiable of praise and
ever willing to tell strangers of the superiority of the
American way of life. (Redfield 1953; 1963 repr.,
p. 232f.)

    Redfield suggested that our national habit needed to be
balanced by listening:
I do not think that we listen enough to what other people
are trying to say to us about themselves, and I do not
think we listen enough to the sound of what we say in the
ears of him to whom we say it. We are guided chiefly in
deciding what to say by the conceptions we have of what
those others ought to like about us if they were just
like us. And they aren't. (p. 233)

    The art of listening to other peoples and the art of
talking need to be cultivated for our own safety:
Mutual security depends on mutual understanding, and for
understanding you have to have a conversation. A conversation is not two people talking loudly at each other,
and certainly it is not one person with a megaphone. It
is first one person listening while the other talks, and
then that one talking while the other listens. In the
Big Room where all peoples meet much of the talk is just
the loudest voices shouting what they mistakenly imagine
the others might find impressive to hear. (pp. 233f.)

    The Big Room is a Hall of Nations in which each people
is conceived of as if it were a single person.
Of course each of these is really a multitude of voices
(except perhaps the Russian); each is a myriad voices
coming to us from real individuals of many sorts speaking

through books, travel, newspapers, and personal contact.
The differences among individuals I for the moment ignore, because it is also true that in general ways each
nation, each people, has a character of its own; each
taken as a whole is saying something that stands for all
the separate individuals that make it up; we can learn to
listen to the nation as if it were one person. (p. 234)

As we listen to the nations in the Big Room, what should
we listen for? Redfield suggested three things (pp. 234-37):
National Character ("the collective personality or the group
heritage or perhaps just the persisting peculiarities that
make the people distinguishable from their neighbors"), Mood
("the response they make to a marked turn in their for-
tunes"), and Human Nature ("the qualities that all men share
with one another...: pride, shame, enjoyment of the company
of those who are near and dear, delight in children, and
laughter, a certain satisfaction in one's work well done,
anger in the face of an injustice--however justice may be
conceived...").

While today some of us reassert the traditional American
emphasis on self-reliance, striving to keep the control
of our affairs in our own hands and out of the control of
either powerful business or bureaucratic government, we
can use this human impulse of ours to understand the mood
of those Asiatics and Middle Easterners who want to keep
the control of their affairs in their own hands--and out
of ours. Their situation has at least this additional
cause for calling up the human disposition to run one's
own life: we to them are foreigners and, as part of
Western industrial civilization, conquerors. (p. 237)

Redfield believed that improving the art of carrying on
the "little conversations" with the peoples of the world
would combine with the more organized discipline of the
"great conversation" carried on by great books and plain and
sensible conversation which maintain and enlarge the company
of the free mind. As between two individuals, so a conversation between two nations must be based on the percep
tion of both difference and likeness:

To talk as free men each must in effect say: "You have a
different view from mine, but we are both reasonable and
human creatures, and I should like to know what your view
is". That this ideal is not usually realized in life
makes its influence on us no less. Our country, in peril
in the Big Room, needs all the strength that reason can

give to our powers of understanding. To indulge hateful
passion for political advantage is to drive ourselves
downward toward that dark reliance on force which today
is Russia's. At home and abroad to talk and then to listen, to listen with the help of reason and then reasonably to talk, is to strengthen us just where we can be so
much stronger than the Soviets. It is to build the community of free minds, "the civilization of the dialogue."
(p. 240)

When Redfield published this article in 1953 in the
Saturday Review he had already launched a cooperative scholarly effort to study the differences and likenesses among
some of the world's civilizations and cultures (Chinese, Is-
lamic, Indian, Middle American) with a view both to improving the "little conversations" among them and to building
the "civilization of the dialogue" from the carrying on of
the "great conversation" among their "great traditions". It
is notable that this effort, to which he devoted the last
seven years of his life, extended his earlier studies (in
Tepoztlán and Yucatan) of what happens to the folk society
and culture in a modern, urban setting. The integration of
the earlier and later approaches was achieved in his conception of a "social anthropology of civilizations" and in a
conversation of cultures implied by that concept.

Redfield's development of a social anthropology of civilizations contributed to a revision of the classical anthropological and sociological theories of cultural and social change. As I have pointed out elsewhere (1976, p.
247f.), he "demonstrated the importance and feasibility of
looking at the process of modernization from the point of
view of the traditional societies, their own values and
world views, their changing moods and biographies....In his
later thought Redfield came to see that the struggle for
independence and the desire to recover some continuity with
their ancient indigenous civilization was for the traditional non-Western societies an inseparable part of the
process of modernization."

Although Redfield's research and thinking antedated the
structural and symbolic theories of the 1960s and 1970s, his
definitions of culture and society were implicitly structural and semiotic (for further discussion of Redfield's struc-
turalism, see Singer 1976, pp. 222-29).
In so far as any defined human aggregate is characterized

by social relations, it is a society; in so far as it is characterized by conventional understandings, it exhibits a culture; and in so far as it may also be said to occupy a territory, it is a community. (Redfield 1941, p. 15f.)

In one of his last writings, "Art and Icon" (1962), Redfield explicitly applied Peirce's icon-concept to the interpretation of a Dogon carving of twins, in order to illustrate the difference between ethnographic and aesthetic analysis of exotic cultural objects.

Another and more specific semiotic cultural analysis of the conversation of cultures is Geertz's Person, Time and Conduct in Bali. Utilizing Schutz's (1962, The Problem of Social Reality 1967 ed., pp. 139-214) framework of phenomenological distinctions between the directly experienced social reality of "consociates" in a face to face situation of a "we -relationship" and the indirectly experienced social reality of "contemporaries" "predecessors", and "successors", Geertz showed that Balinese society "dampens the intimacy implicit in face-to-face relationships" by ceremonializing social intercourse, pulverizing the flow of time into an absolute present, and depersonalizing concrete individuals into stereotyped faceless persons. The result is "a glancing hesitant confrontation of anonymous persons brought physically very close and kept socially very distant" (Geertz 1966, p. 60).

That this represents a cultural transformation of Schutz's conceptual scheme is noted by Geertz (op. cit., p. 42):
The most striking thing about the culture patterns in which Balinese notions of personal identity are embodied is the degree to which they depict virtually everyone-- friends, relatives, neighbors and strangers; elders and youths; superiors and inferiors; men, women, chiefs, kings, priests, and gods; even the dead and unborn--as stereotyped contemporaries, abstract and anonymous fellowmen.
These patterns represent "the symbolic de-emphasis, in the everyday life of the Balinese, of the perception of fellowmen as consociates, successors, or predecessors in favor of the perception of them as contemporaries" (p. 53).

While this is a dominant cultural pattern supported by Balinese perception of people, time, and conduct, Geertz

admits that there are subdominant counter-patterns in close
fit with Schutz's scheme:

> Of course people in Bali are directly, and sometimes
> deeply involved in one another's lives; do feel their
> world to have been shaped by the actions of those who
> came before them and orient their actions toward shaping
> the world of those who will come after them. (p. 43;
> emphasis in original).

But it is not as consociates or "their immediacy and individuality, or their special, never to be repeated, impact upon
the stream of historical events...[which are] emphasized: it
is their social placement, their particular location within
a persisting, indeed an eternal metaphysical order" (ibid.).

The illuminating paradox to which Geertz calls attention is that Balinese formulations of personhood are, in our
terms, depersonalizing. We might also ask whether the formulations of a Balinese phenomenologist would omit Schutz's
category of "consociates" altogether.

The interest of Geertz's study is not exhausted by
these general comments, but resides just as much in the
ethnographic details and their explanatory value. He points
out, for example (p. 20) in Balinese naming-patterns it is
the conventionalized public titles, human and divine, which
"comprise the present expression of the Balinese concept of
personhood in the image of what they consider themselves at
bottom to be". Compared to these, other symbols of personhood are secondary: personal names are secret, birth-order
names are used mainly for children and adolescents, kinship
terms are not used in face-to-face situations, parents
address one another by their children's names, and status
titles form a pure prestige system.

The Balinese sense of shame and the absence of climax
in interpersonal relations in that culture are also given
ingenious explanations by Geertz in terms of this dominant
cultural pattern. Rather than summarize these explanations
here, I prefer to draw one or two implications of the semiotics of dialogue for a semiotics of culture.

In order to understand and participate in the kind of
"conversations of cultures" described by Redfield, one would
need to know national character, changing national moods,
world-view and value systems, group personality types, and
great and little traditions of a civilization. Geertz's

conversation with Balinese culture, although more particu-
larized, requires almost as wide-ranging knowledge of nam-
ing-systems, conceptions of time and its calendrical expression, the etiquette of ceremonial conduct, kinship terminology, political organization, the psychology of social relations. If we are going to communicate with people from other cultures, we shall need to know how their social and cultural structures and organizations extend and transform the
canonical situation of utterance in a face-to-face situation.   This kind of knowledge is more specialized than that
provided by Peirce's general theory of signs and a semiotics
of dialogue based on that theory. It calls for the results
of such special disciplines as linguistis, ethnology, social
and cultural anthropology, geography.

Peirce readily acknowledged the difference between
semiotico as a general theory of signs on the one hand, and
on the other its application to specialized fields. Although he had an imposing knowledge of many languages and
had read widely in history and geography, he undertook few
original cultural studies comparable to his studies in
astronomy, physics, mathematics, logic, or psychophysics.
(His studies of Shakespearean pronunciation and of the psychology of great men are exceptions to this general observation.) Nevertheless, his general theory of signs offers many
fruitful suggestions for social and cultural anthropology
and for linguistic anthropology. This is especially true of
his semiotic analysis of dialogue and its application to a
conversation of cultures. Without trying to discuss the applications already made of Peirce's semiotic to a study of
dialogue and conversation, I should like to summarize those
features of a semiotic of dialogue which still provide a
novel framework of concepts and hypotheses for empirical research on personal and socio-cultural identity.

By relating personal identity and corporate personality
to their linguistic expression (especially in particular
pronouns such as "I" and "We") Peirce raised the problem to
a semiotic level of analysis, directing attention to a phenomenological and pragmatic approach to the self--and away
from transcendental, psychophysical, and psychophysiological
approaches.

His interpretation of the use of personal pronouns (as
well as proper names and definite descriptions) as indexical
signs of, or pointers to, individual and group utterers-

and-interpreters of the signs makes it possible to analyze a
dialogue as a five-termed relation of utterer, sign, object,
interpretant, and interpreter. Such a formulation also makes
possible the location of individual and social identities as
objects of, as well as participants in, a dialogue.

Peirce's observations that Ego and non-Ego are experienced practically simultaneously (along with the opposition
between them), and that the non-Ego is experienced as something external and strange, provides a basis for distinguishing an inner dialogue of "I" and "Me"; an outer dialogue of "I" and "You"; and a dialogue of corporate identities, of "We" and "They". Since this observation, in
Peirce's analysis, is also the foundation for self-consciousness and the consciousness of others, it provides the
point of departure for the structure of inferences that un-
derlies his theory of the self.

The pronouns (and other signs) form systems that may
grow indefinitely. These systems not only consist of discrete lexical sets, but are also socio-cultural patterns and
systems whose meanings are limited by the experience and
habits of the actors. Pairs of pronouns such as "I - me",
"I - you", "we - they", etc. represent a notation for kinds
of dialogues; in Peirce's terms, they are "iconic diagrams",
whose relational structure is similar to the structure of
social relations among the individuals or groups denoted by
the pronouns.[11]

As systems, the pairs (or triads and tetrads) of pronouns that occur in dialogues include iconic signs and symbols as well as indices. The inclusion of icons and symbols
provides the link for Peirce to feelings and concepts:
A concept is not a mere jumble of particulars;--that is
only its crudest species. A concept is the living influence upon us of a _diagram_, or _icon_, with whose several
parts are connected in thought an equal number of feelings or ideas. The law of mind is that feelings or ideas
attach themselves in thought so as to form systems. (CP
VII:467)
The pragmaticist grants that a proper name (although it
is not customary to say that it has a meaning) has a certain denotative function peculiar, in each case, to that
name and its equivalents; and...he grants that every
assertion contains such a denotative or pointing-out
function. In its peculiar individuality, the pragmati-

cist excludes this from the rational purport of the assertion, although the like of it, being common to all assertions, and so, being general and not individual may enter into the pragmaticistic purport. (PW, p. 263; emphasis in original)

While Peirce's youthful interest in "I", "It", and "Thou" was associated with his desire to write a natural history of words—and then with his search for names for his three categories of Firstness, Secondness, and Thirdness—he also saw the possibility of using the pronouns as names for individual and social types. This possibility is envisaged in his prophecy of the coming of a tuistical age, which will succeed the "sensate" generation of the idistical age and the "me" generation of the egotistical age. Whether Peirce's prophecy comes to be fulfilled or not, his doctrine of tuism has already shown us the path to a semiotic analysis of thinking, conversation, and social relations generally. The road to a semiotics of culture winds through the semiotics of dialogue.

EPILOGUE

One bridge between a Peircean semiotics of dialogue and a semiotics of personal and social identity in culture and society has already been started in the work of several anthropologists. I have in mind not only contributions such as those of Redfield and Geertz to a conversation of cultures, but also the neglected and pioneering contributions of Lloyd Warner to a semiotic anthropology, especially in his monograph dealing with an Australian tribe (A Black Civilization, 1937) and in the last monograph of his "Yankee City" series (The Living and the Dead, A Study of the Symbolic Life of Americans, 1959). Although lacking the linguistic sophistication of a Silverstein or a Lyons, Warner's early formulation of the dialogical nature of symbolic and social interaction approximates fairly closely Lyons's definition of a "canonical situation of utterance". Warner analyzes the social situation (1959, p. 470) as a mutual and reciprocal exchange of signs between two actors, a sender and a receiver, within a context of culturally defined sign interaction. The context is one in which the actors interpret and attribute meaning to the signs and to the objects indicated by them, and thus "invest themselves into the signs".

The signs exchanged include gestures, actions, houses and gardens, photographs, and emblematic systems—as well as words and other kinds of signs (Warner 1959, pp. 469f., 474, 476, 477, 484;, see also Singer 1977, 1981a).

While Warner's model allows the interaction between two individuals to represent the "whole web of society's relations", he also discusses (1959, p. 468, 471-73) how possible extensions of the model permit "delayed sign exchange" between the "here and now" of the immediate action-context in face-to-face interactions and remoter contexts in the past and future. His classification of the different types of action contexts into moral, supernatural, and technical, and of the associated symbol-systems (e.g., duties and rights, myths and rituals, skills and tools) suggests how each action-context can be viewed as part of larger action-systems, the totality of which makes up the social system of the community (op. cit., p. 479f.).

For two reasons, the questions of a "private" language of thoughts and of a "private" self do not pose epistemological problems for Warner's model: 1) private and individual interpretations of a sign are "largely dependent on the previous use of the sign in public exchange" (p. 465); and 2) each actor interprets the meaning of the sign to himself as he communicates it to the other actor (p. 464). "Hidden signs"—including for example the manifest content of dreams, reveries and visions, and supernatural experiences— can take objective form in concrete visible symbols (such as a cross or an animal totem) or remain as invisible signs within the "internal conversation" of one individual (pp. 468-70).

Warner sometimes calls the concrete, visible symbols "emblems" or "emblematic systems" (pp. 266, 474). In this usage he is following Durkheim, who developed the analogy between such emblems as flags and heraldic designs and totems. Extrapolating from Durkheim's conception of totems and emblems as sacred collective representations, Warner interprets myths and rituals as largely evocative symbol systems which express and refer to a collective identity. "Such a collective representation symbolizes for men what they feel and think about themselves as animals and persons" (p. 485). The sacred emblems link the individual to a collective identity that takes on a supernatural reality.

> The sacred world is not just a reified symbolic expression of the realities of the society, but also an expression of the ongoing life of the human animal. Men can fully realize all they are as members of a species and a society at the supernatural level. Here they can love and hate themselves as gods and be loved and hated by the deities they have created. (p. 489)

Although he regarded his own work as a work of science, using science's technical tools and logical referential symbol systems, Warner did not seem to share the impression of many scientists that "science will ultimately conquer the whole world of religious life" (p. 489).

> The individual who has lost his faith can no longer express his hope and fears, his sense of belonging and togetherness and thereby his feeling of 'wholeness', for the sacred symbols which combine the emotional world of the species and the moral world of the society are the only ones now available that can function in this manner. (p. 490)

I have discussed Warner's application of Durkheim's emblem theory of totemism to the sacred and secular symbolic life of a new England urban community in another paper (Singer 1981a) I should like to conclude the present paper with a few comments on the relation of Warner's model for a semiotics of culture to Peirce's general theory of signs and his dialogical analysis of sign action. The number of elements in Warner's model that incorporate something of Peirce's general theory is quite striking: his analysis of sign-action into signs, objects, and interpretations in a social situation that consists of at least two actors (as senders-and-receivers of the signs) has already been noted. In both there is also a wide range of signs beyond the verbal signs, and an inclusion of feelings and values as well as denotative and referential meanings. That no sign can be interpreted in isolation but only as part of a system of signs and their meanings ("symbol systems" for Warner) is another shared feature between the two thinkers.

Warner's statement (1959, p. 467) that "The attribution of meaning to an object by an individual depends on previous experience of the individual with the object itself or with signs of the object" and the corollary (op. cit., p. 473) that "signs of the future cannot reach much beyond the present and past meanings on which they are founded" are virtual

restatements of Peirce's principle of "collateral information". Peirce's idea that individual organisms acquire
selves in the course of interacting with one another in
sign-situations, and that selves so formed are not restricted to the "box of flesh and blood" but encompass the
"loosely compacted persons" from one's "circle of society",
finds fuller elaboration in Warner, (op. cit., pp. 449-51),
who, for his model of "social personalities" in symbolic interaction, draws on the ideas of Durkheim and Mauss, Malinowski and Radcliffe-Brown--as well as on Freud, Jung, Piaget, and G.H. Mead, among others.

The echoes of Peirce in Warner are all the more remarkable considering that Warner nowhere mentions Peirce. Since
Warner was quite conscientious about acknowledging and cit-
ing his sources, we must assume that Peirce was transmitted
to him indirectly through Ogden and Richard's The Meaning of
Meaning (1923) and some of the American pragmatists (including Mead and Morris, whom Warner does cite). Through his
reading in these and the other authors he mentions, Warner
might well have picked up the Peircean doctrine that man is
a symbol-system, and the suggestion that human symbol-systems such as Yankee City Memorial Day ceremonies and Australian totemism evoke and express the emotions of hate, fear,
pity, and love much as a Greek drama did for its audience
(Warner 1959, pp. 476f., 506). "Man in his species totality,
as social and animal being, is the ultimate environment of a
symbol" (op. cit., p. 463).

For Warner--as for Peirce, Royce, Cooley, and Mead--the
meaning of any given system of signs depends on the existence of a community of interpreters and a community of interpretation, as well as on a specific social situation of
utterance (Warner 1959, p. 456). Successful communication
between a speaker and a listener therefore presupposes some
shared interpretations of the signs they exchange (op. cit.,
p. 457). This core of meanings that is shared by a speaker
and a listener is precisely Peirce's cominterpretant or commens:
> a determination of that mind into which the minds of the
> utterer and interpreter have to be fused in order that
> any communication should take place....It consists of all
> that is, and must be well understood between utterer and
> interpreter at the outset, in order that the sign in
> question should fulfill its function.... (SS, p. 196f.;
> see also Singer 1980, p. 494)

Successful communication accordingly implies that utterer and interpreter, speaker and listener, bring to any
context of communication some acquaintance with the given
signs and objects, based on their respective previous experience. Consistent with modern psychology, anthropology, and
sociology, Warner believes that (1959, pp. 449-51) "the basic core of meanings for most signs and objects is acquired
in infancy, childhood and adolescence" and constitutes a
community's "cultural heritage". But he also believes, in
common with Peirce, that this heritage changes, that "the
meanings of signs and objects shift throughout the individual's and society's existence", just as the meaning of the
Cross has changed from the year 33 to 1954 A.D. (See Warner
1959, p. 467; also Singer 1980, p. 488.)

ACKNOWLEDGEMENTS

To Bernard Weissbourd, who has created in the Center
for Psychosocial Studies a "civilization of the dialogue", I
am grateful for the opportunity to join him and the unusual
group he has assembled to help build the semiotic foundations of social and psychological studies. This project, as
it happens, has also given me an incentive to continue my
research and writing on the semiotics of the self, of identity, and of urbanism.

I have benefited much from the versatile talents of
Benjamin Lee, who conceived and organized the 1979 Conference on New Approaches to the Self and compiled this volume
of conference papers, as part of his work in helping organize and conduct the Center's program of research and semin-
ars.

To the University of Chicago's Department of Anthropology, I am indebted for the secretarial staff's efficient
and genial help with the typing of and reproduction of my
paper, and for support from the Lichstern Fund; a Rocke-
feller Foundation Humanities Fellowship for 1978 supported
some of the research for the paper.

I am grateful to Joseph Errington, Max Fisch, Paul
Friedrich, Clifford Geertz, Maya Hickmann, Christian
Kloesel, Marta Nicholas, Richard Parmentier, Gene Rochberg-
Halton, Thomas Sebeok, Michael Silverstein, Helen Singer,

and Bernard Weissbourd for careful readings of the manuscript and some helpful comments on it. These readers do not
necessarily agree with my interpretation of Peirce, or sub-
scribe to the theory of personal and social identity developed in the paper.

Helen Singer found in Tennyson's (1850) "In Memoriam
A.H.H." the following lines. They express in verse a conception of personal identity in some respects similar to
that of Peirce, Royce, and Cooley.

>The baby new to earth and sky,
>   What time his tender palm is prest
>   Against the circle of the breast,
>Has never thought 'that this is I':
>
>But as he grows he gathers much,
>   And learns the use of 'I,' and 'me,'
>   And finds 'I' am not what I see,
>And other than the things I touch.
>
>So rounds he to a separate mind
>   From whence clear memory may begin,
>   As thro' the frame that binds him in
>His isolation grows defined.
>
>This use may lie in blood and breath,
>   Which else were fruitless of their due,
>   Had man to learn himself anew
>Beyond the second birth of Death.

(In Memoriam XLV)

ENDNOTES

1. These discussions were held at the Center and were
attended by Maya Hickmann, Benjamin Lee, Addison Stone,
Bernard Weissbourd, and James Wertsch.

2. The social and dialogical nature of hermeneutic interpretation is emphasized in Royce's application of
Peirce's semiotic. Royce, however, seems to have identified the sign to be interpreted with the object
(Royce 1913, II:240-45, 286-91). Also:

> Psychologically, interpretation differs from percep-
> tion and from conception by the fact that it is, in
> its intent, an essentially social process. It
> accompanies every intelligent conversation....It is
> used whenever we acknowledge the being and the inner
> life of our fellowmen. It transforms our own inner
> life into conscious interior conversation wherein we
> interpret ourselves. (op. cit., p. 159).
> Two individuals trying to share experiences do not
> so much imitate each other's responses to things as
> they attempt to interpret one another, through the
> medium of conversation, what they see, feel and
> think in regard to such objects. (op. cit.,
> p. 120).

3. "We may take it for certain that the human race will
    ultimately be extirpated."

4. Michael Silverstein comments on this issue as follows:
    so-called "honorific pronouns" are really triplex (at
    least) indexicals. The German Sie, for example, refer-
    ring to second-person interlocutor, combines its refer-
    entiality, Tuism, and honorific marking in a way that
    is not isomorphic to its surface-form or categories.
    He would also distinguish the level of speaking inter-
    personally ('I'/'Me' speaks to 'You', the pragmatic
    level) from the development of intention to speak in-
    terpersonally through the inner dialogue of 'I' with
    'Me' ('I' discusses with 'Me' how to speak to a 'You',
    the metapragmatic level). For further discussion of
    these two levels of analysis and related functions see
    Silverstein 1976, 1979.

5. Porter's analysis (1979:21) of Richard II finds that
    the first person dominates Richard's speech, even his
    use of the royal plural. This finding is not a confir-
    mation of Lyon's egocentricity principle, but, as Por-
    ter says, "a characteristic of Richard's mind noticed
    by many readers of the play, one having much to do with
    his apparent tendency toward solipsism" (p. 24), and
    toward soliloquy and isolation but directed toward a
    general non-specific public (p. 40).
        Porter's interpretation of Richard's egocentricity
    seems right:
    > In Richard's pronouns and presumably in his mind,
    > person is a single feature....There is for him only

one person, with its negation—that ego is the simple negation of other, and vice versa. (pp. 23f.;
italics in original)
Porter makes it clear, however (pp. 42-47), that Richard's egocentric speech is the peculiarity of one king
—not characteristic of all kings, let alone of all
speakers in the dramaturgy of speech acts.
        For further discussion of the relation of first-,
second-, and third-person pronouns to deixis and social
roles in Indo-European languages, see Benveniste 1971,
p. 195ff., 217ff.; Hamp 1980; Friedrich 1966.

6.   In the last of his Lowell lectures (1866), Peirce com-
     pared his "divine trinity" of object, interpretant, and
     ground with the Christian Trinity—with the object as
     the Father, the interpretant the Son, and the sign the
     Mother. Fisch points out (1979b) that although Peirce
     was brought up a Unitarian, he was converted to Episco-
     palianism in 1862 through the influence of his first
     wife and adopted her feminist interpretation of the
     Trinity.

7.   William James wrote in one of his notebooks in 1862:
         The thou idea, as Peirce calls it, dominates an en-
         tire realm of mental phenomena, embracing poetry,
         all direct intuition of nature, scientific in-
         stincts, relations of man to man, morality, etc. All
         analysis must be into a triad; me and it require the
         complement of thou. (quoted in Fisch Introduction,
         p. 14; cf. SS, pp. 189-94, 196f.)

8.   See, for example, Lee in the present volume, Lyons
     1977, McNeill 1979, Porter 1979, Silverstein 1976, Bean
     1978, Fillmore 1972. The social and psychological sig-
     nificance of pronomial usage is discussed in two clas-
     sical studies (Brown and Gilman 1960, Friedrich 1966.)

9.   James usually wrote the pronouns in italics or in cap-
     itals as names of the different aspects of the self, as
     well as names for the linguistic expressions—a prac-
     tice also followed by Peirce and most of the later sym-
     bolic interactionists. Cooley was one of the first to
     write the pronouns with quotation marks as names for
     linguistic expressions.

10. Mead found in Dewey, "the philosopher of America", the culmination of that movement of thought that began with Peirce's "laboratory habit of mind" (Mead 1930b, p. 225) and James's biological and psychological individualism (op. cit., p. 227), a movement that eliminated an antecedent social and natural universe as precondition for the moral act and the cognitive act: "As it is shown in the former that it is in social participation that the peculiar character of the moral appears, so in the latter it is through the participation that is involved in communication, and hence in thought itself, that meaning arises" (op. cit., p. 229).

In both cases, a method is developed for eliciting the intelligence "implicit in the mind of the American community" by stating ends in terms of means and their social consequences (op. cit., p. 231). For the relation of Peirce to American, German, and Indian transcendentalism see Singer 1981b, pp. 115-119.

11. The use of pronoun pairs as units of analysis that affect the meaning of the constituent pronouns was noted by Buber (1970 ed.:54) "There is no 'I' as such but only the 'I' of the basic word 'I' - 'You' and the 'I' of the basic word 'I' - 'It'."

REFERENCES

Baldwin, J.M. (ed.) 1901-1905. Dictionary of Philosophy and Psychology, 3 vols. 1957 ed., Gloucester: Peter Smith.
Bean, S.S. 1978. Symbolic and Pragmatic Semantics: A Kannada System of Address. Chicago: University of Chicago Press.
Benveniste, E. 1971. Problems in General Linguistics. Coral Gables, Fla.: University of Miami Press.
Borgstrom, B.E. 1980. "The Best of Two Worlds: Rhetoric of Autocracy and Democracy in Nepal". Contributions to Indian Sociology, n.s 14:35-50.
Brown, R. And A. Gilman 1960. The Pronouns of Power and Solidarity. In T. Sebeok (ed.) Style in Language, pp. 253-76. Cambridge: MIT Press.
Buber, M. (1923). I and Thou. 1970 ed. (A New Translation with a Prologue and Notes), New York: Charles Scribner's Sons.

Burks, A.W. 1949. "Icon, Index, and Symbol". Philosophy
     and Phenomenological Research, IX:673-89.
Cherry, C. 1966. On Human Communication. Second Edition,
     Cambridge: MIT Press.
Cooley, C.H. 1908. "A Study of the Early Use of Self-Words
     by a Child". The Psychological Review, n.s. XV,
     6:339-57.
Cooley, C.H. 1909. Social Organization, A Study of the
     Larger Mind. 1929 ed., New York: Charles
     Scribner's Sons.
Cooley, C.H. 1922. Human Nature and the Social Order. New
     York: Charles Scribner's Sons.
Fillmore, C.J. 1972. "Toward a Theory of Deixis", mimeo.
Firth, R. 1973. Symbols: Public and Private. Ithaca:
     Cornell University Press.
Fisch, M.H. 1978. "Peirce's General Theory of Signs". In
     Sight, Sound, and Sense (ed. by T.A. Sebeok,
     Bloomington: Indiana University Press), pp. 31-
     70.
Fisch, M.H. 1979a. 3 pp. draft (to be revised and
     expanded) of Preface to multi-volume edition
     Writings of Charles S. Peirce [see listing under
     Peirce].
Fisch, M.H. 1979b. 17 pp. draft (to be revised and
     expanded) of Introduction to Vol. I (1857-1866),
     of Writings of Charles S. Peirce [see listing
     under Peirce].
Fisch, M.H. 1979c. Presidential address to the Semiotic
     Society of America, Bloomington, Indiana, October
     6; 6pp. draft. To be published, in revised and
     expanded form, in American Journal of Semiotics.
Freud, S. (1927). The Ego and the Id. London: The Hogarth
     Press.
Freud, S. (1930). Civilization and Its Discontents. Lon-
     don: The Hogarth Press.
Friedrich, P. 1966. "Structural Implications of Russian
     Pronomial Usage". In W.O. Bright (ed.) Socio-
     linguistics, pp. 214-59. The Hague: Mouton.
Fuss, P. 1965. The Moral Philosophy of Josiah Royce.
     Cambridge: Harvard University Press.
Geertz, C. 1965. Person, Time and Conduct in Bali. New
     Haven: Yale University Southeast Asia Studies.
Goudge, T.A. 1959. The Thought of C.S. Peirce. Toronto:
     University of Toronto Press.
Groddeck, G. 1923. The Book of the It. 1961 ed., New
     York: The New American Library.

Grossman, C.M. & S. 1965. The Wild Analyst: The Life and Work of George Groddeck. New York: George Brazziller.

Hamp, E. 1980. "Unrecognized Deixis in the Indo-European Pronouns". In Parasession on Pronouns and Anaphora (ed. by J. Kreiman & A.E. Ojeda, Chicago: Chicago Linguistic Society), pp. 147-50.

Jakobson, R. 1973. "The Place of Linguistics among the Sciences of Man". In Main Trends in the Science of Language London: George Allen and Unwin.

James, W. 1892. Psychology, the Briefer Course. 1961 ed., edited by G. Allport, New York: Harper.

Kipling, R. 1940. Rudyard Kipling's Verse (Definitive Edition). Garden City: Doubleday.

Levi-Strauss. 1976. "The Scope of Anthropology". In Structural Anthropology Vol. II (New York: Basic Books), pp. 3-32.

Lyons, J. 1977. Semantics (2 vols.). Cambridge: Cambridge University Press.

McNeill, D. 1979. The Conceptual Basis of Language. New York: Halsted Press.

Mead, G.H. 1922. "A Behavioristic Account of the Significant Symbol". Journal of Philosophy, XIX:157-63.

Mead, G.H. 1925. "The Genesis of the Self and Social Control". International Journal of Ethics, XXXV:251-77.

Mead, G.H. 1929. "National Mindedness and International-Mindedness". International Journal of Ethics, XXXIX:385-407.

Mead, G.H. 1930a. "Cooley's Contribution to American Social Thought". American Journal of Sociology XXXV:693-705.

Mead, G.H. 1930b. "The Philosophies of Royce, James and Dewey in their American Setting". International Journal of Ethics XL:211-31.

Morris, C.W. 1946. Signs, Language, and Behavior. New York: Prentice Hall. 1955 ed., New York: G. Braziller.

Murphey, M.G. 1961. The Development of Peirce's Philosophy. Cambridge: Harvard University Press.

Ogden, C.K. & I.A. Richards. 1923. The Meaning of Meaning. 1946 ed., New York: Harcourt, Brace and World.

Peirce, C.S. Collected Papers [cited in present paper as CP]. 8 Vols., by topic; Vols. I-VI ed. by Hartshorne and Weiss (pub. 1931-35), Vols. VII and VIII ed. by Burks (pub. 1958); Cambridge:

Harvard University Press. [N.B.: In the present
paper, Arabic numerals in citations of this set
of volumes refer to sections, not pages.]

Peirce, C.S. Philosophical Writings of Peirce [cited in
present paper as PW]. Orig. pub. 1940; 1955
edition ed. by J. Buchler, New York: Dover.

Peirce, C.S. Charles S. Peirce: Selected Writings [cited in
present paper as SW]. Ed. By P.P. Wiener, New
York, Dover, 1966.

Peirce, C.S. Semiotic and Significs: The Correspondence of
Charles S. Peirce and Victoria Lady Welby [cited
in present paper as SS]. Ed. by C.S. Hardwick,
Bloomington: Indiana University Press, 1977.

Peirce, C.S. Writings of Charles S. Peirce (A Chronological
Edition). M.H. Fisch, general editor; Bloomington: Indiana University Press, in press.

Porter, J.A. 1979. The Drama of Speech Acts. Berkeley:
University of California Press.

Redfield, R. 1953. "Does America Need a Hearing Aid?" The
Saturday Review, xxxvi:11-45; 1963 repr. in The
Social Uses of Social Science (Chicago: Univer-
sity of Chicago Press), pp. 232-402.

Redfield, R. 1962. "Art and Icon". In Human Nature and
the Study of Society (Chicago: University of
Chicago), pp. 468-89.

Royce, J. 1913. The Problem of Christianity (Vol. II).
New York: Macmillan.

Royce, J. 1970. The Letters of Josiah Royce. Ed. with an
Introduction by J. Clendenning, Chicago: University of Chicago Press.

Schutz, A. (1962). "The Problem of Social Reality".
Collected Papers, Vol. I, ed. by M. Natanson,
The Hague: Martinus Nijhoff. Also in 1967, The
Phenomenology of the Social World, trans. by
G. Walsh & F. Lehnert, Evanston: Northwestern
University Press.

Sebeok, T.A., A.S. Hayes and M.C. Bateson (eds.). 1964.
Approaches to Semiotics. The Hague: Mouton.

Silverstein, M. 1976. "Shifters, Linguistic Categories,
and Cultural Description". In Meaning in Anthropology (ed. by K. Basso & H. Selby, Albuquerque:
University of New Mexico Press), pp. 11-55.

Silverstein, M. 1979. "Language Structure and Linguistic
Ideology". In The Elements: A Parasession on
Linguistic Units and Levels (ed. by P.R. Clyne,

W.F. Hanks, & C.L. Hofbauer; Chicago: Chicago
Linguistic Society), pp. 193-247.

Singer, M. 1961. "A Survey of Culture and Personality
Theory and Research". In Studying Personality
Cross-Culturally (ed. by B. Kaplan, Evanston:
Row, Peterson), pp. 8-90.

Singer, M. (ed.) 1966. Krishna, Myths, Rites and Attitudes. Honolulu: University Press of Hawaii.
1968 repr., Chicago: University of Chicago Press.

Singer, M. 1972. When a Great Tradition Modernizes: An
Anthropological Approach to Indian Civilization.
1980 repr., Chicago: University of Chicago Press.

Singer, M. 1976. "Robert Redfield's Development of a So-
cial Anthropology of Civilizations". In American
Anthropology, The Early Years (ed. by J.V. Murra,
St. Paul: West Publishing Co.), pp. 187-259.

Singer, M. 1977. "The Symbolic and Historic Structure of
an American Identity". Ethos, V:428-54.

Singer, M. 1978. "For a Semiotic Anthropology". In Sight,
Sound and Sense (ed. by T.A. Sebeok, Bloomington:
Indiana University Press), pp. 202-37.

Singer, M. 1980. "Signs of the Self: An Exploration in
Semiotic Anthropology". American Anthropologist,
LXXXII:485-507.

Singer, M. 1981a. "Emblems of Identity: A Semiotic Exploration". In Symbols in Anthropology (ed. by J.
Maquet, Malibu: Undena Publishers).

Singer, M. 1981b. "On the Semiotics of Indian Identity".
American Journal of Semiotics. I,1.

Turner, V. 1969. The Ritual Process, Structure and Anti-
structure. Chicago: Aldine Publishing Co. See
especially Ch. V.

Warner, W.L. 1937. A Black Civilization, A Study of an
Australian Tribe. 1964 ed, New York: Harper.

Warner, W.L 1959. The Living and the Dead: A Study of the
Symbolic Life of Americans. New Haven: Yale University Press.

Wiley, N. 1979. "Notes on Self-Genesis: From Me to We to
I". In Studies in Symbolic Interaction, (Green-
wich, Conn.: JAI Press), II:87-105.

THE SELF, THE THIRD, AND DESIRE

Vincent Crapanzano

Queens College and the Graduate
Center of the City of New York

I have the intention of carrying out a particular
task and I make a plan. The plan in my mind is supposed
to consist in my seeing myself acting thus and so. But
how do I know, that it is myself that I'm seeing? Well,
it isn't myself, but a kind of a picture. But why do I
call it the picture of <u>me</u>?

"How do I know that it's myself?": the question
makes sense if it means, for example, "how do I know that
I'm the one I see there?" And the answer mentions
characteristics by which I can be recognized.

But it is my own decision that makes my image
represent myself. And I might as well ask "how do I know
that the word 'I' stands for myself?" For my shape in
the picture was only another word "I".

Ludwig Wittgenstein
(<u>Philosophical Grammar</u>, paragraph 62)

"The fact that the dreamer's own ego appears several
times, or in several forms, in a dream", Freud wrote in his
1925 revision of <u>The Interpretation of Dreams</u> (1954 ed.,
p. 12), "is at bottom no more remarkable than that the ego
should be contained in a conscious thought several times or
in different places or connections—e.g., in the sentence
'when <u>I</u> think what a healthy child <u>I</u> was.'"[1] Freud was
referring to the various representations the dreamer's ego
can take in a dream. Implicit in his rather unwieldy sentence is a "psychology" that is neither immediately nor necessarily associated with his explicit psychology.[2] This

179

implicit psychology serves as the ground for his thought.
It serves, too, I suggest, as the ground for my own contribution, and the other contributions, to this volume.

Freud here presupposes a fundamental distinction
between dream and conscious thought. The dream is where
appearances occur; conscious thought contains. In its
ordinariness, conscious thought apparently has a certain
priority over the dream. Freud assumes also a particular
spatialization and temporalization of both mental phenomena.
The ego can "appear" several times in a dream and is "contained" several times in conscious thought. It can "appear"
in "several forms" in the dream and is "contained" "in different places or connections" in conscious thought. (One
wonders whether or not such transformations of the ego can
occur in conscious thought as well as in the dream.) What
exactly does Freud mean by the "ego" here?[3] I should point
out that it is not the ego of his typology Id, ego, and
Superego. It is the ego of "egotistical". ("Dreams are
completely egoistical", he writes at the beginning of the
paragraph which our "The fact..." sentence ends.[4]) It
appears to be synonymous with, or a referent of, the two
"I"s in the final phrase "when I think what a healthy child
I was".[5]

Freud is calling attention to the identity of the ego
over time—and not to its linguistic determination. He is
not interested, in this context, in the fact that the continuity of the ego is brought into question through a language which has a particular and, as we know, by-no-means-
universal orientation toward time. Would the same question
arise in Whorf's Hopi? The ego of the past or past tense
and the ego of the present or present tense—not to mention
the ego of the future or future tense—are, paradoxically,
both one and the same and yet different. They are one and
the same, to use William James's (1890) metaphor, in the
stream of thought or consciousness, in its non-reflexive
moments. They are different in those reflexive moments when
the stream (to pursue the metaphor) is turned back upon itself. Time is arrested; identity becomes problematic; differences become, or can become, paramount. The ego, or the
self, becomes the object of scrutiny. With a certain surgi-
cal incisiveness, Flaubert (see Steegmuller 1972) articu-
lates this temporal arrest and objectification of the self,
this schism between the ego then and now, when he writes in

his notes on the Orient: "Between myself of that night and
myself of tonight, there is a difference between the cadaver
and the surgeon doing the autopsy ". He had been rereading
an unsent letter of departure to his mother.

My aim in quoting Freud here is twofold. On the one
hand, I simply want to emphasize the degree to which our
explicit psychologies are founded on the implicit psychological assumptions of our idiom. To what extent is our subject matter—the self and the congeries of associated concepts: "person", "personage", "personality", "consciousness", "psyche", "subject", and "ego"—a precipitate of our
particular cultural idiom? To what extent does it make
sense to talk of the "self" in other idioms? These questions are of course fundamental to all anthropological considerations. They have perhaps greater weight (illusory to
be sure) in the consideration of "psychological" concepts
which, as Berger and Luckmann (1967) have noted, tend to realize themselves in the phenomena they purport to describe.

On the other hand, I want to raise the question, implicit in Freud's sentence, of the relationship between an
idiom (language, understood broadly in the sense of the German _Sprache_ or the French _discours_) and the self (Crapanzano
1977). I will argue in the following pages that the "self"
is an arrested moment in an on-going dialectical movement
between self and other; that this arrest depends upon the
typification of self and other, through language; that the
typification of the other depends upon a Third—who, as a
guarantor of meaning, permits the play of desire.

My argument, I hope, will have more than a bearing on
the question of the self. My primary concern is with the
relationship between what can be called the ideology of
language and particular modes of articulating reality (see
Silverstein 1979). By "the ideology of language", I mean
those assumptions—explicit and implicit—about the nature
of language that determine its usage and the attitudes taken
toward it. This ideology is incorporated into the wider
notion of idiom. In this paper I am particularly interested
in the relationship between a linguistic ideology, going
back at least to Aristotle, that gives priority to the naming, referential, denotative function of language (over such
other language functions as the indexical) and to the arrest
through typification of the dialectical process.

This ideology (here, traditional grammar--which de-
clares a pronoun a noun-substitute; and includes in the same
grammatical category first-, second-, and third-person personal pronouns) masks the indexical function of the first-
and second-person personal pronouns I and you, exploiting
what I call their anaphoric potential. This ideology of
language also supports an essentially stationary (shall I
write "nominalizing"?) picture of the world: the world of
Parmenides in which identity over time is of primary concern
and reflects a certain Angst before the non-stationary, mo-
bile, fluid, or processual--the world of Heraclitus. Words
(and by extension, sentences and propositions) posit reali-
ties, fix them, pinion them even--in a spatio-temporal continuum that is itself linguistically fixed. The extent to
which this ideology reflects the grammar and structure of
the language in which it is expressed must remain an open
question. (See Benveniste 1966 Silverstein 1979). Certainly it is reflected in the kinds of questions anthropologists and other social and psychological scientists pose,
and in their construction of the objects of study.

In accordance with this interest, I have chosen to present my argument in a blatantly non-conventional fashion. I
speak not directly but instead rhetorically--through those
others who have determined my thoughts about the self, language, and its ideology. Although they use different theoretical models that are by no means consistent with one
another, they are, I believe, all subject to similar idio-
matic determinants. I am cognizant of the fact that even as
I pass the reader (to use one of Jacques Lacan's figures)
through the "defiles" of these others, I am not escaping the
determinants of my/their language. I can hope only to call
attention to some of these determinants, embedded as they
are in the particular genres and conventions at our dispos-
al--the genres and conventions that produce "information",
speed-reading, and naive empiricisms--and to suggest that
all anthropological writing is, despite its pretense, meta-
commentary. Ironically given the discipline's focus on the
primitive there is no single primitive text. "In the beginning was the word ...."; and yet to be "the word" (logos),
the word logos had to be taken (should I write "understood"?) as such.

My argument, but obviously neither its language nor its
approach, has been inspired by A.I. Hallowell's (1967)
observation that the self is both a social and a cultural

product. It seems to me that this dual origin of the self
(grounded, of course, in an idiomatically determined analytic distinction) has been one of the sources of the very considerable confusion, at least in anthropological theory,
about the genesis and nature of the self.[7]

    Hallowell--who is rather more careful than some writers
to distinguish between self-awareness and self-conceptuali-
zation--takes self-awareness to be a generic human trait
which cannot however be regarded as an isolated psychological phenomenon.
    For it is becoming increasingly apparent that this pecu-
liarly human phenomena is the focus of complex, and fundamentally dependent, sets of linguistic and cultural
variables that enter into the personal adjustment of
human beings as members of particular societies.
    (Hallowell 1967, p. 75)
Among these "linguistic and cultural variables" are man's
reflections about himself and his relationship to the
world--his concepts of the self, the world, and the relationship between them. An individual's self-image and his
interpretation of his own experience, Hallowell suggests,
"cannot be divorced from the concept of the self that is
characteristic of his society" (1967, p. 76).
    For a differentiated sense of self-awareness to emerge it
    must be possible for the individual to react to himself
    as an empirical object, to identify himself and refer to
    himself, to appraise himself, and so on. Such reflexive
    processes imply a concept and the use of symbolic means
    of representation, and reference. (Hallowell 1967,
    p. 82)
There is both a conceptual and a perceptual aspect of self-
awareness. Concomitant with it is the "awareness of a
contrasting world of articulated objects, experienced as
'other-than-self'". What Hallowell does not make clear is
exactly how self-concepts and other symbolic means of representation and reference function in self-awareness and the
awareness of a contrasting world that is other-than-self.

    If the symbolically mediated concepts of the self
affect self-awareness and if these concepts vary from society to society, then it follows that self-awareness--or at
least its style--will vary from society to society. Although this argument seems to follow from Hallowell's position, he himself is unwilling to accept all of its implications.   He prefers to talk loosely in terms of selves and,

at times, self-images. He is critical of the suggestion
that self-awareness is less developed among primitive peoples, and he attributes the not-infrequent observation that
"primitive man is unable to distinguish clearly between the
'subjective' and the 'objective'" to differences in their
behavioral field.

>   Since the self is also partly a cultural product, the
>   field of behavior that is appropriate for the activities
>   of <u>particular</u> selves in <u>their</u> world of culturally defined
>   objects is not by any means precisely coordinate with any
>   absolute polarity of subjectivity-objectivity that is
>   definable. (loc.cit, p. 84)

Hallowell admits, nevertheless, that the line between subjectivity and objectivity does at times seem to be blurred.
This results in part, he argues, from the fact that the
polarity cannot be adequately conceived in linear terms but
"only with reference to the total pattern of the psychological field" (1967, p. 85). He quotes (ibid.) MacLeod (1947)
that "subjectivity and objectivity are properties of an
organized perceptual field in which points of reference are
selves (subjects) and objects, and the 'degree of articulation' in this dimension may vary greatly"; and he suggests
that variations in the degree of articulation are due to
cultural factors "directly relevant to the psychological
field of the individual". Hallowell's argument is circular,
and we are left with no reason to assume that self-awareness
and the line between subjectivity and objectivity cannot
vary from society to society.

There is (to speak far too simply) a contradiction
between two Western positions regarding the self, and it is
reflected in anthropological treatments of the subject—including Hallowell's. (I am using "self" here loosely, for
so it has been used—to refer not only to the self, self-
awareness, self-image, self-conception but also to that congeries of related concepts that include the personage and
the person.) The self is regarded as a fundamental category
of human thought; the self is seen to evolve (to individu-
ate) over time.

The former position has its roots in Aristotle, is
brought into question by Kant, and is established by Fichte
(Mauss 1973). (In contemporary Anglo-American philosophy,
Strawson (1959) argues that the "person" is a logically
primitive, presumably universal, concept.) The latter is

deeply rooted in Western mythology and is explicitly articulated with Romanticism, Symbolism, and the evolutionary
theories of the second half of the nineteenth century. Do
these two positions reflect a "tension" between the stationary, Parmenidian position, supported by an ideology of reference, and the processual, Heraclitian position, which is
masked by an ideology of reference?

     To cite an influential example of the evolutionary
approach: Jacob Burckhardt wrote (1867) that "at the close
of the Thirteenth century Italy began to swarm with individuality".
     In the Middle Ages both sides of human consciousness--
that which was turned within and that which was turned
without--lay dreaming or half-awake beneath a common
veil. The veil was woven of faith, illusion, and childish prepossession [Kindesbefangenheit] through which the
world and history were seen clad in strange hues. Man
was conscious of himself only as a member of a race, people, party, family, or corporation--only through some
general category. In Italy the veil first melted into
air; an objective treatment of the State and of all the
things of this world became possible. The subjective
side at the same time asserted itself with corresponding
emphasis; man became a spiritual individual and recognized himself as such. (1955 ed., p. 81; in German, 1926
ed., p. 119)
Explaining the birth, or rebirth, of the individual in terms
of the political circumstances in Italy, Burckhardt noted
that a similar individuation had taken place in Greece (the
Greek distinguishing himself from the Barbarian) and among
the Arabs.

     A more systematic, developmental history (Entwicklungs-
geschichte) of the self was elaborated by the controversial
German historian Karl Lamprecht (1900). The Seelenleben
(the psychic life) of a people (Volk) was said to pass
through two basic modes of existence: the fettered and the
unfettered, each of which was divided into specific phases.
In the first phase of the fettered mode man was immersed in
his environment and had no awareness of himself as a separate individual. In the final phase of the unfettered mode
of existence, man is fully an individual and imposes himself
on an external reality to which he is strikingly sensitive.
(See also Weintraub 1966)

Literary historians have noted a similar movement--
whether in a single literature (usually ancient Greek) or in
the entire course of Western literature. The gradual alienation of the individual from his environment, in these evolutionary approaches, appears at times to be an "histori-
cized" version of the flight from the Garden of Eden, with
"primitive" or "early" man as Adam and Eve before they par-
took of the fateful fruit of the Tree of Knowledge. They
enter the world of time and mortality; their identity falls
in question; and referentiality itself becomes problematic.

The contradiction between the universal and the evolutionary approach to the notion of the self is found in Marcel Mauss's 1938 Huxley Memorial lecture, "Une catégorie de
l'esprit humain: la notion de personne celle de 'moi'",
which has inspired a number of subsequent studies. (See,
for example, Dieterlin 1973). Mauss states that he and his
colleagues have been interested in preparing a social history of the categories of the human mind (esprit humain).
These categories are taken tout simplement et provisoirement
from Aristotle. In his lecture, Mauss exemplifies a certain
evolution in the category personne-moi--from Zuni, Northwest
Coast Indians, and Australian aborigines to nineteenth-century philosophical theories. He is careful to state that
his study is neither linguistic nor psychological (though in
fact both approaches are implicit in it) but conceptual.
The phenomena he embraces ambiguously by personne and moi
(person and self/ego/me)--the ambiguity is marked in the title by an absence of a comma between personne and celle
de 'moi'--to develop from the personage (de rôle rempli par
l'individu dans ces drames sacrés comme il joue un rôle dans
la vie familiale) through the person as a mask, a name, a
moral but non-metaphysical entity, a moral and metaphysical
entity to the moi, a conscious self-reflective ego.
    Cependant, la notion de personne devait encore subir une
    autre transformation pour devenir ce qu'elle est devenue
    voici moins d'un siécle et demi, la catégorie du moi.
    Loins d'être l'idée primordiale, innée, clairement
    inscrite depuis Adam au plus profond de notre être, voici
    qu'elle continue, prèsque de notre temps, lentement à
    s'édifier, à se clarifier, à se specifier, à s'identifier
    avec la connaissance de soi avec la conscience psycholo-
    gique. (1973, p. 359)
The movement here--explicitly conceptual--includes a turning
inward, a reflexivity, a self-consciousness, and an emphasis
on inner space that is clearly related to the emphasis on

self and innerness in Romanticism and which serves as the
ground, as Foucault (1966) might well observe, for the
development of psychology and phenomenology and the other
human-centered sciences of the nineteenth century. Did
earlier man, without a concept of the moi, lack self-awareness? Was his self-awareness differently articulated? Mauss
ignores these questions, at least explicitly.[8]

Mauss's Huxley lecture is less bound by the social determination of the categories of the mind than is his earlier work with Durkheim (1963) and Durkheim's own work (1964,
1965). In these, it can be argued, "society" is the media-
tor between the universality of the categories of the mind
and their varied expression or representation (between the
universal and the particular, between essence and appearance, between the named and that which resists naming). In
the Huxley lecture, the Aristotelian categories serve rather
as guides for potential research; they are, nevertheless,
Mauss assumes, to be found, at least primordially, in all
cultures.[9]

Maurice Leenhardt (the missionary-anthropologist who
succeeded Marcel Mauss to chair of History of Primitive
Religions at the École Pratique des Hautes Études) accepts
somewhat ambivalently an evolutionary approach to the study
of the self--in his terms (1953), the person. In his work
on the Canaque of New Caledonia--with whom he spent the
first two and a half decades of this century--he raises the
problematic of the person and challenges the usual anthropological presumption of a center of identity (an ego) which
is reified in the personage (or the person, the self, personality, or character) and is located in the body. In Do
Kamo (1979) his most mature work, a sweeping study of what
might be called the ethnophilosophy of the Canaque, he lays
out (not always very consistently) the parameters of the
Canaque's notion of the person.

As I have pointed out elsewhere (Crapanzano 1979),
Leenhardt approaches the notion of the person in two princi-
pal and not necessarily coordinate ways: the relational and
the existential. Both rest on the notion of kamo, literally
the "which living" (le qui-vivant)--the "personage", as
Leenhardt translates it. Kamo, "the living human ensemble",
indicates life but implies neither contour nor nature. It
is flexible, and it enables the Canaque to follow "the living" through its various metamorphoses. Animals, vegeta-

bles, and mythological subjects can be taken for kamo provided they are invested with humanity. The personage "is
not perceived objectively, it is felt."

In an existential approach, Leenhardt (1979) attempts
to relate the Canaque to his environment. In a manner
reminiscent of Burckhardt and Lamprecht, and of course his
friend and mentor Lucien Levi-Bruhl, he argues that the
(pre-contact) New Caledonian was not individuated; he was
not yet a person but still a personage. He was still embedded in his mythically determined surroundings. Self and
other, self and environment—like subject and object and
word and thing—were not sharply differentiated for him.
His world was one of participation. It was cosmomorphic.
He did not spread out over nature, but was invaded by nature. There was no distance between people and things. In
the eyes of the Canaque, Leenhardt tells us, "rocks, plants,
and the human body originate in similar structures; and
identity of substance blends them in the same flux of life."
From the cosmomorphic stance toward the world, the individual moves through anthropomorphism (already self-centered)
to more analytic and empirical stances toward the world. The
movement is one of individuation.

In the relational approach to the person, Leenhardt
suggests, the Canaque knew himself only through the relations he maintained with others. The kamo was poorly defined for self and other; he was aware of his body only as a
support and not a source of identity over time. (For Leenhardt, as for Mauss—both, in this respect, well within the
Cartesian tradition—the body is a source of personal identity). There was no center that could be marked by a fixed
ego, but rather a series of relations that surrounded an
empty space. One like personage could be substituted for
another. The personage had no single name, but a manifold
of ancestral names that accorded with his relations. His
participation in the personality of these ancestral names,
Leenhardt suggests, implied identity and repetition. They
enabled him to participate in the lived myth, a sort of unspoken cognitive-affective paradigm that grounded his reality.

In Do Kamo and in his other writings, Leenhardt frequently confused the phenomenological and conceptual
approach to the study of the person. In part, this confusion is a result of his refusal to grant the personage, inso-

far as it is non-reflexively embedded in its surroundings--
the privileged, transcendental locus that enables world-con-
struction. The New Caledonian kamo, was, so to speak, truly
a personage in a textless script, the mythe vécu, which he
did not create but only lived. The reciprocal relationship
between man and world, between subject and object (as determinants of each other), that enables the differentiation of
experience and concept, of self and "self", were absent in
the cosmomorphic stance, in the mythe vécu. This myth did
not mediate subject and object as symbols are said to do; it
was the coalesced reality in which experience and concept
were one and the same. It was rather like the Symbolist
poets' longed-for unity of symbol and symbolized (that is,
if I understand Leenhardt correctly).

Leenhardt's position is radical, and he cannot fully
sustain it. (Is this a result of his idiom?) "The human
awareness of 'being there'", the Dutch philosopher-anthro-
pologist Wilhelm Dupré notes (1975, p. 124),
   is an indefinite experience that becomes definite through
   the particular situation in which we live, and that defines the same situation by the modality of its presence.
Not only is human existence (insofar as its presence is
total and universal in outlook) total and universal but
   since it achieves this totality and universality only in
   company and union with definite and particular beings, it
   is equally a heterothetic existence, an existence that is
   real by 'positing' (Gr. thesis) an other (Ger. heteron)
   against itself as the limitation of an otherwise undeter-
   mined modality. (loc. cit., p. 121)
It is not, however, the discovery of otherness that causes
the person to emerge from the personage, I would argue, but
the discovery of his own otherness.

Hallowell, Leenhardt, and Burckhardt (at least where he
remarks that the ancient Greeks discovered themselves
through the barbarian) all recognize an awareness of some
sort of otherness for the emergence of the self (of the person, in Leenhardt's terms). They conceive of the relationship between self and other in static terms rather like the
figure-ground relationship in a perceptual field. They cannot, I believe, account for reflexivity. The notion of the
self requires, as I observed, not simply an awareness of a
contrasting world but a recognition, to speak awkwardly, of
one's own otherness in that world. It requires a particular
notion of possession.

George Herbert Mead's dialectical approach to the self
addresses itself to the problem of reflexivity. The self
for Mead (1934) is a social product. It "has the characteristic that it is an object to itself, and that characteristic distinguishes it from other objects and from the body"
(p. 136). The individual experiences himself as a self

not directly, but only indirectly, from the particular
standpoints of other individual members of the same
social group, or from the generalized standpoint of the
social group as a whole to which he belongs. (p. 138)

Why the individual must take only the standpoint of "other
individual members of the same social group" is not, however, clear.

For Mead, the development of the self procedes in two
stages.[10] First, one responds "to one's self as another
responds to it, taking part in one's own conversation with
other, being aware of what one is saying to determine what
one is going to say thereafter" (p. 140). Conversation—
communication "which is directed not only to others but also
to the individual himself" (p. 139) plays a paramount role
here. "The vocal gesture gives one the capacity for answer-
ing to one's own stimulus as another would answer" (p. 66).
For there to be a unity of self, a "full self", the individual must also take the part of the whole community, of the
generalized other.

He must also, in the same way that he takes the attitudes
of other individuals toward himself and toward one another, take their attitudes toward the various phases or
aspects of the common social activity or set of social
undertakings in which, as members of an organized society
or social group, they are all engaged; and he must then,
by generalizing these individual attitudes of that organized society or social group itself, as a whole, act
toward different social projects which at any given time
it is carrying out, or toward the various larger phases
of the general social process which constitutes its life
and of which these projects are specific manifestations.
(pp. 154f.)

Mead notes, in an interesting footnote (p. 154), that "it is
possible for inanimate objects...to form parts of the generalized and organized—the completely socialized—other for
any given human individual insofar as he responds to such
objects socially or in a social fashion. The "organized set
of attitudes of the others" is incorporated into the self,

Mead suggests somewhat obscurely, as the me. This me, which
seems to correspond at times to the object of self-reflection and at other times to the incorporated generalized
other, contrasts with the I which is the immediate "response
of the organism to the attitudes of the others" (p. 175).
The response of the I is always uncertain.   "There is a
moral necessity but not a mechanical necessity for the act"
(p. 178). The I reflects a certain freedom the individual
has.

    If the dialectical movement that generates the self is
continuous, then it follows that the self is continually
being created—or recreated—in accordance with its "conversations" with others.   (Mead's behavioral approach to
language always stresses the evocative function of language
at the expense of the informative.)   The self appears to be
in continual flux, in this view. It is subject to the con-
tingencies of the individual's life and the whims of those
he encounters. Obviously such a view is neither phenomenologically "realistic" (we do usually perceive a certain per-
manence, a unity and continuity—a resistance even—in our
selves) nor is it socially "realistic".   It is the generalized other (and its incorporation as the me) that serves,
for Mead, to give the self unity and continuity.

    It is not exactly clear how the generalization and
organization of the attitudes of the other, of the community
that produces the generalized other, comes about.   How are
the attitudes symbolized or typified?   What is the status of
the generalized other?   Mead moves here, as elsewhere in his
writings, from high theoretical abstraction to oversimpli-
fied, concrete examples (e.g., a political party) which do
not seem to do justice to his theoretical position.   The
notion of the generalized other, or even a hierarchy of such
others, is, at any rate, too simple.   It demands a social
homogeneity, I would insist, that is not to be found in even
the "simplest" of societies.   In Mead's argument, the generalized other functions as an anchor for the self and provides a constant in different social situations.   Mead is,
therefore, unable to grant it rhetorical flexibility.   As
the me (insofar as it is the me), the generalized other represents the unity of the self, its constancy and continuity,
and is set against the I, the representative of uncertainty.
In Mead's schema there is no explanation for the uncertainty
of the I.

Mead's approach may account for the reflexivity that is
necessary for the emergence of the self, for what Hallowell
would call the social production of the self. It does not
account, though, for its cultural production. The social-
behavioral approach to symbolism (the symbol being a stimulus to the individual as well as a response)—to conversation and communication, more generally—is not in my estima-
tion, sufficient for this. Conversation and communication
may well be necessary for the possibility of reflexivity;
but they are not sufficient, as Mead understands them, for
the emergence of the self.

With the possible exception of the mirror—and this is
rather more dubious than Mead appears ready to admit—it is
only through language that the individual reaches the position "where he responds to his own gestures as other people
respond" (Mead, p. 66; compare Lacan's (1966) mirror phase).
It is of course not altogether clear why Mead insists that
the individual respond to his vocal gestures, or his image,
in the mirror, as others do (except to maintain a particularly homogeneous vision of social life and a peculiarly
simplistic view of human personality). The individual, I
would suggest, need only have the illusion—indeed, such an
illusion may be a social inevitability—that he is responding as his counterpart responds. Together they negotiate a
reality and accommodate to each other; they enter a conspir-
acy of "understanding". They generate the selves they chose
by choosing their counterparts; that is, they typify the
other, label him, name him, characterize him, take possession of themselves. The individual and his counterpart
become rhetorical figures for each other.

It is this play, this casting the other to cast oneself
(to use a theatrical metaphor), that Mead cannot explain.
Nor can he account for those forays into fantasy, those
folies-à-deux, those multiple follies that characterize so
much of social life. Nor, finally—and this is most important—can he account for the absence of lucidity, for those
blind spots in consciousness that we have come to identify
with that late nineteenth-century invention, the unconscious. It is with good reason that Lacan has aphoristical-
ly declared the unconscious "the discourse of the other".

Emile Benveniste, a linguist who is frequently quoted
by the contributors to this volume, adopts a dialectical-
dialogical approach to the constitution of the subject. His

argument has considerable bearing on our discussion of the
self.[11]   He writes (1971, p. 224; 1966, p. 259):
> C'est dans et par le langage que l'homme se constitue
> comme sujet; parce que le langage seul fonde en réalité,
> dans sa réalité qui est celle de l'être, le concept
> d'"ego".

> It is in and through language that man constitutes
> himself as a subject, because language alone establishes
> the concept of "ego" in reality, in its reality which is
> that of the being.

This sentence is significant on two scores: on what it
states, its argument; and on what it reveals, shows (in
Wittgenstein's sense of the word).   It states that the
subject is constituted in and through language. It reveals
that the constituted subject (I accept for the moment sujet
as a primitive appellation) is immediately named, however
obscurely,   even by a foreign nominalized pronomial locution
that is, Benveniste would argue, essentially indexical in
function--namely, ego.

    Subjectivity is, for Benveniste (1966), the ability of
the speaker to posit himself as "subject."   ("La subjecti-
vité, dont nous traitons ici, est la capacité du locuteur à
se poser comme 'sujet'" (p. 259).   N.B. the reflexive se
poser!).   Subjectivity is defined not by the feeling (le
sentiment) of being oneself, but as the psychic unity which
transcends the totality of actual experiences of consciousness (con science). This subjectivity is nothing more than
the emergence in a being of a fundamental property of language.   "Est 'ego' qui dit 'ego'" (p. 260).[12] Subjectivity is determined by the linguistic status of the person.

    Whence the person?   However labeled, it seems for
Benveniste to emerge through dialogue (1971, p. 225; 1966,
p. 260).
> La conscience de soi n'est possible que si s'éprouve par
> contraste. Je n'emploi je qu'en m'addressant à quelqu'un
> qui sera dans mon allocution un tu. C'est cette con-
> dition de dialogue qui est constitutive de la personne,
> car elle implique en réciprocité que je deviens tu dans
> l'allocution de celui qui à son tour se désigne par je.
> C'est là que nous voyons un principe dont les consé-
> quences sont à dérouler dans toutes les directions.

> Consciousness of self is only possible if it is experi-
> enced by contrast.   I use I only when I am speaking to
> someone who will be a you in my address. It is this con-

dition of dialogue that is constitutive of person, for it
implies that reciprocally I become you in the address of
the one who in his turn designates himself as I. Here we
see a principle whose consequences are to be spread out
in all directions.
The speaker's I becomes the listener's you. As such, he is
rendered external to himself--objectivated, we might say--
capable finally of being named (whether specifically or as a
generality) as person, ego, or self, or finally reflexively.
This naming, I suggest, is supported by a referentially centered ideology of language.[13]

The polarity between the I and the you, Benveniste
notes, is unique. It signifies neither equality nor sym-
metry. Ego is always in a position of transcendence with
respect to you. But neither I nor you can be conceived of
without the other. They are complementary, opposed as
interior to exterior, reversible, and reflected in such
dualities as "self" and "other" or "individual" and "society". It would be erroneous, Benveniste insists, to reduce
the duality to a single, original term: the ego.[14] And
yet, a point Benveniste does not take up: within the language and thought of the West at least (we must always note
Leenhardt's Canaque), primacy is always given to one of the
terms: the I.

Seemingly oblivious to the implications of what he
himself has written Benveniste goes on to note that the I
and the you (and not the he and she) must be distinguished
from all other linguistic designations. They refer neither
to a concept nor to an individual. They are linguistic
forms which indicate "person" (1971, p. 276; 1966, p. 262):
À quoi donc je se-réfère-t-il? À quelque chose de très
singulier, qui est exclusivement linguistique: je se réf-
ère à l'acte de discours individuel où il est prononcé,
et il en désigne le locuteur. C'est un terme qui ne peut
être identifié que dans ce que nous avons appelé ailleurs
une instance de discours, et qui n'a de référence actu-
elle. La réalité à laquelle il renvoie est la réalité du
discours. C'est donc l'instance de discours où je
désigne le locuteur que celui-ci énonce comme 'sujet'.
Il est donc vrai à la lettre que le fondement de la sub-
jectivité est dans l'exercice de la langue...
Then what does I refer to? To something very peculiar
which is exlusively linguistic: I refers to the act of
the individual discourse in which it is pronounced, and

by this it designates the speaker. It is a term that
cannot be identified except in what we have called elsewhere an instance of discourse and that has only a momentary reference.   The reality to which it refers is the
reality of the discourse. It is the instance of the discourse in which I designates the speaker that the speaker
proclaims himself as the "subject". And so it is literally true that the basis of subjectivity is in the exercise of language.
Subjectivity rests then in the instance of the discourse.
The I does not name the subjectivity which it constitutes
through discourse. It refers simply to the speaker in a
specific utterance.

    Taken as indices of the instance of discourse, the
first- and second-person personal pronouns are themselves,
albeit functionally significant, referentially hollow. They
demand, if you will, nominalization; and Benveniste, inevitably, in his text provides such nominalization--immediately
by the very terms he seeks to account for (sujet and subjec-
tivité), and mediately with ego and those other terms (person and self) which are the subject of our consideration.

    But we must ask: Is there any sense in asking to whom
an I refers? Can we point to an I?   Or are we already
pointing to a me? Can we point to a subject, a person, a
personage, a self in certain of their non-corporeal accepta-
tions? Do our questions posit an illusory reality?[15]   Is
the "reality" not an artifact of our language? Of any language? Is it not supported by a particular linguistic ideology that lays stress on the nominal and gives the nominal
an object? We have insisted for centuries now that a pronoun is a substitute for a noun--a noun's name.

    Although the first-and second-person pronouns are in-
dexical, they are not necessarily understood as such.   They
are understood as somehow extending beyond the instance of
discourse to other previous and future discourses; they are
somehow transcendent. Without wishing to deny the indexical
function of the I and you, I would like to suggest that they
also have--or are given--an anaphoric potential. They refer
not just to the speaker and hearer, the addressor and
addressee, of a particular utterance; they also refer back
to other instances of the I (and you) uttered by the same
speaker (or interlocutor). They are, in Halliday's (1976)
sense, endophoric. (Their final reference may be conceived

of as a noun, even a proper noun. Consider the privileged
status of such nouns in our language and its grammar!)

It is precisely this anaphoric potential (which some
linguists, given to taking the sentence or the repartee as
their largest units of analysis, have been all too ready to
dismiss) that permits, in the constitution of the self, the
play both with the other--the you--and with the retrospec-
tive I (embodied in previous utterances by the speaker) and
the prospective I (yet to be embodied). We must not forget
the function of suspense in the constitution of the self,
and the anxiety that accompanies such suspense. Narrative
suspense and (conventional) dialogical suspense are constrained suspenses which create an already-mastered anxiety,
the mastery of which is (conventionally) denied or ignored.
The I, retrospectively and prospectively, is an other. (Or
are these "I"s already "me"s?) It is the anaphoric potential of the first- and second-person pronouns that enables
self constitution, transference phenomena (or at least their
analyses--implicit and explicit, licit and illicit), discussions of identity, and the autobiographical enterprise itself. It permits the adhesion of a single speaker's, a single I's utterances--and, if you will, the possibility of
neuroses.

We should note the rarity of playing with the homonym-
ity of the "I" and "you" of two speakers. We should note
too that when such word-games occur in the West, they are
frequently between a child learning to speak and an adult;
and they are stopped not when the child grows tired or confused but when the adult suffers a semantic vertigo. Finally, we should note the terror of regarding those most-sacred
of designations, the I and the you, as only indexical. And
we must ask, nevertheless and despite that terror, whether
the anaphoric potential of which I write is a reaction to
precisely that terror. (Note that I have, in my discussion
of this potential switched from an analytic modality to a
hermeneutical one: "Although the first- and second-person
pronouns are indexical, they are not necessarily understood
as such.") Am I not succumbing to an ideology that insists
that the I and you, like the he and she, are noun-substi-
tutes with determinant antecedents? Am I not rendering them
a "one" (French "on") or a "man"? We do make such transformations and must account for them.

The individual is born into a world of words--into the Symbolic order, as Lacan would put it--which makes him what he is. "Man speaks but it is because the symbol has made him a man" (Lacan 1966, p. 276). Here, in language, as Lacan understands it,

> ce qui domine, c'est l'unité de signification, laquelle s'avère ne jamais se résoudre en une pure indication du réel, mais toujours renoyer à une autre signification. C'est à dire que la signification ne se réalise qu'à partir d'une prise des choses qui est d'ensemble.
>
> What dominates is the unity of signification which establishes itself as never becoming resolved into pure indication of the Real, but always as referring to another signification. This is to say that if the signification "grasp" the things, it is only by constituting their set by enveloping it in the signifier. (quoted in Wilden 1968, p. 122)

Lacan's approach to meaning is radically diacritical, and, despite occasional protestations to the contrary, essentially referential in orientation.[16] Words need not of course signify what they are thought (conventionally) to signify. There is, as Lacan would have it in his play on the Saussurian algorithm, a bar or barrier between the signifier and the signified. Words--signs--may serve as symbolic substitutes for that which resists signification--the repressed (structured as it is by language). They may, I would suggest, also give the illusion of reference where there is no reference, or is only an attenuated referential potential (as in the case of the pronominal indexicals of which I have been writing). They enable man to typify and symbolize (in ways in which he may not even be aware) the other and thereby him-self; they enable him to generalize these others and incorporate their responses in what Mead would call his me --and Freud, in a different sense, his superego. This same world of words gives order to his typifications, generalizations, and incorporations. It is both systemic--governed, Lacan maintains--by the relations between signifying elements and antecedents to his significations. (It is reinforced in every act of signification.) It both deprives the individual of his unbounded freedom and gives him the only meaningful kind of freedom: that is, freedom within an order. The signifying chain, the Symbolic order, culture, and grammar we might say, serves to stabilize the relations between self and other by functioning as a Third.

According to Lacan (1966, pp. 93-100), a child's entry
into the Symbolic order occurs not with the first babbling,
naming, or sentence-construction (however "correct") but
during the first Oedipal phase. It is preceded by the
development of a primordial reflexivity during the mirror
stage--the stage at which the child, between his sixth and
eighteenth month, discovers himself in his mirror image, in
his counterpart, his semblable. It is during the Oedipal
phase, if I understand Lacan correctly, that the name-of-
the-father [17]--his verbal authority or, perhaps better,
his authority through the word--fixes the child's relationship to the word; he is "grasped" by the word. Through the
primordial reflexivity of the mirror phase and the entrance
into language (and the reflexivity granted thereby), the
child--the individual--becomes inevitably alienated, Lacan
suggests, from himself. He discovers himself as an other in
the mirror; he loses himself in Language (langue) like an
object. He can picture himself--and name himself. But he
is, so to speak, doubly alienated from himself. This alienation of the "self" from the self or subject is repeated, I
would suggest, in our every self-reflection.

What is of interest to us here is not Lacan's particular approach to the genesis of the self but a particular
movement in the development of the self that is given "mythical" expression in Lacan's work. It is implicit in Mead's
as well. It is the movement from a dual relationship between
self and other, to a triadic relationship which is achieved
in and through language. In psychoanalytic developmental
terms, it is the movement from the symbiotic mother-child
relationship to the triadic relationship of mother, father,
and child. The father-qua-symbol (Lacan's name-of-the-
father) is himself the symbolic matrix[18] for a series of
other symbols (i.e., authority, law, and God--as Freud
noted--and language, culture, and convention). He represents
the locus of meaning and truth. This Third may be the voice
of conscience (the incorporation of the father's authority,
in Freud's scheme); by various demons who may be "present"
at any human interchange: by God, in his omniscience and
omnipotence; by the community, the party, and the cause; and
most interestingly, by the other as the subject of transference.

There is of course an instability in any triadic relationship, as Sartre (1945) brilliantly showed in No Exit and
as is constantly exemplified in familial Oedipal dramas.

There is a constant shifting of alliances and objectifying gazes. There is a splitting of symbolic functions. In analyzing my use of a field assistant in some of my work in Morocco (Crapanzano 1980), I found that my assistant was the controller of the word. He could mediate between me and my informant—and became, thereby, a symbol of constancy and continuity. He was not, however, the initiator of the word; that lay with me. Nor was he the giver of the word; that lay with my informant. (I am obviously simplifying here.) The three functions of the Oedipal father—the initiator, the giver, and the controller of the word—were split among us. (Compare the trinitarian conception of the Christian God.) Of course, there was in our relationship a certain stability, for it was framed by our intention. We three had accommodated to one another and developed our own idiosyncratic conventions which were supported by our self-interests.

It is precisely convention, a determining frame, that is missing from Sartre's No Exit (and from his Being and Nothingness as well) that produces the "hell" of instability. There are thirds but no Third in Sartre's Godless hell. The Oedipal crisis itself can be viewed, I suppose, as a struggle for a determining frame, convention, law, grammar, and authority—all symbolized by the "father". Convention, Law, Grammar, and Authority—become the Third; they stabilize the dual relationship, much as Mead's generalized other stabilizes the relationship between self and other.[19]

The Third[20] permits a certain freedom in any dual relationship. It is no longer a life-and-death struggle, as in Hegel's (1931) depiction of the master-slave relationship. Within certain limits prescribed by the Third, self and other are able to cast each other in order to cast themselves as they each desire. And this is most important: the Third affords the space of desire. What is sadly lacking in Mead's approach is a dynamic that can explain the freedom of the I. Desire, too, is lacking in Leenhardt's personage who follows by rote his textless script. He cannot take possession of it. Then perhaps, the personage would become a person.

Desire, Lacan has written, is "an effect in the subject of that condition which is imposed upon him through the defiles of the signifier" (quoted in Wilden 1968, p. 185).

Need is directed toward a specific object, is unmediated by
language, and, unlike desire, can be satisfied directly.
(Desire must always be satisfied, insofar as it can be
satisfied, by symbolic substitutes for that which it can
never possess; see Crapanzano 1978). To become a self, the
individual must seek recognition by demanding the other to
recognize him-self--or his desire.[21]   To name him, to
acknowledge at least the noun (the name) as a (grammatical-
ly) legitimate Anlage for the I--and the you. He must take
possession of his own otherness--and not be aware simply of
the otherness about him.

    A possessive reflexivity, one mediated by desire, and
not simply a mechanical reflexivity, is required for the
emergence of the self and indeed of self-awareness. "The
Empirical Self of each of us", William James observed nearly
a century ago (1890),

    is all that he is tempted to call by the name me. But it
    is clear that between what a man calls me and what he
    simply calls mine the line is difficult to draw. (1950
    ed., p. 291)
And Burckhardt, it will be remembered, referred to the
"veil" of pre-Renaissance man as woven of "childish prepossession" (Kindesbefangenheit).

    It is only after we have recognized the fundamental
role of desire in the genesis of the self that we can begin
to explain the positing of those others: the primitive, the
fettered, the personage, and that host of slightly less-
stereotyped others to which anthropologists and psychia-
trists, for that matter, refer--those others against which
or at least through which we constitute our own highly "individuated" selves.   (Is the discovery of those others not
one of the anthropologist's and the psychiatrist's unspoken
functions?)   It is only after this recognition of desire
that we can begin to appreciate our occasional (if not our
permanent) nostalgias for such Edenic conditions--or our
ruthless denial of such Edens.

    It is only then that we can begin to understand why
Freud used the phrase (so revealing really) "when I think
what a healthy child I was" to illustrate his point about
the continuity of the ego, or why Flaubert chose to write
"Between myself of that night and myself of tonight, there
is the difference between the cadaver and the surgeon doing
the autopsy...." He wrote less, I suppose to emphasize his

own discontinuity than to scandalize his reader--and perhaps
even himself. To coin a proverb: Il faut un bourgeois pour
s'épater. Is that bourgeois our Third?

ENDNOTES

1. For readability, I have given an explication of the
   Strachey translation. For the purposes of my argument,
   insofar as the translation makes sense to the reader,
   it reflects the implicit psychology to which I am
   referring. The German reads (Freud 1942 ed., p. 328):
   > Dass das eigene Ich in einem Traume mehrmals vor-
   > kommt oder in verschiedenen Gestaltungen auftritt,
   > ist im Grunde night verwundlicher, als dass es in
   > einem bewussten Gedanken mehrmals und an verschie-
   > denen Stellen oder in anderen Beziehungen enthalten
   > ist, z.b. im Satz: wenn ich daran denke, was fur
   > gesundes Kind ich war.
   We find the same fundamental distinction between dream
   (Traum) and conscious thought (bewusster Gedanke). But
   in the German, there is not the same emphasis on
   appearance in the dream as in the English translation.
   The ego vorkommt--comes forth, occurs, appears (on the
   scene). Or it auftritt--steps forth, presents itself,
   appears (on the scene). There is rather more emphasis
   on the movement of the ego--coming or stepping forth--
   in the dream than in conscious thought, which contains
   the ego (enthalt das Ich). Both vorkommen and auftre-
   ten may be used in a theatrical context to mean "to
   appear". This fits in well with Freud's reference to
   the dream as another stage (ein anderer Schauplatz).
   Conscious thought, insofar as it contains the ego,
   appears in any case to have more control than the
   dream. The Ich as ego and the ich in the final phrase
   are of course homonyms in German and lend, therefore,
   greater credence and panache to Freud's point.

2. For the distinction between implicit and explicit psychology, see Crapanzano 1975.

3. Strachey (1961) notes that Freud uses dass Ich ("ego",
   here) in two senses in his earlier writings: It may
   "distinguish a person's self as a whole (including,
   perhaps, his body) from other people"; or it may denote

a particular part of the mind characterized by special attributes and functions.

4. "Traume sind absolut egoistisch." Note Freud's usage of the Latin derivative "egoistisch" instead of the German selbstisch.

5. It is impossible in the context to determine whether the ego is synonymous with, or a referent of, the two "I"s. At the time, Ferdinand de Saussure's work on the sign had not yet been elaborated—or at least, was not yet published.

6. The dialectical process seems to reflect the dialogical.

7. It is reflected, for example, in the frequent confusion (or blending) of self-awareness with self-conceptualization and of the phenomenological approach with a conceptual one. This confusion results, I think, from a failure to account for the relationship between self-awareness and self-conceptualization.

8. Compare his questions at the end of his lecture (p. 362): "Qui sait ce que seront encore les progrès de l'Entendement sur ce point [the development of the concept of the self]? Qui sait même si cette 'catégorie' que tous ici nous croyons fondée sera toujours reconnue comme telle?"

9. Compare Aristotle: "Spoken words are the symbols of mental experience and written words are the symbols of spoken words. Just as all men have not the same writing, so all men have not the same speech sounds, but the mental experiences, which these directly symbolize, are the same for all, as also are those things of which our experiences are the images." (De Interpretatione 16a1; McKeon ed. p.40)

10. Mead's stages seem to be at times situationally determined (in play, in a game) and at times developmental.

11. Benveniste's argument in fact proceeds in two directions at once. On the one hand, he is concerned with the emergence of subjectivity through discourse; and on the other hand, he is implicitly concerned with the de-

notations of subjectivity: <u>subject</u>, <u>ego</u>, <u>subjectivity</u>, <u>person</u>, etc. Despite the rigor of his argument, Benveniste's use of the terms reflects the same (symptomatic) "promiscuous" usage we have observed in the treatment of the self in the other authors we have considered.

12. Compare with Freud's notion of the ego in our first quotation.

13. Note even the question Benveniste poses in his article "The Nature of the Pronoun" (1966 1971): "What then is the reality to which <u>I</u> or <u>you</u> refers?" (See also note 15 below.)

14. Compare Leenhardt's (1979) understanding of the dual.

15. We should note that in asking what the <u>I</u> refers to--a question that is from Benveniste's own perspective meaningless--he is forced to posit a reality, which he identifies with "'objective' positions in space and time" (1966, p. 252; 1971, p. 219). Of course the <u>I</u> and <u>you</u>, he argues, do not always refer to the same objects in the spatio-temporal continuum but rather to "utterances unique each time". Aside from considering the obvious point that such utterances are also objective occurrences in <u>reality</u>, Benveniste fails to consider that the speaker who uses <u>I</u> and <u>you</u> and his interlocutor who understands <u>I</u> and <u>you</u> would be unwilling to limit their reference to such instances of discourse.

16. I would suggest that many obscure passages in Lacan are the result of his insistance on an essentially referential model of language. The <u>béance</u>, to play on Lacan's term, between reference and index affords him the space for much of his language play.

17. Lacan uses this awkward phrase to stress the fact that it is the father-qua-symbol that is in question here. <u>Nom</u> in <u>nom-de-père</u> is also more or less homonymous with <u>non-de-pere</u>, the father's "no".

18. In Freudian thought, <u>father</u> and <u>mother</u> serve as full stops in the otherwise unending chain of symbolic references and cross-references. Their special position

within the psychoanalytic hermeneutic is rationalized
by chronological and developmental priority.

19. Mead himself does not explicitly recognize the generalized other as a Third in the relationship between   self
and other.

20. My   use   of   the <u>Third</u> here is   probably not altogether
dissimilar to Pierce's (1931) notion of <u>thirdness</u>,   at
least in certain of his usages.   I am thinking, specifically, of where he relates thirdness to meaning,
thought, and law—and to the possibility of generality.
He notes, interestingly, that

    the   dream   itself has no prominant thirdness; it is
    on the contrary, utterly irresponsible; it is   what-
    ever it pleases.   The object of experience as a re-
    ality is a second recant.   But the desire in writing
    to attach the one to the other is a third, or
    medium. (p. 173)

The third, I suppose, enters the dream with the question of meaning.   Peirce's observation that genuine
triadic relations can never be built out of dyadic
relations is of singular importance to my argument.   It
is reflected, in the Oedipus myth and other myths   having to do with the genesis of the genuine triad.

21. Lacan's Hegelianism is apparent.

REFERENCES

Aristotle. "De Interpretatione". In <u>The Basic Writings of
Aristotle</u> (ed. by Richard McKeon, New York:
Random House, 1941), pp. 40-61.
Benveniste, E. 1966. <u>Problèmes de Linguistique Générale</u>.
Paris: Gallimard.
Benveniste, E. 1971 trans. <u>Problems in General Linguistics</u>.
Miami Linguistic Series No. 8 Coral Gables: Uni-
versity of Miami Press.
Berger, P.L. and Luckmann, T. 1967. <u>The Social Construc-
tion of Reality: A Treatise in the Sociology of
Knowledge</u>. Garden City, New York: Anchor Books.
Burckhardt, J. 1867. <u>Die Kultur der Renaissance in Ital-
ien.</u> 1926 ed., Leipzig: Alfred Kroner.

Burckhardt, J. 1955 trans.: The Civilization of the Renais-
     sance in Italy, London: Phaidon.
Crapanzano, V. 1975. "Saints, Jnun, and Dreams: An Essay
     in Moroccan Ethnopsychiatry". Psychiatry,
     XXXVIII:145-59.
Crapanzano, V. 1977. Introduction to Case Studies in Spir-
     it Possession (ed. by V. Crapanzano and V. Garri-
     son, New York: John Wiley), pp. 1-40.
Crapanzano, V. 1978. "Lacan's Ecrits". Canto, II:183-91.
Crapanzano, V. 1979. Introduction to Do Kamo (by M. Leen-
     hardt, Chicago: University of Chicago Press) pp.
     vii-xxix.
Crapanzano, V. 1980. Tuhami. Chicago: University of Chi-
     cago Press.
Dieterlin, G. 1973. La Notion de Personne en Afrique
     Noire. Paris: Editions: C.N.R.S.
Dupre, W. 1975. Religion in Primitive Cultures: A Study
     in Ethnophilosophy. The Hague: Mouton.
Durkheim, E. (1914). "The Dualism in Human Nature". In
     Essays on Sociology and Philosophy (ed. by K.
     Wolff, New York: Harper and Row, 1964) pp. 325-
     40.
Durkheim, E. (1915) 1965 trans.: The Elementary Form of the
     Religious Life. New York: Free Press.
Durkheim, E. and Mauss, (1903) 1963 trans.: Primitive Class-
     ification Chicago: University of Chicago Press.
Foucault, M. 1966. Les Mots et Les Choses. Paris: Galli-
     mard.
Freud, S. (1925, rev. of 1900). "Traumdeutung". In Gesam-
     melte Werke 2/3. Frankfurt am Main: Fischer,
     1942.
Freud, S. 1954 trans.: The Interpretation of Dreams. Lon-
     don: Allen and Unwin.
Halliday, M.A.K. and Hasan, R. 1976. Cohesion in English.
     London: Longman.
Hallowell, A.I. 1967. "The Self and Its Behavioral Envi-
     ronment". In Culture and Experience (New York:
     Schocken) pp. 75-110.
Hegel, B.W.F. 1931. The Phenomenology of the Mind. Lon-
     don: Allen and Unwin.
James, W. (1890). The Principles of Psychology, I. 1950
     ed., New York: Dover.
Lacan, J. 1966. Ecrits. Paris: Seuil.
Lamprecht, K. 1900. Die Kulturhistorische Methode. Ber-
     lin: Gaertner.
Leenhardt, M. 1953. "Quelques eléments communs aux formes

inférieures de la religion". <u>Histoire des Religions</u>, I:83–110.

Leenhardt, M. 1979. <u>Do Kamo: Person and Myth in the Melanesian World.</u> University of Chicago Press.

MacLeod, R.B. 1947. "The Phenomenological Approach to Social Psychology". <u>Psychological Review</u>, LIV: 193–210.

Mauss, M. 1973. <u>Sociologie et Anthropologie.</u> Paris: Presses Universitaires de France.

Mead, G.H. 1934. <u>Mind, Self, and Society.</u> Chicago: University of Chicago Press.

Peirce, C.S. (1931). "Principles of Philosophy". In <u>Collected Papers of C.S. Pierce</u>, I. (Cambridge, Massachusetts: Harvard University Press, 1974) pp. 3–363.

Sartre, J.P. 1945. <u>Huit Clos</u> (Eng. <u>No Exit</u>) Paris: Gallimard.

Silverstein, M. 1979. "Language, Structure, and Linguistic Ideology". In <u>The Elements: A Parasession on Linguistic Units and Levels</u> (ed. by Paul R. Klyne et. al., Chicago: Chicago Linguistic Society), pp. 193–247.

Steegmuller, F. 1972. <u>Flaubert in Egypt.</u> London: The Bodley Head.

Strachey, J. 1961. Editor's Introduction to "The Ego and the Id". In <u>S. Freud, Standard Edition</u>, Vol.xix (London: Hogarth) pp. 3–11.

Strawson, P.F. 1959 <u>Individuals.</u> London: Methuen.

Weintraub, K.J. 1966. <u>Visions of Culture.</u> Chicago: University of Chicago Press.

Wilden, A. 1968. <u>Language of the Self.</u> Baltimore: Johns Hopkins Press.

Wittgenstein, L. 1978. <u>Philosophical Grammar.</u> Berkeley: University of California Press.

LIST OF CONTRIBUTORS

Arnold Goldberg, M.D.
    Training and Supervising Analyst, Chicago Institute for
        Psychoanalysis, Chicago, Illinois
    Attending Psychiatrist, Michael Reese Hospital, Chicago,
        Illinois
    Clinical Professor of Psychiatry, The Pritzker School of
        Medicine, The University of Chicago, Chicago, Illinois

Ernest S. Wolf, M.D.
    Associate Director, Center for Psychosocial Studies,
        Chicago, Illinois
    Training and Supervising Analyst, Chicago Institute for
        Psychoanalysis, Chicago, Illinois
    Assistant Professor of Psychiatry, Northwestern Univer-
        sity, Evanston, Illinois

Robert A. LeVine
    Former Director, Center for Psychosocial Studies, Chicago,
        Illinois
    Roy E. Larsen Professor of Education and Human Development,
        Harvard University, Cambridge, Massachusetts

Raymond D. Fogelson
    Professor of Anthropology and Behavioral Sciences, The
        University of Chicago, Chicago, Illinois

Anne S. Straus
    Teaches Native American Studies, University of Illinois,
        Circle Campus, Chicago, Illinois

Milton Singer
    Advisory Fellow, Center for Psychosocial Studies, Chicago,
        Illinois
    Professor Emeritus of Anthropology, The University of
        Chicago, Chicago, Illinois

Vincent Crapanzano
    Professor of Comparative Literature and Anthropology,
        Queens College, C.U.N.Y., New York, New York

SUBJECT INDEX

Action, 14-15
    man of: Radin's notion of,
        82
Agent, self as, 7-9
Aggression, 40-41, 46
Aggressive drive, 38, 39
Alienation
    of individual from en-
        vironment, 186
    of the self from the self,
        198
Ambition, pole of: Kohut's
    notion of, 35
American Indians, 111
    masking and ceremonial
        performance among, 75-
        77
    See also Cherokees; Chey-
        enne culture; Iroquois,
        the; Ojibwa, the
Ametane, 113-117
Anaphoric potential of per-
    sonal pronouns, 182,
    195-196
Anthropology
    of civilizations, social,
        160
    semiotic, 165
    study of the self and, 67-
        100, 111, 181-184
        Mary Black, 84-85
        Cherokees, 87-92

Anthropology (continued)
    cultural perspectives on
        the self within American
        anthropology, 80-88
    dramaturgical model of
        social interaction,
        75-77
    future strategies, 88-89,
        92-94
    A. Irving Hallowell, 82-85
    Thomas Hay, 86-87
    historical overview, 67-75
    identity concept, 77-80
    Anne Straus, 87-88
Apperception, 68, 95
Assertion, self-: among the
    Gusii, 49, 58-60, 62,
    63
Autobiography, 81, 96-97
Autonomy, 14, 63

Balinese culture, 161-163
Bipolar self, Kohut's con-
    cept of, 23-41
Boasting, among the Gusii,
    49, 58
Body
    Canaque concept of, 188
    Cheyenne view of, 115, 116,
        119, 124
    See also Mind/body problem

213

Death
  Cherokee beliefs about, 90-
    91
  Cheyenne view of, 116-117
Deference, among the Gusii,
  48-49
Deixis, 141-142
Depersonalization, 87, 162
Depression, empty, 36, 37
Desire, 181, 199-200
Dialectical approach to the
  self, 181, 190-192
Dialogue
  civilization of, 160
  personal and social identi-
    ty in, 129-173
  corporate personality
    and collective identi-
    ty, 148-157
  first, second, and third
    persons, 141-144
  inner and outer dialogue,
    137-138, 141, 146, 147,
    151, 152, 164
  private and public personal
    identity as, 138-141
  pronouns of personal and
    interpersonal identity,
    145-148
  social and semiotic psycho-
    logy of personal identi-
    ty, 131-133
  Warner's model of inter-
    action, 165-169
  semiotics of, 133-137,
    162, 163, 165
  subject's emergence
    through, 192-194
  See also Conversation
Disclosure, self-: among
  the Gusii, 49-51
Drama (dramaturgical model),
  192
  personal pronouns and,
    143-145
  social interaction as,
    45-46, 75-77

Dreams, 179, 180
Drives, 12, 19, 38-39

Ego, 8, 11, 14, 97, 179, 180
  American Indian notions of,
    82
  Durkheim on, 69-70
  Peirce on consciousness of
    non-ego and, 139-140,
    164
Egocentricity, assumption of,
  143, 144
Ego identity, Erikson's con-
  cept of, 77, 78
Emblems (emblematic systems),
  166
Embodiment, 5
Emergence, Gusii ceremony of,
  52
Emergence of the self
  anthropological studies and,
    69, 70, 72
  awareness of one's own
    otherness and, 189
  communication and, 192
  desire and, 200
  evolutionary view of, 185-
    186
  Kohut's view of, 32, 34-35
  Peirce on, 139
  See also Individual emer-
    gence of
Empathy, 30-32, 34, 45, 54, 62
  63
  See also Introspective- em-
    pathic data collection
Empirical observation, self
  of psychoanalysis and,
    16-17, 20, 36
Empirical vs. conceptual
  approach to the self,
    6, 10, 15
Entity (thing)
  self as, 6, 9, 10, 13, 14
  See also Reification of
    the self